Rousseau's Politics of Taste

For August

Rousseau's Politics of Taste

Jared Holley

EDINBURGH
University Press

Edinburgh University Press is one of the leading university presses in the UK. We publish academic books and journals in our selected subject areas across the humanities and social sciences, combining cutting-edge scholarship with high editorial and production values to produce academic works of lasting importance. For more information visit our website: edinburghuniversitypress.com

© Jared Holley, 2024

Edinburgh University Press Ltd
13 Infirmary Street
Edinburgh EH1 1LT

Typeset in 10.5/13pt Bembo
by Cheshire Typesetting Ltd, Cuddington, Cheshire

A CIP record for this book is available from the British Library

ISBN 978-1-3995-2115-4 (hardback)
ISBN 978-1-3995-2117-8 (webready PDF)
ISBN 978-1-3995-2118-5 (epub)

The right of Jared Holley to be identified as the author of this work has been asserted in accordance with the Copyright, Designs and Patents Act 1988, and the Copyright and Related Rights Regulations 2003 (SI No. 2498).

Contents

Acknowledgements	vi
Abbreviations	ix

Part I

1. Introduction: A Taste for Virtue	3
2. Modern Epicureanism: Between Sociability and Atheism	25
3. Rousseau's Epicureanism: From Atheism to Aesthetics	54

Part II

4. The Problem of Modern Liberty: Sociability, Taste, Commerce	89
5. The Foundations of Political Judgement: *Amour-propre*, General Taste, General Will	128
6. The Memorial Practice of Happiness: Temperance, Sensuality, and Rousseau's System	166
Afterword: Revisiting Rousseau's Paradoxes	200

Selected Bibliography	208
Index	217

Acknowledgements

This book has had many beginnings. One of these was a marginal comment I received at the University of Cambridge on one of my early essays about Rousseau's *Reveries*: 'Is this Epicureanism?' My doctoral supervisor, Duncan Kelly, asked the question and has, ever since, guided my attempts to answer it with his intellectual rigour and unique combination of theoretical precision and historical erudition. At the same time, Chris Brooke challenged me to be able to say why 'this' wasn't Stoicism, and Mike Sonenscher helped me to come to see the range of modern political views lurking behind these ancient labels. The same is true of the late István Hont, whose willingness to read and discuss my work with his deeply critical eye has left an indelible imprint on this book despite his untimely passing. Duncan, Chris, and Mike have been kind and consistent interlocutors without whose generous criticisms and encouragement this book would not have been possible.

In another sense, this book began in a set of undergraduate lectures at the University of Victoria. Jim Tully first introduced me to political theory, to Rousseau, and to the importance and challenges of studying both in their historical contexts. He also taught us that Rousseau was both a radical critic of commercial society and a radical democrat. If the best gift you can give your teacher is to disagree with them, then I hope he will see this book as an attempt to retain what is true about those lessons while respectfully parting ways with parts of them.

In the most fundamental sense, however, this book began with my family in Ladysmith. My parents, Mike and Sue Holley, nurtured my interests in reading, writing, and learning, and always supported me as those interests shifted to things that must have seemed quite strange. That they have come genuinely to care about those things – and what I think about them – is staggering. Sarah Holley is my sister. I cannot imagine a better one. My Gramma, Illaena Rudy, once told me that if I was going to study Rousseau then I would have to study

ACKNOWLEDGEMENTS vii

the Greeks. Though a voracious reader, she did so seemingly without ever having read either Rousseau or the Greeks. This is both the most and the least relevant of the memories of her to which I often return with great happiness.

I have been fortunate to develop my thoughts about Rousseau in many other places with many other people. For discussions, criticisms, and comments on parts of this work, I thank Richard Bellamy, Benjamin Fong, Rafeeq Hasan, Birte Löschenkohl, Mihaela Mihai, Jennifer Pitts, Tim Stuart-Buttle, Paul Sagar, Mathias Thaler, Richard Whatmore, and Waseem Yaqoob. Special thanks to Sankar Muthu, who supported the book's initial development from a dissertation with a richness of both knowledge and enthusiasm; and to Robin Douglass, who provided comments on the entire draft manuscript and encouraged its publication in ways far beyond mere professional courtesy. Jennifer Pitts offered generative criticism at various points, most recently when it was much needed. Duncan Bell encouraged me to return to the manuscript when I was close to abandoning it. A book written across so many institutions is an index of the precarity early-career scholars increasingly face. The generosity of these dialogue partners helped to make Cambridge, Chicago, Florence, Berlin, and now Edinburgh also feel like home.

This book is a collective effort. Earlier versions of Chapters 2 and 3 were published in *History of European Ideas*; parts of Chapter 4 were published in *European Journal of Political Theory*; parts of Chapter 5 in *British Journal for the History of Philosophy*; and an earlier version of Chapter 6 in *History of Political Thought*. I am grateful to the current editors and publishers for allowing the reproduction of this material and to the editorial team at University of Edinburgh Press for helping me to turn it into *Rousseau's Politics of Taste*. Ersev Ersoy responded enthusiastically to the first draft manuscript and expertly guided the revision process. Beatrice Lopez provided additional guidance and Sam Johnson steered me through the final submission. Responding to the critical comments provided by two anonymous reviewers has improved the text immensely and reinvigorated my sense of its value. During the production phase, I wish to thank: Geraldine Lyons for copy-editing; Stephanie Derbyshire for the cover design; Grace Garland for proof-reading; Amanda Speake for indexing; and Joannah Duncan for guiding the whole process.

Special thanks to the National Gallery for allowing me to use Luca Giordano's *Allegory of Temperance* for the book's cover. In the early 1860s, Giordano prepared this oil study for a ceiling fresco in the Palazzo Medici Riccardi in Florence. It provides a useful illustration of the various approaches to pleasure discussed in this book. The central figure represents Temperance as a young woman, in some ways not unlike the heroine of Rousseau's novel *Julie*. In her right hand, Temperance holds a bridle to indicate restraint −

viii   ACKNOWLEDGEMENTS

as the bridle controls the horse, so Julie controls her will. In her left hand, Temperance holds a clock to indicate patience – as the clock knows the time, so Julie knows when to enjoy and when to abstain. Temperance is supported here by an elephant, which was then understood to be the most temperate of animals. Elephants apparently never consume more food than they need. And they are capable of foregoing even the strongest sexual drives because of their unique sense of modesty – which Rousseau (in)famously identified as a natural capacity that allowed women to bridge the gap between the physical and moral effects of love, and to control men.

In other ways, however, the Christian Platonism informing Giordano's *Allegory* differs markedly from Rousseau's refined Epicurean approach to pleasure. In the painting, Temperance is joined by other figures of beauty and moderation: Meekness (pouring honey from a jar) and Sobriety (holding a key), the latter of which Rousseau always rejected as too austere – too Stoic – to facilitate true enjoyment. He would have shared Giordano's depiction of Temperance triumphing over the effects of intemperance: Sloth, on the left, solitary and miserable; Envy, in the centre, embraced by a snake; Hunger, on the right, chewing on a bone with a ravenous wolf. Flying above, we see: Tranquillity, with a cornucopia representing abundance, and a bird's nest representing the soul; Youth with incense and a serpent-ring, a symbol of eternity; and Voluptuousness holding a winged sphere and fishhooks, to symbolise the motions of the world and the snares of seduction. In the final fresco, Temperance looks upward to Voluptuousness, from which she is protected by Youth. For Rousseau, conversely, the seductive snares of worldly pleasure are instead to be combatted by bringing temperance and voluptuousness closer together. Indeed, he makes voluptuousness the very foundation of the theory of taste that I reconstruct in this book.

While multiple beginnings beget multiple ends, there is only one that matters. Birte Löschenkohl has been my most careful reader and incisive critic – her boundless creativity has improved every idea in this book and her patience has ensured that it is (finally) out in the world. Vastly more important, she is the most loving partner and exemplary co-parent. The arrival of our son, August, inspired the final stages of writing; his joyful wonder sustains the rest. I dedicate this book to him.

Abbreviations

Parenthetical references are to the following works by Jean-Jacques Rousseau.

DSA *Discourse on the Sciences and the Arts*
DI *Discourse on the Origin and Foundations of Inequality Among Men*
SC *Of the Social Contract*

These refer to *The Discourses and other early political writings* and *Of the Social Contract and other later political writings*, trans./ed. Victor Gourevitch (Cambridge: Cambridge University Press, 1997).

C *The Confessions*
D *Dialogues*
E *Emile*
J *Julie*
LD *Letter to d'Alembert*
LM *Letters to Malesherbes*
R *Reveries*

These refer to *The Collected Writings of Rousseau*, 13 vols, ed. Christopher Kelly and Roger D. Masters (Hanover, NH: University Press of New England, 1990–2010).

All other texts refer to volume and page number of the *Collected Writings* (abbreviated as *CW* through the book).

All English references are followed by references to volume and page number of the *Oeuvres complètes de Jean-Jacques Rousseau* (abbreviated as *OC*), 5 vols, ed. Bernard Gagnebin and Marcel Raymond (Paris: Gallimard, 1959–1995).

For Rousseau's correspondence, I refer to *Correspondence Complète de Jean-Jacques Rousseau* (abbreviated as *CC*), 52 vols, ed. Ralph Alexander Leigh (Geneva: Institut de Musée Voltaire, 1965–1971; Oxford: Voltaire Foundation, 1972–1977).

Unless otherwise noted translations of French texts are my own.

I have silently modified some translations of Rousseau.

Part I

1

Introduction: A Taste for Virtue

Shortly after the publication of his *Discours sur l'origine et des fondemens de l'inégalité parmi des hommes* (second *Discourse*), Jean-Jacques Rousseau was asked his opinion on the establishment of a new periodical press in his native Geneva. He responded in early April 1755, with withering scepticism:

> Believe me, Sir, this is not the sort of work that suits us. Serious and profound works would honour us; all the baubles of the fashionable little philosophy would harm us. Great objects, like virtue and liberty, elevate and strengthen the mind; small ones, like poetry and the fine arts, give it more delicacy and refinement. A telescope is needed for some, a microscope for others; and men accustomed to measuring the sky do not know how to dissect flies. That is why Geneva is the land of wisdom and reason, and Paris is the seat of taste. Let us leave the refinements to those myopic men of letters who spend their lives gazing at the tips of their noses; let us be more proud of the taste we lack than are they of that which they have. And while they will have newspapers and pamphlets for the alleys, let us try to make books that are useful and worthy of immortality.[1]

Rousseau's readers recognise the set of distinctions he employs here. We are familiar with his trenchant critique of the pretensions of modern philosophy, the refinement of the arts, and the corruption of Paris. Just as we are aware of his defence of a more profound wisdom, his celebration of political virtue, his lionisation of Geneva's republican liberty. Whatever else we may like or dislike in his thought, we know that Rousseau presents us with alternatives, lays bare

---

[1] 'Rousseau à Vernes, le 2 avril, 1755', *CC*3:115–117.

4 ROUSSEAU'S POLITICS OF TASTE

their fundamental opposition, and forces us to confront the stark reality that, tragically, we must choose between them.

This book is an attempt to show why this familiar picture is wrong. To be sure, Rousseau frequently appeals to binary oppositions. This is part of what he meant when he repeatedly referred to his thought as 'paradoxical'.[2] Some of the most interesting and indeed best interpretations of Rousseau have been generated precisely by attending to such binaries.[3] But too narrow a focus on them can be radically misleading. For, especially in his political thought, Rousseau was not only concerned to elucidate the parameters of a series of stark either/or choices. He was also, and even primarily, concerned with the possibility of keeping both – with keeping, that is, what was necessary and even good about modern politics, while avoiding what was unnecessary and bad. If the familiar picture is not wrong, simply, it leaves far too much outside the frame.

This book is also an attempt to clarify Rousseau's system from the perspective of the 'taste for virtue'. The phrase is one of several that Rousseau used to express the idea that, I argue, forms the core of his account of moral and political freedom. One of these was the equally – and equally deliberately – paradoxical 'temperate sensuality'. Another was the less paradoxical 'Epicureanism of reason', which grounds his more deeply paradoxical conclusion that 'every consistent Epicurean is necessarily a Stoic' (E:682/4:874). Attending to his paradoxes is an especially fruitful way of reading Rousseau because he consistently deployed them as a rhetorical device with which to grab his reader's attention, inviting and challenging them to grasp the idea behind the expression. In this case, each paradox was a way of describing a hedonist theory of temperance, or self-control, through which individuals learned to avoid the false pleasures of vanity and instead pursue real pleasures rooted in nature. Grounding temperance in taste in this way meant that virtuous conduct could be achieved through enjoyment rather than through asceticism, provided one learned how to enjoy. And because temperance or moderation supported material equality, it also meant that both moral and political freedom came to

---

[2] E:226/$OC$4:323; 'Letter to Philopolis', $CW$3:127–128/$OC$3:231–232. Cf. Edmund Burke, *Selected Writings and Speeches* (Transaction Publishers, 1963): 89; *Reflections on the Revolution in France*, ed. William R. Todd (New York, 1959): 211; Stephen G. Salkever, 'Interpreting Rousseau's Paradoxes', *Eighteenth-Century Studies* 11:2 (1977): 204–226; Felicity Baker, 'La Route Contraire', in *Reappraisals of Rousseau*, ed. Harvey et al. (Manchester: Manchester University Press, 1980): 132–62.

[3] Two of the best are Leo Strauss, 'On the Intention of Rousseau', *Social Research* 14:4 (1947): 455–87 and Jacques Derrida, *Of Grammatology*, trans. Gayatri Charkravorty Spivak (London: Johns Hopkins University Press, 1974).

INTRODUCTION

depend in important ways on sensual pleasure and aesthetic judgement. The idea behind all the terms was that moral and political freedom alike required a balance, or equilibrium, between those features synecdochally represented by 'Geneva' and 'Paris' in the above extract: wisdom *and* the fine arts, literature *and* liberty, microscopes *and* telescopes.

Notoriously difficult to define, when we hear the word *taste* it is natural to turn to Kant or to think in terms of what would come to be called aesthetic judgement.[4] Rousseau preferred to describe it with a visual metaphor: taste gives 'spectacles to reason'; taste is 'the microscope of judgment'. The metaphor was designed to capture the way that taste seems uniquely able to bridge the physical world of sensations or sentiments and the moral world of honour or shame. Taste was not judgement per se, he wrote, but 'it is taste which brings small objects within our reach, and its operations begin where those of the latter end' (*J*:47–48/2:58–59).[5] To take a simple, physical example: our experience of our tongue contacting sugar or citrus peel generates respectively sweet or bitter sensations, which we then express as the value judgement 'jam is superior to marmalade'. These personal judgements come to ground our evaluations of our own and others' actions and can, in turn, be generalised into norms of propriety reinforced by cultural sanctions. If sufficiently many people feel that jam is superior to marmalade, then they may come to consider a preference for marmalade a sign of perversion of which one ought to feel shame, and a preference for jam a mark of nobility worthy of esteem. Rousseau did not distinguish between bitter and sweet confitures. In his view, 'all the jams of the earth' were unnatural relishes, inferior to natural goods like 'idleness' or natural 'commodities' ranging from snails and beetles to acorns and turnips.[6] A preference for jams, whether bitter or sweet, was a mark of one's 'taste for luxury', not a 'taste for virtue'. Taste is like a microscope, then, because it links something small, like jam, to something great, like virtue. His metaphorical description of taste concluded that, to cultivate taste, one had 'to practice seeing as well as feeling, and to judge the beautiful by inspection as well as the good by sentiment' (*J*:48/2:59). There was nothing wrong with dissecting flies, in other words, provided one kept sight of the sky.

One might, finally, say that this book attempts to show Rousseau thinking through the implications for moral and political freedom of the mind's curious ability to function as both microscope and telescope. His reflections on this

[4] Paul Guyer, *A History of Modern Aesthetics: Volume 1 – The Eighteenth Century* (Cambridge: Cambridge University Press, 2014): 289–302.

[5] Rousseau, *The Complete Dictionary of Music*, trans. W. Waring. (London: J. French, 1779): 428–429/*OC*5:842–43.

[6] 'Rousseau à M. D'Ivernois, le 15 aout, 1765', *CC*26:218–219.

ability led him to conclude that one could 'say taste or morals indifferently: for although the one is not the other, they always have a common origin and undergo the same revolutions' (*LD*:264/5:18). Rousseau scholars have overlooked the significance of this conclusion for Rousseau's political thought. But it is crucial for understanding his other widely cited conclusion: that 'those who want to treat politics and morals separately will never understand anything of either of the two' (*E*:389/4:524). The common element of the conclusions was the imagination. Unique among the mental faculties for its ability to mediate between mind and body, the imagination allows us to relate physical inputs from a particular sensation (like bitterness) to a general idea (like marmalade) and to turn general ideas into sentiments with emotional content (like shame). His main interest in taste was political, in how this imaginative transition could be given institutional expression. He was especially concerned with taste's complicated interaction with the institutions of political economy and the law. But he was no less intrigued by both formal and informal institutions of censorship. By publicly articulating the locally approved sentiments informing moral and political action, censorial institutions allowed certain societies to promote certain types of behaviour and to proscribe others. We generally recognise that we cannot understand Rousseau's political thought without understanding his moral thought. As I hope to show in this book, we fail to understand either of the two if we neglect his reflections on taste. The remainder of this introduction sketches the contours of my wider argument.

The Consistency Dilemma

Any investigation of Rousseau must begin with his repeated insistence that his writings amounted to what he called a system. The earliest such claims came in response to critics of the first *Discourse*. In 1753, he referred to his 'sad and great system' for the first time. But he also conceded that his method of presenting it had tended to obscure both its parts and the whole.[7] When he subsequently addressed the widespread impression that he advocated returning to the 'barbarism' of the Middle Ages, he wrote 'it is impossible to imagine anything more contrary to my system'.[8] Returning to the practice of public self-defence in 1762, he identified the first and second *Discourses* along with *Emile* as his 'three principal writings', which are 'inseparable and together form the same whole' (*LM*:575/1:1136). And in a public epistolary exchange with the presiding Archbishop of Paris the following year, he wrote that, once an author

[7] Rousseau, 'Letter to Bordes', *CW*2:183–185/*OC*3:103–105.
[8] Rousseau, 'Preface to Narcisssus', *CW*2:190/*OC*2:964.

INTRODUCTION

has clearly established his sentiment on a matter, 'his writings then explain each other, and the latest, when he is methodical, always presuppose the earliest. That', he continued, 'is what I have always tried to do, and have done'.[9]

Despite this repeated insistence on his system, to this day there persists an image of Rousseau as an inconsistent, incoherent, or unsystematic thinker. To a large extent, this has to do with what having a philosophical 'system' subsequently came to mean, particularly in German idealism.[10] This view informed the customary twentieth-century reading of Rousseau's thought as being structured by a series of irreconcilable binary oppositions. Paradigmatically, Judith Shklar and Leo Strauss both advanced versions of what I will call the 'incompatibility thesis': the claim that Rousseau's personal and political ideals are incompatible and, further, that precisely the incompatibility or tension between them is Rousseau's central insight, which renders his system coherent.[11] For Shklar, Rousseau intended to demonstrate the necessity of a tragic choice between individual and political flourishing; for Strauss, Rousseau's preference for the individual over the political ideal was tragically or ironically undermined by his accepting a modern materialist natural philosophy. More recently, Rousseau's readers have pushed back against this incompatibility thesis. In direct response to Shklar, egalitarian philosophers Joshua Cohen and Frederick Neuhouser have offered different versions of what has been called the 'social autonomy interpretation' of Rousseau. Within this view, Rousseau's work constitutes a coherent system. But that coherence is provided by an ideal of 'rational agency' that unifies Rousseau's accounts of moral and political freedom by transcending the practical tension between them on which Shklar insisted.[12] Especially among political theorists, these are in many ways the leading interpretive positions in contemporary approaches to Rousseau.

---

[9] Rousseau, 'Letter to Christophe de Beaumont', *CW*9:39/*OC*4:951.

[10] See Leo Catana, 'The Concept "System of Philosophy": The Case of Jacob Brucker's Historiography of Philosophy', *History and Theory* 44:1 (2005): 72–90.

[11] Judith N. Shklar, *Men and Citizens: A Study of Rousseau's Social Theory* (Cambridge: Cambridge University Press, 1969); Strauss (1947). My bringing Shklar and Strauss together in this way may surprise many readers, and perhaps offend a few. But cf. Richard Fralin, 'The Evolution of Rousseau's View of Representative Government', *Political Theory* 6:4 (1978): 517–536, who notes that both 'stressed the unity of Rousseau's political thought to the point of excluding virtually all development' (518). As this suggests, the 'systematic' question of Rousseau's coherence bears significantly on the 'historical' or biographical question of his intellectual development.

[12] For 'social autonomy', see Joshua Cohen, *Rousseau: A Free Community of Equals* (Oxford: Oxford University Press, 2010). Cf. Frederick Neuhouser, *Rousseau's Theodicy of Self-Love: Evil, Rationality, and the Drive for Recognition* (Oxford: Oxford University Press, 2008).

8 ROUSSEAU'S POLITICS OF TASTE

This consistency dilemma provides the first of three central questions to which this book is a response. If any general interpretation of Rousseau's political thought must address it, one must nevertheless approach it with caution. It is perhaps the perennial issue in Rousseau interpretation, having been asked in various terms in different contexts. Where previous generations worried about the 'psychological' and the 'intellectual' dimensions of his system, or compared its 'Romantic' and 'Rationalist' tendencies, contemporary political theorists ask whether Rousseau's account of political freedom through popular sovereignty is consistent with his account of moral freedom through personal autonomy. This iteration of the dilemma owes much to Ernst Cassirer's discussion of what he called 'the problem of Jean-Jacques Rousseau' – namely, how to reconcile Rousseau's critical account of private property, *amour-propre*, and revolution with the more positive vision of the sovereignty of the general will. For Cassirer and others following in his neo-Kantian wake, Rousseau's 'answer' is a secular theodicy in which the development of human reason offsets the loss of physical independence by enabling moral autonomy and the rule of law, yet keeping morality and politics separate.[13] Other iterations share this structure of a dilemma with its horns. But as I have already indicated, too narrow a focus on binary oppositions can be radically misleading. I am not the first to suggest that the answer to this particular 'either/or' dilemma is, indeed, 'both'. Many others have sought the unity of Rousseau's system in his intention, his 'method or orientation', or in one or another of his ideas.[14] Yet others downplay the dilemma but generally assume that Rousseau is indeed consistent in his ultimate message, whether that be the task of achieving emotional and democratic 'transparency' or of combining sovereignty and government

---

[13] Ernst Cassirer, 'Das Problem Jean-Jacques Rousseau', *Archiv für Geschichte der Philosophie*, 41 (1932): 177–213, 479–513; *The Question of Jean-Jacques Rousseau*, trans. Peter Gay (New York, Columbia University Press, 1954). Cf. Jean Starobinski, *Le remède dans le mal* (Paris: Gallimard, 1989).

[14] I borrow this categorisation from Blair Campbell, 'Montaigne and Rousseau's First Discourse', *The Western Political Quarterly* 28:1 (1975): 7–31. An especially fruitful recent interpretation of the unity of Rousseau's thought, which my account largely supports, is Jason Neidelman, *Rousseau's Ethics of Truth: The Sublime Science of Simple Souls* (London: Routledge, 2017). Campbell helpfully distinguishes among earlier competing accounts of Rousseau, many of which remain classics in the field: (a) unity of 'intention': Bertrand Jouvenal, 'Rousseau, évolutioniste et pessimiste', in *Rousseau et la philosophie politique*, ed. Pierre Arnaud, Annales de philosophie politique 5 (Paris: Presses Universitaires de France, 1965): 1–19. (b) unity of method or orientation: Albert Schinz, *La Pensée de Jean-Jacques Rousseau* (Paris: Librairie Felix Alcan, 1929), Charles W. Hendel, *Jean-Jacques Rousseau: Moralist* (Indianapolis: Bobbs-Merrill, 1934); (c) unity of ideas: Ernest D. Wright, *The Meaning of Rousseau* (London: Oxford University Press, 1929), Roger D. Masters, *The Political Philosophy of Rousseau* (Princeton, NJ: Princeton University Press, 1968).

INTRODUCTION 9

given the tension between morals and politics.[15] For these reasons, it is important not to become myopically focused on either the dilemma itself or the terms in which it is presented at any given time.

With these precautions in mind, I hope to provide a genuinely new answer to the consistency dilemma. First, I approach it through a historiographical lens. Historicising the dilemma as a problem can help to reveal the interpretive concerns of different readers in different contexts. For instance, Strauss' claim that Rousseau's thought is unified by a fundamental tension between the life of philosophy and the life of politics was part of his attempt to reassess the theoretical foundations of the modern state by rethinking the intellectual history of liberalism, an approach he shared with contemporaries like Michael Oakeshott, Carl Schmitt, and Hannah Arendt.[16] Second, I deploy this historicised consistency dilemma as a sort of ideological flashlight. Once we see that its various formulations derive from certain background assumptions in different contexts, we can better see what those formulations and assumptions leave out of the picture. In the contemporary context, the dilemma is framed by a dominant approach to political theory that has been criticised as having at least three blind spots. That is, contemporary liberal-egalitarian political theory is said: first, to be insufficiently 'realistic' in its approach to practical politics; second, to be insufficiently attentive to the 'affective' and 'aesthetic' dimensions of political judgement and agency; and, third, to operate in a strikingly 'ahistorical' mode.[17] The approach to Rousseau's system developed in this book deepens the critique of these overlapping and intersecting shortcomings, and pushes back against the normative positions they imply.

There is one further respect in which I approach the consistency dilemma somewhat differently. If the terms of the incompatibility thesis and the social autonomy interpretation are approached from the kind of sceptical perspective I

[15] Robert Derathé, *Jean-Jacques Rousseau et la science politique de son temps* (Paris: PUF, 1950); *Le rationalisme de Jean-Jacques Rousseau* (Paris: PUF, 1948); Richard Tuck, *The Sleeping Sovereign: The Invention of Modern Democracy* (Cambridge: Cambridge University Press, 2015).

[16] For a different way of historicising the dilemma, which emphasises its importance for political-economic and legal-philosophical thought in nineteenth-century Germany, see Michael Sonenscher, *Jean-Jacques Rousseau: The Division of Labour, the Politics of the Imagination and the Concept of Federal Government* (Leiden: Brill, 2020).

[17] Compare, for example, Raymond Geuss, *Philosophy and Real Politics* (Princeton, NJ: Princeton University Press, 2008), Linda M. G. Zerilli, *A Democratic Theory of Judgment* (Chicago: Chicago University Press, 2018), John Dunn, *Setting the People Free: The Story of Democracy* (London: Atlantic Books, 2005). Rawls of course took his famous idea of a realistic utopia from Rousseau: see Céline Spector, 'Rousseau at Harvard: John Rawls and Judith Shklar on Realistic Utopia', in *Engaging with Rousseau: Reaction and Interpretation from the Eighteenth Century to the Present*, ed. Avi Lifschitz (Cambridge: Cambridge University Press, 2016): 152–167.

10   ROUSSEAU'S POLITICS OF TASTE

am advocating, they can indeed elucidate Rousseau's system in certain respects. Michael Sonenscher has aptly noted that it is more fruitful to search for consistency rather than inconsistency in Rousseau's work because Rousseau appears genuinely to have been engaged in 'a sustained effort to try to get things right', at least to his own satisfaction; but it is even more fruitful to start by accepting that 'the subject-matter of Rousseau's thought was, simply, difficult'.[18] It is in this spirit that I attempt in what follows to develop something of a middle position between the two rival camps. On the one hand, I agree with Neuhouser that Rousseau's ideal of political freedom through popular sovereignty is theoretically consistent with his ideal of moral freedom through personal autonomy. On the other hand, I argue that the coherence of Rousseau's thought lies not in any *transcendent* ideal but, rather, in the fact that Rousseau's accounts of moral and political freedom alike embody a materially grounded and more *realistic* goal – not, 'rational agency' but temperate sensuality, refined Epicureanism, or the taste for virtue. This attention to Rousseau's realism, in turn, partially rehabilitates the incompatibility thesis, while reframing it. Taking seriously Rousseau's consistent approach to taste allows us to recognise the complex tensions in his thought – after all, he explained that his system is 'sad' precisely because he composed it without entertaining 'the chimerical pleasure of hoping' that the reformation he encouraged would ever be widely adopted.[19] But it also provides a way of articulating neglected patterns in those tensions and, thereby, a new perspective on what he was trying to do with his political thought.

A Political Theory of the Modern State

However certain he was of its practical implausibility, Rousseau always insisted that one of his primary intentions in composing the various parts of his system was to be 'useful'. In his 'Final Reply' to the critics of the first *Discourse*, he noted that he had not attempted to be merely 'agreeable' but also 'useful', driven to work for others out of his 'intense desire to see men happier, and especially worthy of being so'.[20] He famously identified his reflections on human nature in the second *Discourse* as contributing to 'the most useful and the least advanced branch of knowledge' (*DI*:124/3:122). His pedagogical treatise *Emile* begins with a reference to his hope of reminding the public of the forgotten 'art of

---

[18] Sonenscher (2020): 16 (cf. 13–17). I am grateful to Mike for his willingness to engage over the years in a dialogue that has deeply informed my approach to and enriched my understanding of Rousseau.

[19] Rousseau, 'Letter to Bordes', *CW*2:183/*OC*3:103.

[20] Rousseau, 'Final Reply', *CW*2:112, 129/*OC*3:74,96.

INTRODUCTION

forming men, the first of all useful things' (*E*:157/4:241). And he suggested that his epistolary novel *Julie* would 'be of some use' because it would be read not only in cities like Paris but also in the provinces – for it was essential that one be read in the countryside 'if one wants to be useful' (*J*:13, 16/2:19, 22).[21]

Most significant for the argument of this book, Rousseau's utilitarian intentions extended to the state theory he developed and published as the *Social Contract*. As he explained in his autobiographical *Confessions*, that text is in fact an excerpt from a larger work that he had originally planned to serve as a textbook for tutors of politics and political philosophy.[22] He decided to release it in April 1762, at the height of a constitutional crisis in Geneva, when it would be 'useful to the happiness of the human race, but above all to that of my fatherland'. Its utility consisted in conceptual clarification: what Rousseau called privately his support for 'the re-establishment of the liberty and rights of the bourgeoisie' was expressed publicly through the clear and precise concepts of freedom and law the text provided his compatriots.[23] Importantly, he also clarified that his theoretical innovation was useful because it was empirically grounded. In the first place, it drew on his practical knowledge of the real politics of actually existing states: it was informed by his personal experiences of republican politics in Geneva and as secretary to the French ambassador in Venice. It was also grounded, in the second place, in what Rousseau called his 'historical study of morality' (*C*:340/1:404). The sort of history he had in mind here was the conjectural 'art of choosing among several lies the one best resembling truth'. His scepticism about notions of historical 'facts' and 'truth' led him to prefer ancient to modern historians as guides to moral judgement; among these he preferred Plutarch's biographies of moral 'exemplars' to Herodotus or Thucydides (*E*:393–396/4:527–531). I discuss Rousseau's conjectures further in Chapter 4. Here, it suffices merely to emphasise his contention that the unique combination of theoretical precision, realistic political knowledge, and historical imagination saved his own political theory from the fate of those previous – which were, almost without exception, useless.

---

[21] Rousseau's overriding intention to be useful, and its significance, is largely overlooked. But see Helena Rosenblatt, *Rousseau and Geneva: From the First Discourse to the Social Contract, 1749–1762* (Cambridge: Cambridge University Press, 1997): 269 and Joseph R. Reisert, *Jean-Jacques Rousseau: A Friend of Virtue* (Ithaca, NY: Cornell University Press): 13.

[22] *C*:331, 339, 432/*OC*1:394, 404, 516. The larger work would have been entitled *Political Institutions*, mirroring the textbook on *Chemical Institutions* he had planned as a young enthusiast of the emerging modern science of chemistry. One of the only scholars to have noted the importance of the textbook as a distinct genre and its bearing on Rousseau's work is Bruno Bernardi, 'Pour situer les Institutions chimiques', avec B. Bensaude-Vincent, *Corpus* 36 (1999): 5–38.

[23] 'Rousseau à Mézières, le 10 août 1762', *CC*12:167–170.

12   ROUSSEAU'S POLITICS OF TASTE

Rousseau identified two ways in which political theory could be useless. The first of these was for it to be overly utopian. On the model of Plato's *Republic* or Thomas More's *Utopia*, this was to imagine ideal republics and to make deductions from metaphysical speculations or abstract moral intuitions. Such theories were the product of a vain imagination and belonged in what Rousseau derisively called 'the land of chimeras'.[24] He was clear that the *Social Contract* avoided similar exile because it drew on his knowledge of Geneva's political constitution, history, and culture: it 'depicted an existing object', albeit in a favourable light.[25] But if, to avoid being useless, political theorists had to reason inductively from the historical record and real politics, it was equally important that they not overcorrect. For the second way that a political theory could be useless was for it to be overly empirical. Montesquieu had finally made the study of politics a 'great science', Rousseau wrote, because his realistic approach provided the foundation for a precise definition of the law. But his *Spirit of the Laws* lacked a normative perspective from which to judge whether any *given* law was good or bad – devolving into mere description, it was what Rousseau called 'a useless science' (*E*:649/4:836). The core of Rousseau's understanding of the nature and aims of political theory, then, is his insistence on finding a balance or equilibrium between history and normativity. To be useful, political theory required an empirical, scientific foundation. But the real purpose of political theory was to facilitate critical judgement, and this required transcending local contexts through historical imagination, carefully bounded by rigorous conceptualisation. In other words, to be useful, political theorists required a mind capable of switching between microscope and telescope.

It is often noted that Rousseau's own historical imagination was preoccupied with the politics of the ancient Greek city-states. Less often noted, however, is precisely *why* Rousseau thought that an imaginative return to the ancient world could be useful for anyone looking to understand the world of modern politics. In the first place, such a perspective could serve as a reminder of perennial truths in moral and political life. Among these truths, the most important was that morals and politics had to be considered together, in their reciprocal interaction. Describing the tendency of the general will to be corrupted by factional interest, he unmasked the democracy of Athens as 'in fact not a democracy but a most tyrannical aristocracy governed by learned

---

[24] A chimera is an unreal creature of the imagination, a mere wild fancy; an unfounded conception; a vain imagination. But it is important to note that Emile is still a 'dreamer who pursues his chimera' – in this sense, a chimera can be a useful falsehood, as it is in romantic love where 'everything is an illusion' (*E*:482, 499/*OC*4:636, 656).

[25] Rousseau, 'Letters Written from the Mountain', *CW*9:234/*OC*3:810.

INTRODUCTION 13

men and orators' (*CW*3:144/3:246). Crucially, the Athenians were no better off morally than politically. Far from being morally upright and abstemious, they were an example of luxurious consumption and moral corruption. The point of his frequent references to Athens was that the *moral* corruption of the citizens was inseparable from the corruption of its *political* institutions. On Rousseau's analysis, the Athenians' taste for luxury engendered a devolution from democratic to tyrannical politics because the Athenian constitution allowed anyone to propose a law in the assembly, thereby providing an institutional outlet for corrupt citizens to propose laws that were rooted in factional interest (*DI*:116–119/3:114–117). Sparta, of course, was precisely the opposite. It provided a positive example of the reciprocal interaction of morals and politics. For Rousseau, the Spartans proved the possibility that moral virtue might combine with political wisdom, by practising the sort of ancient austerity that allowed general laws to rule over particular men.[26] While certainly no democracy, Sparta was nevertheless a republic, in no small part because it was composed of men with 'superior virtues' born of their 'happy ignorance'. In his imaginative return to ancient Greek politics, then, both the negative example of Athens and the positive example of Sparta offered proof for Rousseau of the perennial truth one would never understand either politics or morals if they were treated separately.

But there is a second reason that Rousseau found the imaginative return to ancient politics useful. He also invoked the Greeks to emphasise not transhistorical continuity but contextual specificity. There was a vast gulf separating ancient from modern. On the specific terms of the political theory of the *Social Contract*, Athenian politics failed to distinguish between what Rousseau called *sovereignty* and what he called *government*. His discussion of Athens is a critique of what we could call direct democracy: for Rousseau, sovereignty must not be represented, and it must be clearly distinguished – both theoretically and institutionally – from government, which was a delegated form of sovereign power.[27] Athens' failure did not, however, mean that Rousseau wanted his contemporaries to emulate Sparta. For, as he advised his Genevan compatriots in the *Letters from the Mountain*, 'ancient peoples are no longer a model for modern ones'. Far from being austere Spartans, he said, Genevans were

---

[26] See Paul Cartledge, 'The Socratics' Sparta and Rousseau's', *University of London School of Advanced Studies*, History of Political Thought E-Seminars. R. A. Leigh, 'Jean-Jacques Rousseau and the Myth of Antiquity in the Eighteenth century', in *Classical Influences on Western Thought A.D. 1650–1870*, ed. R. R Bolgar (Cambridge: King's College Conference Proceedings, 1977): 155–168.

[27] Richard Tuck, *The Sleeping Sovereign: The Invention of Modern Democracy* (Cambridge: Cambridge University Press, 2018).

14   ROUSSEAU'S POLITICS OF TASTE

'not even Athenians': they were moderns, preoccupied with private interest and material gain.[28] We should not overburden this passage with interpretive weight.[29] But we should acknowledge Rousseau's explanation that this historical distance had little to do with moral laxity. For Rousseau, ancient Spartan austerity had become practically impossible because of the historically unique structural situation of modern politics and the division of labour.

This brief discussion of Rousseau's use of ancient examples serves to introduce the second central question to which this book provides an answer. For my first question of Rousseau's consistency is deeply implicated with the question of whether and to what extent Rousseau should be considered a theorist of the modern state. Shklar argued that Rousseau's personal ideal of 'self-expression' in a 'recreated Golden Age of domestic happiness' is incompatible with his political ideal of 'self-repression' of the 'citizen of a Spartan republic'.[30] Proponents of the social autonomy interpretation concede that Rousseau's ideal of individual human flourishing is incompatible with ancient citizenship. But they argue that Rousseau's political ideal is not, in fact, ancient: for Neuhouser, the principles of political right outlined in the *Social Contract* demonstrate Rousseau's concern with distinctly modern notions of 'respect and esteem' for all citizens.[31] The most advanced historiography largely supports this view of Rousseau's modernity. Contemporary historians of political thought see Rousseau's state theory as a response to his awareness that modern politics had become irreducibly 'commercial' – as 'economics' became, for the first time, a 'matter of state'. The central issues for Rousseau and his contemporaries were thus economic inequality at home, military competition abroad, and the terrifying combination of the two under the increasingly centralised authority of the state. Over the course of the eighteenth century, two central debates raged over the political place of economic growth. On the one hand, there was a debate between the 'moderns' who accepted luxury production and the 'ancients' who simply rejected it. Far more interesting, however, was the debate that occurred amongst the 'moderns' themselves. It concerned whether modern luxury production should be either 'regulated' or 'unregulated'. Here, the question was not whether to accept or reject luxury but, rather, how to make economic growth safe for politics.[32]

---

[28] Rousseau, 'Letters Written from the Mountain', *CW*9:292–293/*OC*3:880–881.

[29] Robin Douglass, 'Tuck, Rousseau and the Sovereignty of the People', *History of European Ideas* 42:8 (2016): 1111–1114 (1113–1114).

[30] Shklar (1969): 5–6.

[31] Neuhouser (2008): 166.

[32] Istvan Hont, 'The Early Enlightenment Debate on Commerce and Luxury', in *The Cambridge History of Eighteenth-Century Political Thought*, ed. Mark Goldie and Robert Wokler (Cambridge:

INTRODUCTION 15

That Rousseau had a realistic assessment of the economic foundations and limits of modern politics is clear in the *Social Contract*. The following passage is crucial for understanding Rousseau and what he was trying to do in his political thought. In the course of drawing his fundamental distinction between sovereignty and government, he wrote:

> Among the Greeks, all the People had to do it did by itself; it was constantly assembled in the public. It lived in a mild climate, it was not greedy, slaves did its work, its chief business was its freedom. No longer having the same advantages, how are we to preserve the same rights? Your harsh climates make for more needs, six months of the year you cannot stay out on the public square, your muted languages cannot make themselves heard in the open, you care more for your gain than for your freedom, and you fear slavery less than you fear poverty. (SC:115/3:430–431)

Rousseau identifies here two ways in which modern states differ from the Roman Republic and Greek *polis*. The first is economic: moderns are more concerned with private interest than with freedom. Importantly, however, this is not because of their moral corruption. Rather, it is because of the greater material effort required to meet individual survival needs in severe northern climates. Indeed, it is also at least partly because modern moral consciousness condemns slave labour. But there is a second difference that Rousseau identifies here between ancient and modern politics. Compared to their ancient forebears, he notes, moderns speak muted and indistinct languages, incapable of eloquence, and lacking the persuasive power to stir patriotic affection for the common good. Whether analytic philosophers or historians of political thought, those of Rousseau's readers accustomed to looking for his critique of modern political economy almost uniformly neglect this cultural or aesthetic dimension of the passage.[33] Noting the connection between them helps us to appreciate more fully Rousseau's sense of the usefulness of the ancient/modern periodisation. In essence, turning back to ancient politics was useful because it helped Rousseau to formulate more sharply the central normative problem to which the *Social Contract* should be seen as an answer – namely, the problem of *modern* liberty. In this way, it served as a reminder both that the ancient world

Cambridge University Press, 2006): 377–418. Michael Sonenscher, 'Property, Community, and Citizenship', in Goldie and Wokler eds (2008): 465–494.

[33] Tuck (2018): 1–3, 141–142. Tuck rightly notes 'Rousseauian democracy was not an idyll of an ancient city-state transported to the present day, but a serious attempt at working out how a modern commercial state might genuinely deserve the title of democracy' (142). My argument is that we fail to understand his attempt if we neglect its aesthetic dimensions.

no longer provided a realistic political model, and that useful political theory demanded serious reflection on how to preserve freedom in the uniquely modern situation of economic necessity and aesthetic impoverishment.

The arguments of this book are grounded in the revisionist account of Rousseau as a modern who recognised the necessity of economic growth but argued for its, sometimes very strict, regulation. The eighteenth century has been called 'the century of taste' in part because the modern discourse of taste was then beginning to flourish, just as the new category of fine art was emerging to classify the drastically increasing number of superfluous commodities generated by the modern division of labour.[34] In this context, taste was one way of making economics safe for modern politics. Under the banner of what would come to be called 'aesthetics' as a new and distinct branch of philosophy, various theories of taste and ideas of 'good taste' were developed by many of Rousseau's contemporaries hoping to provide moral pressure or normative guidance to exercise restraint in consumption. Rousseau's evident distaste for this individualistic, ethical approach to the regulation of economic growth has long been recognised as sharing something with later critiques of the function of taste in 'bourgeois' ideology.[35] But it is critical to note that he did not simply reject taste out of hand.

My attention to Rousseau's account of taste provides a more fulsome perspective on his view of the economic limits of modern politics than most of those currently on offer. A great strength of the revisionist account of the eighteenth-century luxury debates is its clarification of the historical importance of Bernard Mandeville's *Fable of the Bees*. In particular, we have learned to appreciate that the text was most important as an argument against the political economy of the Archbishop Fénelon, rather than as the attack on the Third Earl of Shaftesbury's moral sense theory it is, at least in part, presented as.[36] While there may well be grounds to criticise the revisionist view of Mandeville, I want merely to insist that we not neglect either that Mandeville

---

[34] Paul Oskar Kristeller, 'The Modern System of the Arts: A Study in the History of Aesthetics Part I', *Journal of the History of Ideas* 12:4 (1951): 496–527. Paul Oskar Kristeller, 'The Modern System of the Arts: A Study in the History of Aesthetics (II)', *Journal of the History of Ideas* 13:1 (1952): 17–46.

[35] Pierre Bourdieu, *Distinction: A Social Critique of the Judgement of Taste* (London: Routledge, 2013); Terry Eagleton, 'The Ideology of the Aesthetic', *Poetics Today* 9:2 (1988): 327–338. Cf. Michael Moriarty, *Taste and Ideology in Seventeenth-Century France* (Cambridge: Cambridge University Press, 1988).

[36] Compare Hont (2006) and E. J. Hundert, *The Enlightenment's Fable: Bernard Mandeville and the Discovery of Society* (Cambridge: Cambridge University Press, 1994): 117–126. For reassessment, see Robin Douglass, 'Mandeville on the Origins of Virtue', *British Journal for the History of Philosophy* 28:2 (2020): 276–295.

INTRODUCTION

did in fact attack Shaftesbury, or the manner in which he did so. As is well known, Mandeville grounded his interventions in a defence of the principle of 'utility' as a criterion of moral judgement. But it is crucial to recall that his account of 'the good and the useful' was twinned with and in many ways inseparable from his account of the 'beautiful and the good'.[37] As the passage from the *Social Contract* suggests, and as I argue throughout this book, Rousseau's reflections on economic utility similarly run alongside a concern with aesthetic beauty. To this extent at least, my argument is a defensive one. It is born of the worry that, by focusing too narrowly on the economic *limits* of modern politics, historians of political thought might neglect its aesthetic possibilities.[38]

Rousseau's Epicureanism

Alongside his insistence on the coherence and utility of his system, Rousseau also always insisted on his originality. This was typically an insistence on his uniqueness as both individual and author. He famously described his attempt in *Confessions* to reveal himself 'in all the truth of nature' as 'without precedent'; and he began that attempt by asserting 'I am not made like anyone I have seen; I dare to believe that I am not made like any that exists.' The two claims were mutually reinforcing: personal and authorial originality combined to make *Confessions* a 'unique and useful work' that could provide a point of 'comparison for the study of men' (*C*:5, 3/1:5, 3). In Chapter 6, we will see how, in his autobiographies, radical self-disclosure became the means of comparative evaluation and general observation. Putting oneself in particular under the microscope, as it were, allowed one to observe humanity in general, as through a telescope.

He extended these claims to his philosophical originality as well. While it has gone largely overlooked, *Confessions* also contains an important description

---

[37] Or, in the classical terms Mandeville borrowed from Shaftesbury, the 'honestum et utilitas' went together with the 'pulchrum et honestum'. On this distinction and its afterlife, see Aaron Garrett, 'Hutcheson on the Unity of Virtue and Right', in *Kant and the Scottish Enlightenment*, ed. Elizabeth Robinson and Chris W. Surprenant (New York: Routledge, 2017): 19–35.

[38] In arguing that revisionist historians have underemphasised the importantly aesthetic dimensions of eighteenth-century political thought, I do not mean to suggest that it has been entirely ignored. See, especially, Michael Sonenscher, 'Sociability, Perfectibility and the Intellectual Legacy of Jean-Jacques Rousseau', *History of European Ideas* 41:5 (2015): 683–698 and *Sans-Culottes: An Eighteenth-Century Emblem in the French Revolution* (Princeton, NJ: Princeton University Press, 2008): 71–77. Cf. Istvan Hont, *Jealousy of Trade: International Competition and the Nation-state in Historical Perspective* (Cambridge, MA: Harvard University Press, 2005): 142–144, n. 257.

18   ROUSSEAU'S POLITICS OF TASTE

of his study habits and intellectual development. There, he narrates his gradually abandoning hope of reconciling various competing philosophical systems and authors in 'perpetual contradiction' with one another. Such a syncretic solution, he came to believe, was as 'chimerical' as Plato's ideal republic. Instead, he adopted a strategy of dogmatic engagement: he would 'adopt and follow' a given thinker's ideas without disputing their premises or comparing their conclusions to any others. The method was difficult but merely instrumental. For after several years, it furnished his mind with a store of ideas to recall and combine:

> I would amuse myself by revisiting and comparing what I had read, weighing each item in the balance of reason, and sometimes passing judgment on my masters. I did not find that my faculty of judging had lost its vigour . . . and when I published my own ideas, I was never accused of servility or of being a disciple who could swear only *in verba magistri* (in the master's voice). (C:199/1:237–238)

Progressing from syncretism through dogmatism to eclecticism, he wrote, secured for him in philosophy the self-sufficiency he valued so highly in ethics and politics.

This brief account of Rousseau's methodology points to the third central question to which this book provides an answer. For as with the consistency dilemma, the question of the modernity of Rousseau's state theory is bound up with the question of his relationship to his ancient philosophical predecessors. Unsurprisingly, his readers have always been fascinated by this relationship. The first *Discourse* launched his literary career with a stirring critique of modern luxury through a celebration of ancient virtue: for Socrates, he wrote, to have been forced to live in the modern world would have been a fate worse than death (DSA:14/3:15). The second *Discourse* was instantly recognised as having been greatly influenced by Lucretius' Epicurean poem *De rerum natura*. And just as critics quickly pointed out that Rousseau had excerpted long passages of Montaigne's *Essais* in the first *Discourse*, so was he immediately accused of having plagiarised widely from Seneca in the composition of *Emile*.[39] His claims to formal innovation are generally affirmed. But readers have long questioned whether Rousseau's ability to combine the parts of different systems into an eclectic whole really amounted to anything new, or philosophically original.

---

[39] Jean de Castillon, *Discours sur l'origine de l'inegalite parmi les hommes. Pour servir de reponse au discours que M. Rousseau a publie sur le meme sujet* (Amsterdam, 1756). Dom Joseph Cajot, *Les Plagiats de M. J-J Rousseau de Genève sur l'éducation* (La Haye: Durand, 1766).

INTRODUCTION   19

Disputes about Rousseau's sources and influences are simply characteristic of his reception. Even his admirers disagree about which 'master' of whom he is most helpfully considered a disciple. Those pursuing modern connections typically point to Hobbes, sometimes to Locke, and other times to both.[40] But these disagreements are most pronounced amongst those who interrogate what Rousseau called his 'ancient soul'.[41] There is, in short, simply no agreement about which ancient philosopher – or school, or idea – offers the best perspective from which to view his work. By commentators attracted and repulsed in almost equal numbers, Rousseau was and continues to be identified as a Platonist, an Epicurean, a Stoic, or a Cynic.

This book provides the first monograph treatment of Rousseau's relationship to Epicureanism. One benefit of approaching Rousseau from the perspective of ancient philosophy in general is that it opens up a broader range of ways of thinking about the moral foundations of politics. An ancient orientation, that is, helpfully shifts our attention from seeing Rousseau as primarily a social contract thinker, a conjectural historian, or a critic of natural jurisprudence, and allows us better to see the importance for Rousseau of keeping morals and politics together, rather than separating them. The benefits of approaching his system from the perspective of Epicureanism in particular will become clear over the course of this book. But I should emphasise two benefits from the outset. One is historical and contextual: while some might arrive at the problem of moral foundations through attention to Platonism or Stoicism, the ancient school that resonated early and often among Rousseau's readers is Epicureanism. Because it resonated early, focusing on his relationship to Epicureanism also deepens our understanding of Rousseau's reception by his contemporaries, allowing us to appreciate what they appreciated in his work. This, in turn, deepens our understanding of Rousseau's complicated – and neglected – reception of Epicurean ideas, allowing us to appreciate what he appreciated about them. And because his relationship to Epicureanism has continued to resonate often, this perspective also deepens our understanding of his reception by later commentators, including our contemporaries – and what they (fail to) appreciate about him.

A core claim of this book is that questions of Rousseau's reception *as* an Epicurean and his reception *of* Epicureanism are of more than merely historical interest. The other major benefit of exploring his relationship to Epicurean

---

[40] Richard Tuck, 'Rousseau and Hobbes: The Hobbesianism of Rousseau', in *Thinking with Rousseau*, ed. Helena Rosenblatt and Paul Schweigert (Cambridge: Cambridge University Press, 2017): 37–62. Robin Douglass, *Rousseau and Hobbes: Nature, Free Will, and the Passions* (Oxford: Oxford University Press, 2015).

[41] Rousseau, *CW*11:175/*OC*3:961; *Judgment on the Polysynody*, *CW*11:97/*OC*3:643.

ideas is conceptual and exegetical. Other scholars have generated valuable insights into Rousseau's system by emphasising his other possible masters. Seeing Rousseau as a Platonist, for instance, supports a reading of the general will as constrained by a transcendent notion of justice. My Epicurean approach disagrees fundamentally with such readings, arguing instead that Rousseau saw justice and the general will as conventional. The contrast with other Hellenistic frameworks is less stark. Whereas viewing Rousseau as a kind of modern Cynic foregrounds his emphasis on the limitation of individual and collective needs and emotions, an Epicurean perspective clarifies his celebrations of pleasure and the ethics of enjoyment. Readers interested in Rousseau's proximity to Stoic thought are forced to recognise his rejection of asceticism. My Epicurean account shows that he placed that rejection squarely at the centre of some of his most important ideas, like *amour-propre*. These Hellenistic contrasts perhaps amount mostly to a change of emphasis. But as I have suggested, and as we will see, the Epicurean framework, more than any other, has the further benefit of clarifying the centrality of taste to Rousseau's political thought.[42]

At this point, sceptical readers might ask: If understanding Rousseau's relationship to Epicureanism is so helpful for understanding his political thought, then why is this the first book dedicated to it? That such a lacuna exists is surprising, for the eighteenth century was saturated with discussions of Epicureanism and the Epicurean dimensions of modern political ideas. But it is also unsurprising. For as much as Epicureanism was a subject of eighteenth-century philosophical debate, the terms 'Epicurean' and 'Epicureanism' were used by different authors to refer to different things in different texts and places. They were also terms of abuse. This combination of conceptual variability and polemical purpose makes determining what a given author meant in using the terms 'Epicurean' or 'Epicureanism' very difficult. But it does not make it impossible. Historians of political thought have shown that determining the 'meaning' of indeterminate terms requires contextualising their 'use' by particular authors in particular texts. I have little to add to such methodological discussions.[43] Instead, I simply note that the general point applies to the subjects of this book. And if the label 'Epicurean' has become rather more

---

[42] For the alternative frameworks suggested here, see: David Lay Williams, *Rousseau's Platonic Enlightenment* (University Park: Pennsylvania State University Press, 2007); Sonenscher (2008) and Louisa Shea, *The Cynic Enlightenment: Diogenes in the Salon* (Baltimore, MD: The Johns Hopkins University Press, 2010); and Christopher Brooke, *Philosophic Pride: Stoicism and the Politics of Self-Love from Lipsius to Rousseau* (Princeton, NJ: Princeton University Press, 2012).

[43] See, classically, John Dunn, 'The Identity of the History of Ideas', *Philosophy* 43:164 (1968): 85–104 and Quentin Skinner, 'Meaning and Understanding in the History of Ideas', *History and Theory* 8:1 (1969): 3–53.

INTRODUCTION   21

anodyne in contemporary scholarship, one basic aim of the historical element of my story is to explain why Epicureanism was initially a very hostile term to apply to someone in the eighteenth century.

The account that follows of Rousseau's relationship to Epicureanism reinforces these positions. My argument that Rousseau is helpfully seen as an Epicurean should not be mistaken for an argument that Rousseau was nothing but an Epicurean. Indeed, the lesson to be drawn from his description of his eclecticism is to resist viewing his philosophical influences in exclusive or binary terms. In this book, I endeavour instead to see him as – more complexly, ambiguously, and often frustratingly – Rousseau.

To illustrate my point, I will draw this chapter to a close with a brief discussion of the tensions apparent in the other terms Rousseau used to express 'the taste for virtue' – namely, 'temperate sensuality' and the 'Epicureanism of reason'. My argument that Rousseau should be seen as a modern might seem to rule out the idea of temperance playing an important role in his system. After all, temperance is the fundamental virtue of those ancient Greek polities that Rousseau rejected as a model. Their term for it was *sophrosyne* – literally 'sound-mindedness' – which modern translations variously render as temperance, moderation, or self-restraint. Something of its political importance is indicated by the Temple of Delphi, where the famous inscription 'Know thyself' was paired with another, 'Nothing to excess'. The idea was that Greek citizens were entitled to exercise direct political rule over others only insofar as they were able to control themselves or demonstrate *sophrosyne*. Rousseau similarly linked moderation and freedom: for individuals, 'it is less the strength of arms than the moderation of hearts that makes a man independent and free' (*E*:390/4:524); for states, the political freedom of living according to the general will is grounded on a degree of economic equality that, in turn, presupposes 'on the part of the great, moderation in goods and services and, on the part of the lowly, moderation in avarice and covetousness' (*SC*:78/3:392). Temperance or moderation is thus fundamental to Rousseau's understanding of moral and political freedom in modernity.

We typically understand temperance as a Platonic virtue, not an Epicurean one.[44] Of the many discussions of *sophrosyne* across Plato's work, the best known comes in Book IV of the *Republic*. There, Socrates defines moderation as 'a kind of beautiful order and a mastery of certain pleasures and appetites'. Moderate individuals are those in whom 'that which is better by nature' – reason – is

---

[44] It is also of course widely associated with Montesquieuean virtue. See Aurelian Craiutu, *A Virtue for Courageous Minds: Moderation in French Political Thought, 1748–1830* (Princeton, NJ: Princeton University Press, 2012).

'master of that which is worse' – the passions or appetites, especially those of the body. This rationalist view of moderation supports a paternalist and explicitly anti-democratic politics, in which 'the desires of the inferior multitude and rabble are mastered by the desires and the wisdom of the superior minority'.[45] As the leading historian of *sophrosyne* notes, 'all subsequent interpretations' of moderation are 'the result, in some fashion', of this definition.[46]

The marginal notations Rousseau left in his personal copy of Plato's collected works show that he read the *Republic* very carefully. Scholars pursuing his Platonic affinities have taken his marginalia as evidence that he adopted this definition.[47] But of his twenty-six annotations to the text, there are only two in Book IV, and these are most revealing for *passing over* this famous definition of moderation. After the founding of the ideal city in speech and shortly before the definition, Rousseau wrote 'from here, go immediately to Book V'. The implications of this marginal commentary have not been assessed. It presents an interpretive puzzle: if Rousseau stressed the importance of moderation to freedom and was obviously familiar with Plato's definition, why did he advise that one ignore that definition? Did he reject it, in favour of another?

Two of Rousseau's other annotations suggest a solution to this puzzle. These come in a well-known discussion of *sophrosyne* in Plato's *Phaedo*. As part of the dialogue's striking dichotomy between the true philosopher and the non-philosophical people, Socrates presents diametrically opposed versions of temperance. The first passage Rousseau annotated is a critique of what Socrates calls the 'foolish and ridiculous temperance' practised by the 'multitude and rabble'. These common people, he says, 'renounce one pleasure only for fear of being deprived of other pleasures, which they covet, and which are ascendant over them. It is only their subjection to some predominant pleasures, which makes them discard others.' In this way, Socrates derisively concludes, 'they are only temperate through intemperance'.[48] The opposing view of temperance comes in the second passage Rousseau annotated, which summarises Plato's account of true philosophical virtue:

> The straight road to virtue does not lie in shifting pleasures for pleasures . . . imitating those who change large pieces of money for many small ones. Wisdom is the only true coin, with which we purchase fortitude, temperance,

---

[45] Plato, *Republic*, 430e ff.

[46] Helen F. North, *Sophrosyne: Self-Knowledge and Self-Restraint in Greek Literature* (Ithaca, NY: Cornell University Press, 1966): 150.

[47] David Lay Williams, 'The Platonic Soul of Rousseau's *Reveries*: The Role of Solitude in Rousseau's Democratic Politics', *History of Political Thought* 33:1 (2012): 87–123 (92–93).

[48] *Republic*, 68e.

INTRODUCTION

and justice. In a word, that virtue is always true which accompanies wisdom, without any dependence upon pleasures, grief, fears, or any other passions. Whereas all virtues stripped of wisdom, which run upon a perpetual exchange, are only shadows of virtue. True virtue is really a purgation of all these sorts of passions. Temperance, justice, fortitude, and prudence or wisdom itself, are not exchanges for passions; but cleanse us of them.[49]

By directing us to these passages, Rousseau's marginalia alert us to his engagement with a spectrum of views on *sophrosyne*: from an irrational temperance grounded in the exchange of pleasures to an extreme rationalist temperance involving the outright purging of pleasure. The account in the *Republic* falls somewhere in between as a kind of limited rationalist temperance involving the appropriate ordering of pleasures according to reason.

A similar spectrum lies behind Rousseau's concepts of both temperate sensuality and the Epicureanism of reason. In his autobiographical *Dialogues*, it is 'the mixture in most of his sensations' that allow him to enjoy a sensuality that was 'lively' yet 'never impetuous'. For this reason, he argued, he was best described as 'temperate rather than sober'. Nevertheless, Rousseau recognised that there was something paradoxical in the idea that temperance could be sensual. To clarify his position, he emphasised that 'this term sensuality must be confined to the meaning I give it'. That is, his version of sensuality was compatible with temperance because it could 'not be extended to those voluptuaries who make a vanity of being so, or who in their wish to exceed the limits of pleasure, fall into depravity' (*D*:114/1:807–808).

The same idea appears in his epistolary novel *Julie*. There, *Dialogues'* depraved voluptuaries are branded 'vulgar Epicureans' who, 'by racing after pleasures do not know how to experience it'. He contrasted this position with the 'opposite view' held by Julie. Her 'Epicureanism of reason' allows her to restrain her enjoyment of sensual pleasure whenever 'she enjoys it too much' and, by resuming it later, to 'enjoy it twice'. By so deferring gratification of her desire for pleasure, she 'maintains the control of [her] will' over herself, or practices *sophrosyne* (*J*:444/2:542). With these examples, Rousseau developed a hedonist theory of self-command that he defended from Socrates' derisive conclusion: the use of pleasure to restrain one's desire for pleasure was more than a mere 'temperance through intemperance'.

With these descriptions, Rousseau reconfigured the spectrum of *sophrosyne* he encountered and annotated in Plato. His 'sobriety' replaces Plato's philosophical virtue, the extreme avoidance of pleasure or purging of passion. At

---

[49] *Republic*, 69a.

the opposite end, Rousseau placed vulgar Epicureanism or depraved voluptuousness, an unrestrained libertinism even more extreme than Plato's irrational temperance. And because his temperance is sensual, it falls somewhere in between, as a sort of limited or refined hedonism. From this perspective, we can see why he might have been inclined to pass over the famous account of the virtues of the soul in Book IV of the *Republic*. His own view comes closest to Plato's irrational temperance. But by expanding his spectrum to include libertine hedonism, Rousseau recovered the view that Plato critically summarised as 'temperance through intemperance', re-describing it as 'temperance through sensuality'. In this way, Rousseau's hedonist version of *sophrosyne* avoided the exaggerated faith in the power of reason at the heart of Platonic philosophical virtue, and the paternalist, anti-democratic politics it supported. It was an ancient virtue, repurposed in support of Rousseau's vision of moral and political freedom in modern states.

Recognising the content of this idea allows us to understand why he expressed it in the terms that he did and, thereby, what he was trying to do in his political thought. The critique of vulgar Epicureanism in *Julie* was celebrated in the *Encyclopédie* article on temperance.[50] But Rousseau claimed no originality for it. In an unpublished fragment, which likely served as a draft of that discussion, he explained that he was simply following 'the true conclusion of Epicurus's doctrine' – namely, 'always to keep ourselves to the good that is closest to us'. The depraved voluptuary or vulgar Epicurean who pursues pleasure without restraint is, conversely, 'a madman who does not know what he wants, and does not understand anything in his master's system' (*E*:682/4:874). It was precisely its lack of originality, however, that made his Epicurean account of temperance useful. In this context, recovering a more authentic version of Epicureanism was useful because it functioned as an ideology critique – without lapsing into moralism or relying on unrealistic psychological assumptions, it allowed Rousseau to advocate moderation on the same hedonistic terms as the staunchest defenders of unrestrained consumption. It was also necessary for his system to cohere. For as I have suggested, Rousseau's theory of the modern state is founded on precisely this hedonistic view of moral and political agency. Insofar as the division of labour created structural incentives for the pursuit of self-interest, the moderns were Epicureans. But it remained to be seen what kind of Epicureans they would become.

---

[50] Chevalier Louis de Jaucourt, 'Tempérance', in *Encyclopédie, Ou Dictionnaire Raisonné Des Sciences, Des Arts et Des Métiers*, ed. Denis Diderot and Jean le Rond d'Alembert (Paris: Briasson, 1751–1772): 16:59.

2

Modern Epicureanism: Between Sociability and Atheism

Introduction

There are two standard ways of seeing eighteenth-century moral and political thought as in some sense 'Epicurean'. Most agree that Rousseau and his contemporaries were preoccupied with the problem of how to secure peace in increasingly unequal and divided societies. In one view, this preoccupation should be seen as an 'external' generalisation of the ancient Epicurean concern with 'internal' psychological tranquillity.[1] In another view, the concern with social peace is best seen as the practical motivation behind the development of a new theory of human nature.[2] Here, the central feature of eighteenth-century political thought is said to be the convergence of Augustinian pessimism and Epicurean animalism – the idea that human beings are self-interested and passionate creatures because we are fallen and material ones. This new view of human nature and moral agency is central because it came to underpin political economy as a new discursive framework. Of course, grounds for scepticism remain. Both views can be taken to imply the existence of something like an Epicurean 'tradition' of thought. Yet the uncertain epistemic status of traditions is well known. If understood in a narrow sense as a set of ideas whose essential meaning remains the same over a long stretch of time, then it is not clear that traditions can be said properly to exist as anything other than reified constructions imposed by the historian on the archive.[3] With worries of this

---

[1] Leo Strauss, *Philosophy and Law: Essays Toward the Understanding of Maimonides and His Predecessors*, trans. Fred Bauman (New York: Jewish Publication Society, 1987): 16–17.

[2] John Robertson, *The Case for the Enlightenment: Scotland and Naples 1680–1760* (Cambridge: Cambridge University Press, 2005).

[3] Skinner (1969): 37.

26   ROUSSEAU'S POLITICS OF TASTE

sort in the background, we might well be inclined to question whether 'the idea of an epicurean revival has genuine historical traction' at all.[4]

A response to such worries must begin by noting that Rousseau and his contemporaries frequently presented their positions as modern variants of ancient ones. Many eighteenth-century thinkers received a classical education; most of those who did not, like Rousseau, were familiar with the ancient philosophical schools. Kant noted that, like Montaigne and Hobbes before them, Mandeville and Helvétius had followed Epicurus in founding a morality of self-interest or self-love on internal, physical sensuality.[5] Against these modern Epicureans, Kant positioned the followers of the Third Earl of Shaftesbury, who himself had noted that his moral sense theory was part of the 'secret anti-Epicurean view' he had developed in his engagement with Hobbes and his teacher Locke.[6] From this perspective, the standard ways of approaching eighteenth-century Epicureanism at least partially reflect contemporary thinkers' understandings of their own age and activity. In short, this was the language they spoke. Yet, as the antagonism noted by Kant and Shaftesbury indicates, eighteenth-century thinkers received the ideas of Epicurus and the Epicurean tradition with ambivalence. For some, Epicurean hedonism offered a sanguine assessment of psychological motivation and moral evaluation. It was celebrated as being particularly well-suited to the emerging political-economic realities of commercial society. Precisely its reductive view of human nature, however, led others to view Epicureanism with apprehension. For them, Epicureanism was a pernicious influence on modern moral and political theory – a proto-anarchistic threat to community, social cohesion, and civic virtue.

In this chapter and the next, I reconstruct the context of eighteenth-century Epicureanism. While I take seriously the sceptical worry about reification, I argue that it is indeed possible to specify commonalities in what eighteenth-century authors thought they were doing in writing about Epicureanism or in identifying themselves and others as Epicurean. Such an enterprise, moreover, need not necessarily be committed to a strong but historically dubious notion of an Epicurean tradition. For part of my aim in these

---

[4] Richard Bourke, 'Revising the Cambridge School: Republicanism Revisited', *Political Theory* 46:3 (2018): 467–477 (475).

[5] Immanuel Kant, *Lectures on Ethics*, ed. P. Heath and J. B. Schneewind, trans. P. Heath (Cambridge: Cambridge University Press, 1997): 3, 48, 228, 240. Cf. Immanuel Kant, *Notes and Fragments*, ed. Paul Guyer, trans. Guyer et al. (Cambridge: Cambridge University Press, 2005): 421–425.

[6] Quoted in Lawrence E. Klein, *Shaftesbury and the Culture of Politeness: Moral Discourse and Cultural Politics in Early Eighteenth-Century England* (Cambridge: Cambridge University Press, 1994): 61.

MODERN EPICUREANISM

opening chapters is precisely to demonstrate the variability of – and to chart the shifts in – meanings of Epicureanism across eighteenth-century moral and political argument. When I refer to a tradition, then, I do so in the sense that Michael Oakeshott seems to have had in mind when he wrote:

> The most profound movement in modern political philosophy is, as I see it, a revivification of the Stoic natural law theory achieved by the grafting upon it an Epicurean theory; it springs from the union of the two great traditions of political philosophy inherited by Western Europe from the ancient world.[7]

If we understand tradition in a much broader sense similar to ideas of individual 'character', then the concept of an Epicurean tradition can be a useful way to make sense of the positions 'habitually' taken by thinkers, which avoids essentialism and permits a wide range of possible meanings.[8] And while Oakeshott issued this claim in a discussion of Hobbes, it foreshadows my presentation of Rousseau. For as we shall see, Rousseau argued that the true Epicurean is also a Stoic because a taste for true pleasure demands the exercise of self-command.

The core of my historical argument is that reconstructing this argumentative context is extremely useful for understanding Rousseau's political thought. The second *Discourse* was initially received as an Epicurean pamphlet. And Rousseau also intervened directly in an earlier debate to defend Alexander Pope from accusations of Epicureanism. Understanding his interventions might even be essential for understanding his political thought. He referred to the idea behind temperate sensuality or the taste for virtue as 'the Epicureanism of reason'. Why did he use that term, and what did he mean by it? What is the precise content of the idea behind it and how is it distinct from the 'vulgar Epicureanism' he wanted to reject? These questions can only fully be answered when seen in this context. And because, as I argue, the idea behind the terms demonstrates the consistency of his system, my exegetical argument must be grounded in a historical reconstruction of what it meant to be branded an Epicurean, and to self-identify as a particular kind of Epicurean, in Rousseau's immediate context.

This chapter focuses on contemporary critics of modern Epicureanism in eighteenth-century France. It presents a selective reception history to argue

---

[7] Michael Oakeshott, 'Dr Leo Strauss on Hobbes' (1937), reprinted in *Hobbes on Civil Association* (Oxford: Blackwell, 1974): 1.

[8] Following Duncan Kelly, *The State of the Political: Conceptions of Politics and the State in the Thought of Max Weber, Carl Schmitt, and Franz Neumann* (Oxford: Oxford University Press, 2003).

that the term 'Epicurean' had multiple meanings in the moral and political thought of the eighteenth century. Some critics, typically those who focused on Epicurus' hedonistic moral psychology, labelled Epicurean those thinkers who denied natural sociability – the existence of any strong natural tendency in humans to form social groups, and hence the possibility of durable moral consensus prior to or outside the coercive structure of the state.[9] For others, who instead focused on Epicurus' materialist natural philosophy, to label a thinker Epicurean was to label them an atheist, one who denied the existence of an immortal soul and God's providential governance of temporal affairs.[10] I argue that we should take this sort of polyvalence as a salutary caution against essentialising claims about a tradition of modern Epicureanism per se. But my argument is crucially not merely a sceptical one. For I also argue that precisely our recognition of this polyvalence enables us fruitfully to investigate the engagement with Epicureanism by particular thinkers or in particular texts. I show this by turning to Denis Diderot's *Encyclopédie* entry on 'Epicuréisme', written and published while he and Rousseau were still close friends. A comparative reading of Diderot's entry and his source material in Johan Jakob Brucker and Pierre Bayle demonstrates that Diderot used his discussion of Epicureanism to intervene directly in contemporary theological controversies over the immortal soul and a providential god. In this way, my reconstruction demonstrates that these issues of materialism must not be 'bracketed' when considering either the content of eighteenth-century Epicureanism or Rousseau's relationship to it.[11]

This perspective also allows us more fully to appreciate what was most distinctive about Rousseau's reception of Epicureanism. My reading of Diderot recovers aspects of the eighteenth-century debate that were broadly continuous with earlier discussions in biblical criticism, natural jurisprudence, and the history of science. But the debate was not merely derivative. Beginning in Chapter 3, we will see that important but largely unappreciated developments in the modern reception of Epicureanism did indeed occur in the eighteenth century. As thinkers concerned to identify the peculiarly 'modern' features of modern society increasingly focused on its 'commercial' character, they developed arguments about the imagination, the psychology of inequality, and taste

---

[9] Hont (2005): 39–45. Cf. Eva Piirimäe and Alexander Schmidt, 'Introduction: Between Morality and Anthropology – Sociability in Enlightenment Thought', *History of European Ideas* 41:5 (2015): 571–588.

[10] Leo Strauss, *Natural Right and History* (Chicago: University of Chicago Press, 1953): 266; 107–112, 168–168, 188–189, 169, 279. Cf. Leo Strauss, *Spinoza's Critique of Religion*, trans. E. M. Sinclair (Chicago, University of Chicago Press, 1950): 42–45.

[11] Cp. Istvan Hont, *Politics in Commercial Society* (London: Harvard University Press, 2015): 15.

MODERN EPICUREANISM

that they understood as developments of Epicureanism. There was a shift, in other words, from theology and ethics to aesthetics in the modern reception of Epicureanism – a shift that was in many ways crystallised in Rousseau's work.

Epicureanism in Modern France

Historiographical debates about Epicureanism stem at least in part from the instability that has plagued the philosophy throughout its tumultuous history. First articulated by Epicurus of Samos in fifth-century (BCE) Athens, the classical texts divide Epicureanism into the three 'divisions' of physics, epistemology, and ethics. Epicurean physics is founded on the principle that nothing exists other than matter in motion and the void, and that physical objects are produced by the chance concourse of indivisible and eternal atomic particles.[12] Epicurean epistemology understands perception to derive from particulate film or 'effluvia' emanating from physical objects and making contact with one's sensory apparatus.[13] These perceptions generate sensations of pleasure or pain, and Epicurean ethics deems those actions that procure pleasure to be 'good', while those that produce pain are 'bad'.[14] Rigidly materialistic, radically sensationalist, and resolutely hedonistic, Epicureanism is a systematic doctrine following from intuitive first principles.[15]

Despite its holistic nature, however, the intellectual history of Epicureanism is riddled with partial transmissions and frustrated receptions. Very few of Epicurus' writings are extant: only fragments survive of his twenty-seven-volume magnum opus *On Nature*; our main sources are the 'Letters' and 'Principal Doctrines' transmitted in Book X of Diogenes Laertius' third-century (BCE) *Lives and Opinions of the Eminent Philosophers*.[16] Epicurus' teachings survived as an oral tradition through the decline of Athens and the rise

---

[12] Epicurus, 'Letter to Herodotus', in Diogenes Laertius, *Lives of Eminent Philosophers*, Vol. II, trans R. D. Hicks (Cambridge, MA: Harvard University Press, 2000): 569–571 (§38–41); Lucretius, *On the Nature of Things*, trans. W. H. D. Rouse, revised by Martin Ferguson Smith (Cambridge, MA: Harvard University Press, 1992): 35–37, 43–49 (1.419–444, 503–598); hereafter *DRN*.

[13] Epicurus, 'Herodotus', 575–583 (§46–53), Lucretius, *DRN*, 295–297, 333–341 (4.230–328, 256–268, 722–822).

[14] Epicurus, 'Letter to Menoeceus', 653–657 (§127–132).

[15] For an overview, see A. A. Long, *Hellenistic Philosophy: Stoics, Epicureans, Sceptics* (Berkeley: University of California Press, 1986): 14–74. Cf. Victor Goldschmitt, *La doctrine d'Epicure et le droit* (Paris: Vrin, 1977).

[16] David Sedley, *Lucretius and the Transformation of Greek Wisdom* (Cambridge: Cambridge University Press, 1998): 94–132; Jørgen Mejer, *Diogenes Laertius and his Hellenistic Background* (Wiesbaden: Steiner, 1978).

30   ROUSSEAU'S POLITICS OF TASTE

of Rome, and for centuries the most cited sources of Epicureanism have been Roman ones – yet the only Roman text that can unproblematically be ascribed to a fully-fledged Epicurean, Lucretius' epic poem *De rerum natura*, was lost until its rediscovery in 1417 Florence.[17] Many of the most frequently cited secondary sources are critical interventions from those hostile to his philosophy's perceived religious and political implications. Sympathetic summaries and commentaries are generally faithful in their presentations of Epicurus' doctrines. However, even these often contain eclectic borrowings that tend to emphasise some of Epicureanism's closely integrated positions at the expense or to the exclusion of others. This combination of critical engagement and eclectic emphasis is simply characteristic of the reception of Epicureanism in eighteenth-century moral and political thought.

Take for example the Baron de Montesquieu's celebrated defence of luxury in his *Considerations on the Greatness of the Romans, and of their Decline* (1734). Montesquieu put a polemical twist on a familiar story. Ancient historians had conventionally ascribed the collapse of the Republic to the moral vices of ambition, avarice, luxury, and libido. These analyses were often used to support both Christian and republican critiques of luxurious consumption.[18] Against his contemporary followers of these 'ancients', however, Montesquieu joined the ranks of the modern defenders of luxury. Crucially for my purposes, his justification of luxurious consumption was a partial defence of the pursuit of pleasure he associated with Epicureanism.

> I believe that the Epicurean sect, which was introduced to Rome towards the end of the Republic, contributed much to the corruption of the heart and mind of the Romans. The Greeks had been infatuated with this sect before them; accordingly, they were sooner corrupt. Polybius tells us that in his time no Greek could be trusted on the security of his oath; whereas a Roman was, so to speak, inevitably bound by it.

---

[17] Ada Palmer, *Reading Lucretius in the Renaissance* (Cambridge, MA: Harvard University Press, 2014); Philip R. Hardie, *Lucretian Receptions: History, the Sublime, Knowledge* (Cambridge: Cambridge University Press, 2009); Eleni Kechagia, *Plutarch against Colotes: A Lesson in History of Philosophy* (Oxford: Oxford University Press, 2011); Holger Essler, 'Cicero's Use and Abuse of Epicurean Theology', in *Epicurus and the Epicurean Tradition*, ed. Jeffrey Fish and Kirk R. Sanders (Cambridge: Cambridge University Press, 2011): 129–151; John Ferguson, 'Epicureanism under the Roman Empire' (revised and supplemented by Jackson Hershbell), in *Aufstieg und Niedergang der römischen Welt*, ed. Hildegard Temporini and Wolfgang Haase, Vol. 2 Bd 36, Volume 2 (Berlin: de Gruyter, 1990): 2272.

[18] Barbara Levick, 'Morals, Politics, and the Fall of the Roman Republic', *Greece & Rome* 29:1 (1982): 53–62.

MODERN EPICUREANISM

Epicureanism had thus undermined Roman morals. But it was not a sufficient cause of the Republic's demise. Montesquieu saw the core of Rome's collapse as not a moral but a political failing – not hedonism, simply, but militaristic expansion and over-extension. For him, the 'martial virtues remained after all the others were lost' because Rome's republican institutional structure had enabled it to preserve its 'application to war in the midst of riches, indolence, and sensual pleasures'.[19]

Whereas Montesquieu's text emphasises the political implications of Epicurean hedonism, the original passage from Polybius to which he referred highlights the doctrine's theological implications. Montesquieu noted that 'religion is always the best guarantee one can have of man'.[20] His source, which makes no mention of Epicureanism, was far more effusive in this respect. After referring to their 'laws and customs in relation to the acquisition of wealth', Polybius isolated the Romans' superior moral rectitude in their belief in an afterlife:

> The quality in which the Roman commonwealth is most distinctly superior is in my opinion the nature of their religious convictions. I believe that it is the very thing, which among other peoples is the object of reproach. I mean superstition, which maintains the cohesion of the Roman state.

Because it was impossible that a state be composed entirely of philosophers, the state had to employ 'invisible terrors' and 'pageantry' instead of wisdom to regulate the 'lawless desires, unreasoned passion, and violent anger' of the people. For Polybius, the moral corruption of his contemporaries stemmed from their refusal to follow the Romans' example and institutionalise belief in immortality. Their actions, like those of the Epicureans, therefore lacked the regulative support provided by thoughts of the gods and the 'terrors of hell'.[21]

This subtle shift of emphasis from Polybius to Montesquieu indicates the variety of ways that Epicureanism was deployed in eighteenth-century debate. For some, Epicureanism provided a crucial conceptual armoury with which to advance a solution to the closely related problems of moral obligation and social cohesion under the conditions created by early commercial society. Here, historians of political thought emphasise both a 'convergence' of Epicurean and Augustinian theories of human nature and a general philosophical shift

---

[19] Charles de Secondat, Baron de Montesquieu, *Considerations sur les causes de la grandeur des Romains, et leur décadence* (Paris: Didot, 1802): 84, 86–87.
[20] Ibid.: 85.
[21] Polybius, *The Complete Histories of Polybius*, trans. W. R. Paton (London: Loeb, 1922): 6.56.

32   ROUSSEAU'S POLITICS OF TASTE

in focus from 'the passions' to 'the interests'.[22] This combination fruitfully elucidates the importance of Hellenistic thought to the rise of utilitarianism, political economy, and *doux commerce*; and French contributions to the luxury debates such as Jean-François Melon's *Political Essays on Commerce* (1734) and Voltaire's *Le Mondain* (1736).[23] For others, Epicureanism was the fundamental problem with which modern moral and political theory was forced to grapple. Such was the message the French *philosophes* received from two of their most important seventeenth-century predecessors. I have already noted Shaftesbury's explicit anti-Epicureanism. Similarly, Pufendorf's defence of natural sociability was part of his explicit opposition to the conventionalist account of justice that, he wrote, Hobbes had 'borrowed from Epicurus'.[24] The importance of these 'foreign' sources to the French *philosophes* is one reason to avoid framing the modern reception of Epicureanism through a narrowly national lens.

At the same time, we must avoid seeing discussions of Epicureanism in eighteenth-century France as merely derivative of earlier ones. Intellectual historians of the history of philosophy share my scepticism about reifying Epicureanism as a historical phenomenon: as in eighteenth-century France, so 'no one was an 'Epicurean' in some essentialist sense' in seventeenth-century England. Yet while this revisionist scholarship has correctly noted that the earlier 'historiographical obsession with English "Epicureanism"' is in many ways 'unjustified', it incorrectly argues that eighteenth-century intellectual combat was 'only a faint after-skirmish of the great campaigns of the seventeenth-century'.[25] Similarly, historians of natural philosophy and atheism in France imply that eighteenth-century discussions of Epicureanism are most significant for popularising interpretations developed in far more intellectually sophisticated ways by seventeenth-century authors, most with strong

---

[22] Jean Lafond, 'Augustinisme et épicurisme au XVIIe siècle', in *L'homme et son image: morales et littératures de Montaigne à Mandeville* (Paris: Champion, 1996): 345–368. Jean Lafond, *La Rochefoucauld, augustinisme et littérature* (Paris: Klincksieck, 1977). A. O. Hirschman, *The Passions and the Interests: Political Arguments for Capitalism Before its Triumph* (Princeton, NJ: Princeton University Press, 1977).

[23] For Voltaire, see André Morize, *L'apologie du luxe au XVIIIe siècle et 'Le mondain' de Voltaire; etude critique sur Le mondain et ses sources* (Paris, 1909). For Melon, see J. Bouzinac, *Les doctrines économiques au XVIIIe siècle. Jean-François Melon, économiste* (Toulouse, 1906). For an overview, see Hont (2006): 407–409.

[24] Samuel Pufendorf, *Of the Law of Nature and Nations*, trans. Mr. Carew (London: Knapton, 1729): Vol. 1/8, I.VII.13, 81; *Le droit de la nature et des gens*, trans. Jean Barbeyrac (Amsterdam: Kuyper, 1706): 113.

[25] Dmitri Levitin, *Ancient Wisdom in the Age of the New Science: Histories of Philosophy in England, c. 1640–1700* (Cambridge: Cambridge University Press, 2015): 4, 545–546, 229.

Christian commitments.[26] We should certainly reject the facile use of ancient labels to describe modern philosophical positions. One aim of this chapter and the next is to challenge the equally facile rejection of eighteenth-century uses of Epicureanism as unsophisticated by examining what the authors themselves thought of the ancient school.

When the ideas of Shaftesbury and Pufendorf crossed the Channel and the Rhine, they merged with French literary and philosophical traditions to produce an eclectic reception context. Michel de Montaigne and Pierre Charon are most often identified with the *nouvelle pyrrhonisme* of the sixteenth-century.[27] But Montaigne's *Essais* were also important for exposing eighteenth-century readers to many ideas of Epicurus and the Epicurean tradition.[28] The seventeenth-century 'erudite libertines' liked to add Epicurean arguments to their predecessors' scepticism.[29] Uriel da Costa drew on aspects of Epicurean theology and Pierre Gassendi presented an updated Epicurean physics.[30] Historians of science now consider Gassendi's 'baptized Epicureanism' to have been one of the most significant philosophical developments of the scientific revolution.[31] His harmonising Epicurean materialism with Christian belief in creation may have gone some way to facilitating the 'enlightened Epicureanism' of later religious thinkers who placed the height

---

[26] As implied in Alan Charles Kors, *Atheism in France, 1650–1729, Volume 1 – The Orthodox Sources of Disbelief* (Princeton, NJ: Princeton University Press, 1990), *Naturalism and Unbelief in France, 1650–1729* (Cambridge: Cambridge University Press, 2016), *Epicureans and Atheists in France, 1650–1729* (Cambridge: Cambridge University Press, 2016).

[27] Richard H. Popkin, *The History of Scepticism: From Savonarola to Bayle* (Oxford: Oxford University Press, 2003): 44–66.

[28] Michael Andrew Screech, *Montaigne's Annotated Copy of Lucretius: A Transcription and Study of the Manuscript, Notes and Pen-Marks* (Geneva: Droz, 1998): 24–25, 134–137.

[29] Jean Wirth, '"Libertins" et "Epicuriens": Aspects de l'irréligion au XVIe siècle', *Bibliothèque d'Humanisme et Renaissance* 39 (1997): 601–627. René Pintard, *Le libertinage érudit dans la première moitié du XVIIème siècle* (Geneva: Slatkine, 2000). Olivier Bloch, *Matières à histoires* (Paris: Vrin, 1997): 225–287. Françoise Charles-Daubert, 'Le "libertinage érudit": problems de définition', in *Libertinage et philosophie au XVII siècle*, ed. Antony McKenna and Pierre-François Moreau (Saint-Etienne: Université de Saint-Etienne, 1996): 11–25. J. S. Spink, *French Free-Thought from Gassendi to Voltaire* (New York: Athlone Press, 1960).

[30] Richard H. Popkin, 'Epicureanism and Skepticism in the Early 17th Century', *Philomathes* (1971): 346–357. Cf. Strauss (1950): 53–63.

[31] Margaret J. Osler, *Divine Will and the Mechanical Philosophy: Gassendi and Descartes on Contingency and Necessity in the Created World* (Cambridge: Cambridge University Press, 1994). Thomas M. Lennon, *The Battle of the Gods and Giants: Legacies of Descartes and Gassendi, 1655–1715* (Princeton, NJ: Princeton University Press, 1993). Antonia Lolordo, *Pierre Gassendi and the Birth of Early Modern Philosophy* (Cambridge: Cambridge University Press 2007). Catherine Wilson, *Epicureanism at the Origins of Modernity* (Oxford: Oxford University Press, 2008).

of pleasure in the love of God.[32] It was against this rather Stoic colour given to Epicureanism by Gassendi and his disciple François Bernier that Charles de Saint-Évremond presented the 'sceptical Epicureanism' he shared with Ninon de Lenclos and their many later admirers.[33] It was widely understood that this peculiarly Epicurean inflection of modern French philosophy had only intensified in the eighteenth century.

In this respect, it is especially instructive to consider the reports of foreign commentators on eighteenth-century French philosophical developments. The Irish Catholic Bishop Laurence Nihell, for example, constructed a rudimentary genealogy of modern Epicureanism. He identified several mid-century French *philosophes* as 'malignant wits' who had perverted the ingenious maxims of their master, the Duke de La Rochefoucauld.[34] As Nihell argued in the preface to his *Rational Self-Love*, modern moral philosophy was characterised by a fundamental misunderstanding of the nature of self-love in human motivation. While it was undeniable that, as he put it, 'our own good . . . is always the first object of our pursuit', this self-love was but 'the grand spring which Providence sets in motion to engage the attention of individuals to the great object of the general good'. Nihell attacked modern philosophers like Bernard Mandeville for erecting philosophical systems that were based on self-love but denied God's providential design. This generated the erroneous conclusion that 'our notions of right and wrong are essentially variable, and to be determined only by opinion'. On such a basis, he complained, there could be 'nothing permanent in the sentiment of virtue'. Quoting from John Brown's *Thoughts on Civil Liberty*, Nihell branded Mandeville, and the many modern thinkers that followed him, as having written with 'a pen truly Epicurean':

---

[32] Isaac Nakhimovsky, 'The Enlightened Epicureanism of Jacques Abbadie: L'Art de Se Connoître Soi-Même and the Morality of Self-Interest', *History of European Ideas* 29 (2003): 1–14. Lisa T. Sarasohn, *Gassendi's Ethics: Freedom in a Mechanistic Universe* (Ithaca, NY: Cornell University Press, 1996).

[33] Sylvia Murr, 'Bernier et Gassendi: une filiation déviationniste?', in *Gassendi et l'Europe*, ed. Sylvia Murr (Paris: Vrin, 1997): 71–114. Jean-Charles Darmon, 'Le Gassendism "frivole" de Saint-Évremond', in *Gassendi et l'Europe* (1997): 57–70. Cf. David Bensoussan, 'L'honnêteté chez Saint Evremond : élégance et commodité', in *L'Honnête homme et le dandy*, ed. Alain Montandon (Tübingen: Gunter Narr Verlag, 1993). Émile Magne, *Ninon de lanclos*, Vol. 3 (Paris: Emile-Paul, 1913, 1925, 1948), Vol. 2, 3–91. Edgar H. Cohen, *Mademoiselle Libertine: a portrait of Ninon de Lanclos* (Boston, MA: Houghton Mifflin, 1970): 62–70.

[34] Wit Sivasriyananda, *L'épicurisme de la Rochefoucauld* (Paris: Rodstein, 1939). Antony McKenna, 'Quelques aspects de la réception des Maximes en Angleterre', in *Images de la Rochefoucauld*, ed. J. Lafond and J. Mesnard (Paris: Presses Universitaires de France, 1984): 77–94. Cp. Vivien Thweatt, *La Rochefoucauld and the Seventeenth-Century Concept of the Self* (Geneva: Droz, 1980): 10–14; 150–151.

MODERN EPICUREANISM

'these seducing opinions', he cautioned his readers, 'softly . . . glide into the soul, and assume, in a little time, the appearance of reason'.[35]

Emphasising the irreligious implications of modern Epicureanism, this representation of the doctrine as a seductive intoxicant cleared the ground for Nihell's subtle reworking of a famous image from Lucretius. At the opening of Book IV of *De rerum natura*, Lucretius likened the effect of his beautiful verse to that of the honey placed around the rim of the physician's medicine cup: both were palliatives for the bitter but necessary medicine within. For Lucretius, Epicureanism was the medicine that would cure the psychological intoxication brought on by religious superstition, the central barrier to worldly happiness.[36] It was a typical rhetorical strategy of modern critics instead to present Epicureanism itself as the poison. Playing further on the image, Nihell described *De rerum natura* as 'a work replete with impiety and beauty', one through which Lucretius 'presented the intoxicating cup' of Epicureanism to his Roman audience, who then 'tasted, and drank deep of the delicious poison'.[37] Nihell identified Diderot, La Mettrie, and Helvétius as recent French thinkers to have presented the Epicurean poison in a modern cup. Changing the metaphor, he singled out their respective *Pensées Philosophiques* (1746), *L'Homme Machine* (1747), and *De L'Esprit* (1758) as works that, 'like the spider's web, seem calculated only for the poor and unmanly purpose of ensnaring flies, and taking advantage of the natural curiosity of men to betray them into the pernicious schemes of irreligion, or modern Epicureism'.[38] Nihell signalled his further intellectual debt to John Brown by grounding this genealogy of modern Epicureanism in Mandeville and Hobbes, who took up the 'general principles of the Epicurean philosophy . . . with all their horrid train of errors, and impiety'; all of their work had the 'same general tendency to overthrow morality'

---

[35] Laurence Nihell, *Rational Self-Love; or, a Philosophical and Moral Essay on the Natural Principles of Happiness and Virtue. With Reflections on the Various Systems of Philosophers* (London: W. Griffin, 1770): viii, ix, x, xiii. Cf. John Brown, *Thoughts on Civil Liberty, on Licentiousness and Faction* (Dublin: White and Saint, 1765): 110.

[36] Lucretius, *DRN*: 277 (4.11–23).

[37] Nihell (1770): xiv. Admiration and even imitation of the formal properties of Lucretius' poem did not, of course, entail any necessary adoption of its content: see Wolfgang Bernard Fleischmann, 'The Debt of the Enlightenment to Lucretius', *Studies on Voltaire and the Eighteenth-Century* 25 (1963): 631–643.

[38] Nihell (1770): xxii. Cf. James Steintrager, 'Oscillate and Reflect: La Mettrie, Materialist Physiology, and the Revival of the Epicurean Canonic', in *Dynamic Reading: Studies in the Reception of Epicureanism*, ed. Brooke Holmes and W. H. Shearin (Oxford: Oxford University Press, 2012): 162–198. Charles T. Wolfe, 'A Happiness Fit for Organic Bodies: La Mettrie's Medical Epicureanism', in *Epicurus in the Enlightenment*, ed. N. Leddy and A. Lifschitz (Oxford: SVEC, 2009): 69–84. Pierre Force, 'Helvétius as an Epicurean Political Theorist', in *Epicurus in the Enlightenment*, 105–118.

36 ROUSSEAU'S POLITICS OF TASTE

precisely because they all rest on the same Epicurean foundations.[39] Brown's *Essays* on Shaftesbury had similarly ranked 'Mr. Hobbes, Dr. Mandeville, and several *French* writers' among the 'modern patronisers' of 'the *Epicurean* sect'.[40]

Identifications of Hobbes as an Epicurean in the eighteenth century were just as often intended to highlight not his atheism but his denial of natural sociability. The question of whether or not human beings are naturally sociable has been called 'the great ideological divide of the eighteenth century'.[41] As Mandeville presented the debate, modern Stoics or Christians followed the Aristotelian view that human beings are by nature political animals or *polis* beings (*zoon politikon*), arguing that there is 'in the mind of man a natural affection that prompts him to love his species'. Against this positive or benevolent 'thick' sociability, vulgar Epicureans or Hobbists posited a pure natural unsociability, arguing that humans were 'born with hatred and aversion, that makes us wolves and bears to one another'. Mandeville's own position was part of the more interesting debate that took place between these extremes. Humans do not have any inherent 'love to others'. But their natural self-love and physical weakness (*imbecillitas*) give them a sort of 'thin' sociability: 'the love man has for his ease and security, and his perpetual desire of meliorating his condition, must be sufficient motives to make him fond of society; considering the necessitous and helpless condition of his nature'.[42] Within this view, sociability is 'natural' in the sense that society follows directly from an attribute of human nature. But sociability is 'unnatural' in the sense that society is only indirectly sociable, not intentionally or directly.

In France, the emphasis on Hobbes' Epicurean denial of natural sociability had much to do with Jean Barbeyrac's remarkably influential translation of Pufendorf's *Law of Nature*. Pufendorf had criticised Hobbes for rejecting the traditional distinction between commutative and distributive justice and, instead, advancing 'one single notion of justice to comprehend every kind; making it nothing but a keeping of faith and fulfilling of covenants'.[43] For Pufendorf, Hobbes was simply updating Epicurus' well-known theory of justice as 'a pledge of reciprocal usefulness', 'not a thing in its own right' but 'a pact about neither harming one another nor being harmed'.[44] Moreover, in

---

[39] Nihell (1770): 94, xxiii.

[40] John Brown, *Essays on the Characteristics of the Earl of Shaftesbury* (London: C. Davis, 1750): 170. Cf. Hundert (1994): 43–50.

[41] Hont (2005): 142.

[42] Bernard Mandeville, *The Fable of the Bees: Or, Private Vices, Publick Benefits*, ed. F. B. Kaye, 2 vols (London: Oxford University Press, 1924): 2: 178–180.

[43] Pufendorf (1729): 81; (1706): 113.

[44] Epicurus, 'Sovereign Maxims': 673–675 (§31, 33).

the lengthy history of moral philosophy with which he introduced the text, Barbeyrac himself identified Hobbes as an Epicurean for his denial of natural sociability. For him, Hobbes' *De Cive* contained many 'dangerous errors', all of which derived from endeavouring to establish the 'principle of Epicurus; which makes self-preservation and self-interest . . . the original causes of civil society'.[45] In this way, Hobbes' characterisations of the state of nature as a state of war and his solution of absolute sovereignty were taken to have been erected on an Epicurean foundation.

Barbeyrac's account of Hobbes' Epicureanism was subsequently reproduced almost verbatim in the *Encyclopédie* article on natural right. In the fifth volume, the jurist Antoine-Gaspard Boucher d'Argis followed Barbeyrac and wrote that Hobbes' *De Cive* was constructed on the foundation of 'the moral philosophy of Epicurus' – that 'dangerous opinion . . . that the primary purpose of societies is self-preservation and private utility'. Just as Brown and Nihell would later do with Mandeville, Boucher identified Hobbes' assertions of the essential variability, subjective determination, and impermanence of moral values as evidence of his Epicureanism. Concluding his discussion by dismissing Hobbes' account of the state of nature, Boucher refused even to engage with a 'pernicious system' founded on these 'easily recognized' Epicurean errors.[46]

French writers seeking to reject the vulgar Epicurean or Hobbist denial of sociability often turned to the rich moral psychology of neo-Augustinian political theology. Following Augustine, especially those with links to Jansenism saw original sin as a kind of perverted will rooted in pride, an excessive love of self that was starkly opposed to the love of God. Humans are not naturally sociable because, in our fallen state, we are dominated by pride and self-love.[47] For Pierre Nicole, the Fall so diminished human moral capacities that we are incapable of showing either humility to God or love, charity, and respect to others. But pride can still generate cooperation because it leads us to seek pleasures that are secured by increasing our relative standing in the eyes of others. If pride meant that our fallen nature is unsociable, it was nevertheless a constructive force that stimulated sociability through emulation, exchange, and commerce. But it always remained a destructive force, driving us to injustice and disorder. Like Hobbes, Nicole argued that the double-bind of pride meant that durable sociability required state sovereignty. With disciplinary power in place, we could redirect our pride to other modes of competition and learn

---

[45] Pufendorf (1729): 67; (1706): lxxix.

[46] Antoine-Gaspard Boucher d'Argis, 'Droit de la Nature, ou Droit naturel', in *Encyclopédie* (1755): 5: 131–134 (132–133).

[47] Augustine, *The City of God Against the Pagans*, ed. and trans. R. W. Dyson (Cambridge: Cambridge University Press, 1998): 608–610.

38   ROUSSEAU'S POLITICS OF TASTE

to simulate something like 'morality' to attract the positive appreciation of others.[48]

The other standard way of arriving at this middle position between thick sociability and its vulgar denial was by juxtaposing Pufendorf to Hobbes as representing rival positions in modern natural law theory.[49] Rousseau famously deployed this argumentative strategy in the second *Discourse*:

> Hobbes contends that man is naturally intrepid, and seeks only to attack, and to fight. An illustrious philosopher [Montesquieu] thinks, on the contrary, and Cumberland and Pufendorf also maintain, that nothing is as timid as man in the state of nature, and that he is forever trembling, and ready to flee at the least noise that strikes him, at the least movement he notices. (*DI*:135/3:136)

The degree to which Pufendorf was able to overcome Hobbes' denial of sociability with his own principle of *socialitas* is the subject of disagreement. Indeed, some doubt whether he genuinely intended to do so.[50] Rousseau famously rejected both positions. He insisted that the first humans in the state of nature were radically isolated and self-sufficient. This meant that the combined effect of the physical sentiments of self-preservation and pity would have been sufficient to unite them together in society without the need to introduce any notion of natural sociability (127, 149/3:126, 151).[51] As we will see in Chapter 3, precisely advancing this 'thin' account of sociability and rejecting

---

[48] Pierre Nicole, 'Of Charity and Self-Love', in Bernard Mandeville, *The Fable of the Bees and Other Writings*, ed. E. J. Hundert (Indianapolis, IN: Hackett, 1997): 1–9. Cf. Hont (2005): 47–51.

[49] Richard Tuck, *Natural Rights Theories: Their Origin and Development* (Cambridge: Cambridge University Press, 1979). Cf. David Saunders, 'The Natural Jurisprudence of Jean Barbeyrac: Translation as an Art of Political Adjustment', *Eighteenth-Century Studies* 36:4 (2003): 473–490.

[50] Compare Fiammetta Palladini, *Samuel Pufendorf Discepolo di Hobbes* (Bologna: Il Mulino, 1990) and Istvan Hont, 'The Language of Sociability and Commerce: Samuel Pufendorf and the Foundations of Smith's "Four Stages" Theory', in *Languages of Political Theory in Early-Modern Europe*, ed. A. Pagden (Cambridge: Cambridge University Press, 1986): 271–316 with Richard Tuck, *The Rights of War and Peace: Political Thought and the Intellectual Order from Grotius to Kant* (Oxford: Oxford University Press, 1999): 152, T. J. Hochstrasser, *Natural Law Theories in the Early Enlightenment* (Cambridge: Cambridge University Press, 1994), and Kari Saastamoinen, *The Morality of the Fallen Man: Samuel Pufendorf on Natural Law* (Helsinki: Societas Historica Finlandiae, 1995).

[51] Cf. Robert Wokler, 'Rousseau's Pufendorf: Natural Law and the Foundations of Commercial Society', *History of Political Thought* 15:3 (1994): 373–402 and Gabriella Silvestrini, 'Rousseau, Pufendorf and the Eighteenth-Century Natural Law Tradition', *History of European Ideas* 36:3 (2010): 280–301.

MODERN EPICUREANISM

39

the naturalness of 'thick' ties of friendship and community led to accusations of Rousseau's Epicureanism.

Rousseau's friend Diderot deployed the same bifurcation to side decisively with Pufendorf in a critique of Hobbes. His own entry on natural right appeared in the same volume of the *Encyclopédie* as Boucher's article. In it, Diderot presented a speech from a 'violent interlocutor', a Hobbesian natural man who assumes the natural right of each individual to 'determine the nature of justice and injustice'. In response, Diderot expanded Pufendorf's *socialitas* into the twin notions of a 'society of mankind' and a 'general will' of the human race. In this way, he sought to refute the denial of natural sociability that he, Rousseau, and their contemporaries associated with both Hobbes and Epicurus.[52]

The fifth volume of the *Encyclopédie* offers a unique lens through which to view the reception of Epicureanism in eighteenth-century France. Boucher invoked the Epicurean tradition to discuss sociability in natural law debates about human nature and the foundations of justice. It is significant that, in his parallel discussion, Diderot did not. But he did discuss the doctrine in great detail in the same fifth volume. As we will see in the next section, his article on Epicureanism is animated by his concerns with materialism, the immortality of the soul, and the nature of divinity, rather than his concern with sociability. This is perhaps unsurprising, both biographically and contextually. Diderot's long-standing interest in materialism is well known.[53] In the late seventeenth century, the writings of English theologians and philosophers such as John Toland and Anthony Collins crossed the Channel and combined with continental advances in medical science to produce a materialist vision of human nature that was 'inextricably linked to thinking about the soul'.[54] Moreover, when Diderot was writing at mid-century, suspicion over sensationalism and Locke's 'thinking matter' hypothesis was at a fever pitch.[55] The initial furore

---

[52] Denis Diderot, 'Droit Naturel', *Encyclopédie* 5 (1755b): 115–116. See Jacques Proust, 'La contribution de Diderot à l'Encyclopédie et les théories du droit naturel', *Annales historiques de la révolution française* 173 (1963): 257–286. Cf. Céline Spector, 'De Diderot à Rousseau: La double crise du droit naturel moderne', in *Jean-Jacques Rousseau, Du contract social ou Essai sur la forme de la République: manuscrit de Genève: Textes et Commentaires*, ed. B. Bachofen, B. Bernardi, and G. Olivo (Paris: Vrin, 2012): 141–153.

[53] See Annie Ibrahim, *Diderot: Un matérialisme éclectique* (Paris: Vrin, 2010).

[54] Ann Thomson, *Bodies of Thought: Science, Religion, and the Soul in the Early Enlightenment* (Oxford: Oxford University Press, 2008): 3. Cf. Gabriel Bonno, *La culture et la civilisation britanniques devant l'opinion française de la paix d'Utrecht aux Lettres philosophiques* (Philadelphia, PA: American Philosophical Society, 1948).

[55] John Yolton, *Locke and French Materialism* (Oxford: Oxford University Press, 1991). S. J. Savonius, 'Locke in French', *Historical Journal* 47:1 (2004): 45–79.

arose when Voltaire introduced the hypothesis to a French audience in his *Lettres philosophiques* (1734). After a brief moment of relative calm, the controversy was rekindled when the Faculty of Theology at the Sorbonne passed the Abbé de Prades' thesis (1751), which questioned Christ's miracles and traditional Christian morality from sensationalist premises.[56] The so-called de Prades affair combined with Condillac's updated sensationalism in the *Treatise on Sensations* (1754) to render the sensationalism of the Encyclopédists unacceptable to political and religious orthodoxy alike.[57] Diderot took the need for an *Encyclopédie* entry on Epicureanism as an opportunity to intervene directly in these controversies.

Epicureanism was not a univocal concept in eighteenth-century France. As the foregoing survey demonstrates, the self-interested pursuit of pleasure and other ideas associated with Epicurus and the Epicurean tradition were with almost equal regularity taken to signify a denial of either natural sociability or the immaterial soul and God's providence. While these were understood as different aspects of a coherent doctrine, eighteenth-century writers typically used the term 'Epicurean' itself to refer to one rather than the other, at least in the first instance. My reconstruction of this complex reception context demonstrates that we should reject any essentialist understandings of *an* 'Epicurean' tradition or its revival in 'the Enlightenment'. However, rather than resting comfortably with this merely sceptical conclusion, the following section shows that precisely an awareness of the variability of Epicureanism allows us fruitfully to engage with its use in particular eighteenth-century texts. Such awareness allows us more clearly to understand what, precisely, Epicureanism is doing in and for a given author. Not despite but because of the equivocal nature of Epicureanism in eighteenth-century France, then, I now turn to Diderot's *Encyclopédie* entry 'Epicuréisme ou Epicurisme'.[58]

---

[56] Jeffrey D. Burson, *The Rise and Fall of Theological Enlightenment: Jean-Martin de Prades and Ideological Polarization in Eighteenth-Century France* (Notre Dame, IN: University of Notre Dame Press, 2010). John S. Spink, 'L'Abbé philosophe: l'affaire de J.-M. de Prades', *Dix-huitième siècle* 3 (1971): 145–180.

[57] Avi Lifschitz, *Language and Enlightenment: The Berlin Debates of the Eighteenth Century* (Oxford: Oxford University Press, 2012): 16–39. Although Condillac's 1746 *Essai sur l'origine des connaissances humaines* was arguably more radical for attempting explicitly to go beyond Locke, it occasioned somewhat less controversy than the 1754 *Treatise*.

[58] For brief discussions of Diderot's entry, see Natania Meeker, 'Sexing Epicurean Materialism in Diderot', in Leddy and Lifschitz (2009): 83–100 (91–94) and Thomas M. Kavanagh, *Enlightened Pleasures: Eighteenth-Century France and the New Epicureanism* (New Haven, CT: Yale University Press, 2010).

Diderot on 'Epicuréisme'

Also published in the fifth volume of the *Encyclopédie* in 1755, Diderot's entry on Epicureanism was a direct intervention in contemporary theological debates. Comparing the 'Epicuréisme' article with Diderot's source material demonstrates the controversial intention behind his position on the immortal soul and a providential God. As we will see, Diderot actively edited the source from which he transcribed the majority of his entry, Johann Jakob Brucker's account of 'the philosophy of Epicurus'. In doing so, he foregrounded the materialist premises of Epicureanism aggressively to conclude that 'the human soul is corporeal'.[59] Consideration of the entry on Epicurus in Pierre Bayle's *Dictionnaire Histoire et Critique* further illustrates Diderot's polemical intentions, which were readily apparent to his early critics.

Laurence Nihell had good reason for branding Diderot's *Pensées philosophiques* (1746) an Epicurean text. Diderot engaged extensively with Epicureanism; the influence of Lucretius in particular impelled his reflections upon materialism and determinism to such an extent that it affected every facet of his work.[60] The very aims of the *Encyclopédie* itself embody the Epicurean belief that a careful study of nature leads, in Diderot's words, 'to knowledge which will ensure peace in his soul, frees the mind from all vain terrors, raises him to the level of the gods and returns him to the only real reasons that he has to fulfil his duties'.[61] While Diderot was given a Jesuit education and was received into the clerical order, he had come to identify as a deist by the time he wrote the *Pensées*. He published the work anonymously to protect himself from the storm of criticism he quite rightly anticipated. Of the many sections objectionable to orthodox readers, 'Pensée 15' is of particular relevance for our purposes. For not only does Diderot there address the key points of contemporary religious controversy but, crucially, the monologue with which it begins articulates a distinctly Epicurean critique of religion. Diderot's hypothetical atheist denies outright both the existence of God and creation, and he is sceptical about the immortality of the soul. Even if

---

[59] Diderot, 'Epicuréisme ou Epicurisme', in *Encyclopédie, ou Dictionnaire raisonné des sciences, des arts et des métiers*, ed. D. Diderot and J. d'Alembert, 17 vols (Paris, 1751–1772 (1755a)): 5: 779–785 (782).

[60] See in particular the detailed studies by Moishe Black, 'Lucretius tells Diderot: Here's the Plan', *Diderot Studies* 28 (2000): 39–58 and 'Lucretius's Venus Meets Diderot', *Diderot Studies* XXVII (1997): 29–40. Cf. the more general but particularly vehement studies by the Catholic historian C. A. Fusil, 'Lucrèce et les philosophes du XVIIIe siècle', *Revue d'histoire littéraire de la France* 35 (1928): 194–210. C. A. Fusil, 'Lucrèce et les littérateurs, poètes et artistes du XVIIIe siècle', *Revue d'histoire littéraire de la France* 37 (1930): 161–176.

[61] Diderot (1755a): 783.

42 ROUSSEAU'S POLITICS OF TASTE

some form of intelligent design was to be granted in the *physical* universe, he argues that 'the confusions in the moral order' would nevertheless negate providence. Finally, these disputes over the immortal soul and the intelligent production of a providentially conserved world are said to result from ignorance of the nature of matter in motion: simply 'because I do not see how motion could have caused this universe', the atheist argues, 'it is ridiculous to solve the difficulty by supposing the existence of a being of whom I can have no real conception'.[62]

Writing as the atheist's interlocutor, Diderot offered no defence of theism, orthodox or otherwise. Instead, he argued for the necessity of moving beyond mere philosophical argument to refute the atheist's case. Not 'the vain speculations of metaphysics' but the discoveries of Newton and others had left 'that dangerous hypothesis' of materialism 'tottering'. The 'subtleties of ontology' could, at best, encourage scepticism. Knowledge of nature, alone, belonged to the 'true deists'. Natural mechanism afforded even more conclusive proof of intelligent design than did traditional arguments founded on the premise of human rationality. The latter were susceptible to scepticism insofar as external actions required the further unfounded supposition of rationality. They certainly could not show that reason had been providentially endowed.[63]

Diderot was aware that his text would be received with hostility. He distinguished between atheist unbelief, sceptical doubt, and the deist who 'maintains the existence of a God, the immortality of the soul, and its consequences'. But he knew that orthodox readers would see little more than variations of the same irreligious themes. 'I know the zealots well', he wrote, and they are quick to take offence. Once it was decided that 'this work contains something repugnant to their ideas', he would be excoriated publicly. To only be called 'a deist and wretch' would be to 'get off lightly'. After presenting his text as a link in the great chain of religiously suspect philosophers – 'Descartes, Montaigne, Locke and Bayle' – he offered an explicit profession of faith as a precautionary measure.[64] But its dubious sincerity was evident, and the *Pensées* was burned by the Paris censors for having been found, along with La Mettrie's *Histoire naturelle de l'âme*, to be 'contrary to religion and to good morals'.[65] Only the book's anonymous publication saved Diderot from imprisonment.

---

[62] Denis Diderot, *Diderot's Early Philosophical Writings*, trans. Margaret Jourdain (London: Open Court, 1916): 33.

[63] Ibid.: 34, 35, 38.

[64] Ibid.: 40, 63, 33.

[65] Parlement de Paris, *Arrest de la cour du parlement, qui condamne deux livres intitulez: l'un, Histoire naturelle de l'ame; l'autre, Pensées philosophiques, à être lacerez ûlez par l'exécuteur de la haute-justice, comme scandaleux, contraires à la religion, & aux bonnes mœurs'* (7 juillet, 1746).

MODERN EPICUREANISM

When he published the *Letter on the Blind* (1749), Diderot was emboldened. Exercising no such caution, he issued an eloquent refutation of this very same deist position. Without an equivalent profession of faith and with his name attached, he was famously imprisoned at Vincennes for three months as a result.[66] Late in the *Letter*, the clergyman 'Holmes' visits the blind mathematician 'Saunderson' on his deathbed to debate the existence of God. Holmes begins with an argument from natural design, which of course does nothing to persuade his blind interlocutor. Saunderson's crucial argument is the sceptical one: even if the 'animal mechanism' of nature were 'perfect', its perfection still would not entail the existence of 'a supremely intelligent Being'. The deist experiences nature with 'astonishment' simply because of the human tendency to explain what we do not understand as a 'miracle'. Diderot thus has Saunderson follow Lucretius and Epicurus in deriding the customary recourse to divine intelligence as the work of ignorance, vanity, and pride, not philosophy.[67] Undeterred, Holmes next appeals to authority. He cites 'Newton, Leibniz [and] Clarke' as men of probity who had argued for the existence of intelligent creation on the basis of empirical observation. While Saunderson defers to these illustrious authorities on the 'admirable design and order' in the 'present state of the universe', he insists on maintaining 'liberty of thought' regarding its 'ancient and primitive state'. Without a witness of its origin, there was no guarantee that this order had always persisted. Thus, neither natural design nor appeals to authority can erode Saunderson's Epicurean-tinged scepticism.

Crucially for our purposes, Diderot drew directly on Lucretius' proto-evolutionary arguments to compose Saunderson's counterarguments. First, it was just as likely that the material universe was initially organised with 'defective combinations' that had disappeared, with only those 'whose mechanism was not defective in an important particular' being eventually able to support and perpetuate themselves. Second, even if one granted that the present state of the material world was both perpetual and perpetually governed by Newton's laws, one could not rule out the possible existence of other worlds, in both past and present. Finally, Diderot has Saunderson put forth the basic Epicurean premise that the material world is a 'rapid succession of beings' with a 'continual tendency to destruction'; it exhibits 'a merely transitory symmetry and momentary appearance of order'. The belief that its present stability and reg-

---

[66] See Kate E. Tunstall, *Blindness and Enlightenment: An Essay. With a New Translation of Diderot's Letter on the Blind and La Mothe Le Vayer's 'Of a Man Born Blind'* (London: Continuum, 2011): 115–118 for Epicureanism.

[67] Diderot (1916): 109–110.

44   ROUSSEAU'S POLITICS OF TASTE

ularity was eternal was the result of humanity's limited temporal perspective, our tendency to 'measure duration by our own existence'.[68]

At least two notable conclusions follow from this brief discussion of the Epicurean dimensions of Diderot's early writings. First, though the list is far from exhaustive, Diderot engaged directly with several issues of active theological controversy in mid-century Paris: the existence of God; the act of creation; the immateriality of the soul; the nature of motion; providence; and multiple worlds. Second, we see how these components could be linked together systematically in argument. Intervening in this debate and over these particular issues was an abiding concern of Diderot's in his pre-*Encyclopédie* phase, and he drew heavily on arguments derived from Lucretius in doing so. With this concern and context in mind, we can now examine Diderot's 'Epicuréisme' article in detail. As we will see, he used Epicureanism to challenge the same controversial issues.

As with his relationship to Epicureanism, so is the complex nature of Diderot's role as editor of the *Encyclopédie* beyond the scope of our discussion.[69] What concerns me here and in what follows is Diderot's use of Johann Jakob Brucker's *Historia critica philosophiae* as a source. He is widely acknowledged to have borrowed heavily from Brucker, even translating into French from the original Latin and excerpting long passages verbatim. Diderot made modifications to both the structural presentation of Brucker's article and to more technical points of interpretation.[70] Most importantly, he deliberately and explicitly foregrounded the Epicurean account of the contemporary theological controversies over the material composition of God and the soul, placing them under the new heading 'On Theology'. A detailed comparison of Diderot's entry with his source material in Brucker clarifies the unique contributions of Diderot's entry, the reception of Epicureanism in his immediate context, and especially the polemical intentions behind his own reception of it.

Both Brucker and Diderot introduced the Epicurean sect as the least understood and most slandered in the history of philosophy. This distorting reception history required that Brucker present the doctrines of Epicurus with 'accuracy and diligence' in the hope of enabling his reader to 'form a judgment' freely. Diderot echoed this rationale but went further, placing Epicurus' doctrines in

---

[68] Ibid.: 111–114. Cp. Lucretius, *DRN* (5.783–925): 439–451. Cf. Gordon Campbell, *Lucretius on Creation and Evolution: A Commentary on De Rerum Natura 5.772–1104* (Oxford: Oxford University Press, 2003).

[69] Jacques Proust, *Diderot et l'Encyclopédie* (Paris: A. Colin, 1962). John Lough, *Essays on the Encyclopédie of Diderot and D'Alembert* (Oxford: Oxford University Press, 1968).

[70] Comparing Diderot (1755a) and Johann Jakob Brucker, *The History of Philosophy, from the Earliest Times to the Beginning of the Present Century; Drawn up from Brucker's Historia Critica Philosophiae* trans. and ed. William Enfield (London: J. Johnson, 1791).

MODERN EPICUREANISM

the mouth of the philosopher himself, writing 'it is he who is going to speak in the rest of our article'.[71] Moreover, whereas Brucker had clarified that many of Epicurus' followers had disgraced their sect through licentious behaviour, Diderot's distancing strategy permitted him to claim that all Epicureans 'were exceptionally honourable people' undeserving of their terrible reputation.[72] With this rhetorical strategy, then, Diderot attempted to protect himself from accusations of personal adherence to or sympathies with such statements and the doctrines he adumbrated. The strong claims that he presumed himself able to make take on new resonance when viewed in the light of the valuable history of modern Epicureanism that concludes his entry. Once again, Diderot began by following Brucker; but he borrowed relatively sparingly from the detailed biography of Epicurus, preferring instead to devote more space to recent developments in the Epicurean revival. He characterised these developments as undeniably French, presenting Gassendi in proto-nationalistic terms as doing honour to both 'Philosophy and the nation' by his efforts. Indeed, Diderot's praise that 'there was never a philosopher who was a better humanist, nor a humanist a better philosopher' is wildly exaggerated in relation to Brucker's muted mention of Gassendi's 'uncommon abilities'.[73] After referring briefly to Bernier, Saint-Évremond, and Rochefoucauld, among others, the article finishes with the resounding conclusion: 'Epicureanism has never had more radiance than in France, and above all during the last century.'[74]

Diderot's first direct engagement with the Epicurean arguments concerning the denial of providence and belief in the material soul comes in the article's account of plants and animals. To conclude this section of the article, he followed Brucker and treated Epicurus' famous explanation of body parts and organs – though his more succinct formulations were likely more offensive to orthodox sensibilities: 'the eyes have not been made in order to see, nor feet in order to walk: but the animal had feet, and it walked; eyes, and it saw'.[75] This anti-teleological argument went directly against the orthodox view of the functions, capacities, and faculties of the human being as providentially endowed gifts of a creating God. It also was inextricably linked to the Epicurean treatment of both the *nature* and the *condition* of the Gods. As we will see, it is here that the concerns with sociability and atheism most frequently converged.

Diderot and Brucker both drew on Pierre Bayle's entry on Epicurus in his *Dictionnaire Histoire et Critique*. There, they encountered Bayle's view that

---

[71] Brucker (1791): 446; cf. 451; Diderot (1755a): 779.
[72] Brucker (1791): 456; Diderot (1755a): 779.
[73] Diderot (1755a): 782; Brucker (1791): 466.
[74] Diderot (1755a): 785.
[75] Diderot (1755a): 782; Brucker (1791): 469.

Epicurus taught reverence of the gods because it was right for human beings to 'respect and honour all that is great and perfect'.[76] The crucial idea here is 'perfection'. Because the gods are perfect beings, it follows for Epicurus that they must be perfectly happy. For their felicity to be truly perfect, moreover, it must be constant and unalterable. But providential governance through miraculous intervention in the material world would constitute an alteration of the gods' condition. Therefore, Bayle writes, 'Epicurus confined the divine nature to a state of inactivity [and] took from it the government of the world'. Such is the foundation of Epicurus' teaching that his followers should neither hope for benefits nor fear harm from the gods.[77]

God's providential direction of temporal affairs is obviously a central principle of Christian doctrine. Providence, though, has never been *simply* a theological problem. Or, put differently, providence has always been a theological problem with significant political implications. As Voltaire noted, the 'moral question' of the possibility of a society of atheists was 'set in action' by Bayle's 1682 *Various Thoughts on the Occasion of a Comet*. There, Bayle asserted that, so far as 'manners and civil life' were concerned, a 'commonwealth of atheists' would be no different than a 'commonwealth of pagans'. While a society of atheists would require 'severe and well-executed' laws, this could be said of all societies. Indeed, Bayle continued, it was not religious belief but conventional, human laws that served as the 'foundation of human virtue'.[78] He reiterated this claim in the *Dictionnaire*, presenting Epicurus' philosophical school in Greece as the perfect example of just such a well-ordered community of those who denied providence. Bayle referenced both Epicurus' rejection of the community of goods and the Epicurean account of friendship to directly challenge the idea that believers were more sociable than atheists. The history of modern Europe was a history of religious sects and communities wrought with quarrel and party division. The Epicureans, on the other hand, enjoyed a 'profound peace' in their Garden by following their founder's doctrine without 'dissensions and contradictions'.[79]

Bayle used one of the final notes of his Epicurus entry to emphasise the connection between the doctrines of creation and providence. If it were once admitted that God did not create matter, it was absurd to maintain that he had

---

[76] For Diderot and Bayle, see Pierre Rétat, *Le Dictionnaire de Bayle et la lutte philosophique au XVIIIe siècle* (Paris: Belles Lettres, 1971): 385–403.

[77] Pierre Bayle, 'Epicurus', in *The Dictionary Historical and Critical of Mr Bayle*, trans. P. Desmaizeaux (London: Knapton et al., 1734): 780.

[78] Pierre Bayle, *Miscellaneous Reflections, on Occasion of the Comet Which Appeared in December*, Vol. 2 (London: J. Morphew, 1680): 329, 334.

[79] Bayle (1734): 776.

formed the world, preserves it, and directs it through providence. As such, the idea of an 'Epicurean' who was 'orthodox' was a 'bastard and monstrous production'. Because belief in providence required belief in creation in this way, the revelation of scripture was the only means of secure belief in the 'providence and perfection of god'. From revelation followed the 'sublime' and 'fundamental' doctrines of Christianity. For Bayle, then, the refutation of Epicureanism rested solely on scriptural authority. Thus, in addition to advancing his heterodox position on the possibility of a society of atheists, Bayle's entry provided further ammunition for sceptics with what superficially appears as a critical commentary: for once revelation was questioned, he made clear, Epicureanism was philosophically defensible.[80]

Brucker's account of this connection between Epicurus' denial of providence and his account of divine happiness was more fulsome than that of Bayle. He also made sure to include a scathing commentary.[81] We saw that Bayle had been ambivalent about the philosophical status of revelation. In a similar spirit, he singled out Epicurus' observance of local religious customs and submission to political authority, good or bad, as a commendation of his 'piety'.[82] Brucker, on the other hand, claimed that the charge of impiety launched by Epicurus' legions of detractors 'admits of no refutation'. Indeed, the charge may not have gone far enough, for there was at least some reason to suspect that Epicurus' teaching on the gods was simply a mercenary ploy to deflect the criticism that would attend any outright avowal of his evident atheism. Brucker's commentary is consistent in its explicit criticisms of Epicureanism. But he saved his greatest criticism for Epicurus' teaching of the gods' detached tranquillity, which 'falls infinitely short of the true conception of Deity, as the Intelligent Creator and Governor of the world'.[83]

Unsurprisingly, Diderot can also be seen following Brucker's model in his presentation of the necessarily perfect felicity of the gods and the denial of providence. If he had been inclined to comment on these aspects of Epicureanism, this was the appropriate point at which to have done so. But he did not offer any profession like that of the *Pensées*. Nor did he follow Bayle's recourse to revelation. Instead, he in fact *removed* all of Brucker's critical commentary, leaving the passages on the condition of the gods and the denial of providence to stand on their own.[84] Diderot's entry is audacious in this respect and, as we will see, it was subjected to violent attacks as a result.

[80] Ibid.: 786–787, 789.
[81] Brucker (1791): 473.
[82] Bayle (1734): 784, 785.
[83] Brucker (1791): 451–452, 452, 473–474, 474.
[84] Diderot (1755a): 782.

48   ROUSSEAU'S POLITICS OF TASTE

Here, then, Diderot's editorial innovation came more by way of subtraction than addition.

Diderot's account of the material composition of the gods and the individual soul demonstrates that his real novelty was not simply of the negative variety. Bayle had commented that Epicurus' teaching on the nature of the gods and providence was 'most impious'. He continued to the crucial point:

> authors disagree about the question, whether he taught that the Gods were composed of atoms? If he had taught such a thing, he had robbed the divine nature of its eternity and indestructibility; a monstrous and blasphemous doctrine! But which I think cannot be charged upon him.

Bayle's evidence for his conclusion, supported by reference to Cicero, is that Epicurus instructed his pupils to meditate on the 'immortality and felicity of God'. On Bayle's account, given that Epicurus taught both that all bodies decompose on death and that the gods were immortal, he could not have believed that the gods were composed of atoms.[85] For his part, Brucker had noted Epicurus' contention that the gods were not to be understood as 'gross bodies' of flesh and blood but, rather, as 'thin ethereal substances' with a 'peculiar nature, incapable of decay'. Moreover, and again in contrast to Bayle's sympathetic reasoning, he offered a lengthy excoriating commentary. Because Diderot engaged directly with Brucker's passage, it is worth quoting in full:

> Finding it wholly inconsistent with his fundamental principles to suppose the existence of immaterial beings, yet wishing to ascribe to the gods an incorporeal nature, [Epicurus] seems to have had recourse to an abstract notion of a peculiar substance, in the form of man, of such tenuity as to be intangible, indivisible, and indissoluble; and which he supposed to be endued with perception and reason. What this peculiar nature of Epicurus' divinities was, which was not a body, yet was like a body, we own ourselves unable to explain. The truth seems to have been, that Epicurus, reduced to inextricable difficulties by the absurdity of his system, that he might not wholly discard the idea of divinity, had recourse to the common asylum of ignorance, words without meaning.[86]

Diderot's central innovation was to isolate precisely this discussion of the gods and to emphasise its importance by placing it under its own heading, 'On

---

[85] Bayle (1734): 779, 780.
[86] Brucker (1791): 473, 474–475.

MODERN EPICUREANISM

49

Theology'. There, he summarised the dispute with a rhetorical question posed, recall, by 'Epicurus' himself: 'After having established the principle that there is nothing in nature but matter and the void, what shall we think of the gods? Shall we abandon our philosophy and submit to popular opinions, or shall we say that the gods are corporeal beings?' To state otherwise, as Brucker had noted, would have been a glaring inconsistency. Diderot thus concludes that, while the bodies of the gods are not like those of men, they are nonetheless composed of atoms – albeit in 'a similar but superior combination' that gave them 'a special nature' knowing neither change nor action.[87] With this subtlety, Diderot effectively disagreed with Bayle. Once more the point of his rhetorical strategy is clear: by having Epicurus speak directly to his audience, Diderot presumed to have absolved himself of the responsibility to issue a critical commentary of Brucker's sort. He can therefore be seen as attempting to present one of the most heterodox components of the Epicurean philosophy in such a way as to make it appear reasonably benign.

For Diderot and his contemporaries, discussions of the gods' materiality functioned as a powerful analogy for the materiality of the individual soul – both were particular instances of the general materialist denial of spiritual substance. Diderot's discussion of the soul also diverges from Bayle, whose commentary here had been highly critical.[88] But once more, he offered no qualifying commentary. 'The human soul is corporeal', he asserted forthrightly; those who argue the contrary 'do not hear themselves' or 'speak without having ideas'. He followed Brucker in reducing the debate to the problem of human agency: if the soul was incorporeal, 'it could neither touch nor be touched and consequently could neither act nor suffer'. And if the soul was not the cause of action, it was unclear on what basis humans could be said to determine their own actions. But Diderot went further, polemically asserting that to explain human agency by an 'immaterial principle' was not to resolve the difficulty but only to 'transport it to another object'. One subtle substance widely dispersed throughout the body, the soul exercises its sensible capacity through the bodily organs. As such, sensation is the result of the union of body and soul. For Diderot, *l'ésprit* is but the most subtle part of the soul. Diffused in the substance of the soul and united with it just as the soul is diffused through the body and united with it, the mind is that portion of the soul in which resides, on Brucker's terms, 'the power of thinking, judging, and determining'. Individuals experience through the soul sensations of pleasure and pain that produce those desires and aversions that precipitate action: 'to live',

[87] Diderot (1755a): 783.
[88] Bayle (1734): 779; cp. Brucker (1791): 475.

50   ROUSSEAU'S POLITICS OF TASTE

says Diderot's Epicurus, 'is to feel these alternating movements'.[89] In this way, the Epicurean account of the materiality of the soul was taken to have direct bearing on individual free will, with the subsequent implications on moral and political notions of responsibility and consent. So, too, were the epistemological aspects of Epicureanism understood to have had implications on the philosophical understanding of individual sensation and action.

Diderot's critics quickly homed in on the article. The staunch Jansenist priest Abraham-Joseph de Chaumeix easily saw past his rhetorical ploys.[90] The first and one of the most vociferous critics of the *Encyclopédie*, Chaumeix released eight volumes of his *Préjugés légitimes contre l'encyclopédie* between November 1758 and January 1760. Launched as it was in the context of the controversy surrounding the publication of Helvétius' *De L'Ésprit*, it is unsurprising that Chaumeix singled out the 'Epicuréisme' article for attack.[91] Indeed, in his introductory remarks Chaumeix emphasised that the scandalous claims in Helvétius' book were merely developments of the metaphysical and moral doctrines that had been promulgated for years in the *Encyclopédie*.[92] Addressing Diderot's attempted subterfuge, Chaumeix saw clearly that Epicurus had been introduced to represent the Encyclopédists themselves. The 'Epicurus' that speaks in the article, he commented, had been so well instructed by Diderot that he recites the same sentiments and nearly 'the same words as the author of *L'interpretation de la Nature*, a collection of nonsense'.[93] Diderot's neglecting clearly to distinguish his own views from Epicurus' showed that 'Epicurus is here only a straw-man'. The expressions placed in his mouth 'feel much more like Diderotisme than Epicureanism'. To Chaumeix, it was obvious that the Encyclopédists were 'more Epicurean than Epicurus himself'.[94]

Another critic to see past Diderot's ploy was Jean-Nicolas Hayer. He was an Augustinian friar who edited *La Religion vengée*, a multi-volume orthodox

[89] Diderot (1755a): 782; cp. Brucker (1791): 469–471.

[90] On Jansenists and Jesuits as critics of the *Encyclopédie*, compare Monique Cottret, *Jansénismes et lumières: pour une autre XVIIIe siècle* (Paris: Albin Michel, 1998) and Didier Masseau, *Les enemis des philosophes: l'antiphilosophie au temps des Lumières* (Paris: Albin Michel, 2000) with Dale van Kley, *The Jansenists and the Expulsion of the Jesuits from France, 1757–1765* (New Haven, CT: Yale University Press, 1975).

[91] See D. W. Smith, *Helvétius: A Study in Persecution* (Oxford: Oxford University Press, 1965). Cf. Masseau (2000): 131–141.

[92] Abraham-Joseph de Chaumeix, *Préjugés légitimes contre l'encyclopédie; et Essai de Refutation de ce Dictionnaire*, Vol. 1 (Brussels: Hérissant, 1758): ii.xii. Cf. Neven Leddy, 'Adam Smith's Critique of Enlightenment Epicureanism', in Leddy and Lifschitz (2009): 185–203 (188–190).

[93] The Epigraph to Diderot's 1751 *Interpretation of Nature* was taken from Lucretius' account of vision. See Russell Goulbourne, 'Diderot and the Ancients', in *New Essays on Diderot*, ed. James Fowler (Cambridge: Cambridge University Press, 2011): 13–30.

[94] De Chaumeix (1758): Vol. 2, 208, 213, 217, 223.

MODERN EPICUREANISM

51

defence against impiety that devoted three volumes to *Encyclopédie* criticism in 1760. In contrast to de Chaumeix's passionate and often distracted critique, *La Religion vengée* illustrates clearly what its more astute readers found objectionable in the *Encyclopédie*. Crucially for our purposes, such readers isolated precisely that section that we have seen Diderot foreground from Brucker. The discussion of the formation and composition of the gods in the 'On Theology' section, they wrote, reveals that Epicurus and Diderot are united in an 'impious and extravagant mockery: Gods formed by chance! Gods composed only of atoms! . . . What we admire is that such fools, such rogues, can have apologists in this century of light, and in men who believe themselves to bring it to all minds.' They raised further objection over Diderot's praise of Gassendi as the father of modern Epicureanism. Gassendi had also made Epicurus speak for himself. But whereas Diderot 'only has him speak to applaud his impieties', Gassendi did so 'to combat it and inspire with its horror'. Diderot was thus seen as adopting all of Epicurus' teachings 'with neither limitation nor reserve'. As such, he was labelled a 'shameless impostor' for having claimed, in the *Pensées*, to be a Christian because it was reasonable to be so.[95] Diderot's 'Epicuréisme' article, then, was both intended and received as a direct intervention in the most important theological debates in 1755 Paris.

When both de Chaumeix and Hayer presented the *Encyclopédie* as the plant that bore fruit in Helvétius' *De L'ésprit*, they extended their genealogy back to Locke's *Essay Concerning Human Understanding* as the progenitor of the *philosophes*' Epicureanism. This genealogy must be understood in the context of the aforementioned renewal of suspicion of Lockean sensationalism after 1751. De Chaumeix launched the typical critique that, while Locke's fundamental teaching that our thoughts were generated from sensations was philosophically important, his infamous ambiguity on the materiality of the soul could no longer be excused or explained away. The *philosophes* had exploited this ambiguity and were now promulgating an explicit, atheistic materialism: 'why do we find in Locke's book so much attention given to the spirituality of the soul? Would he not only demonstrate that it is only matter? No, he would have liked to, but even his creative power did not go there. It was reserved for his disciples, the Encyclopédists, to work for this new creation.'[96] Thus, at mid-decade, a sensationalist epistemology and materialist conception of judgement was seen as necessarily culminating in an atheism that de Chaumeix and others characterised as essentially Epicurean.

---

[95] *La Religion vengée ou, Réfutation des auteurs impies vol. X*, ed. Jean-Nicolas Hayer X (Paris: Chaubert, 1760): 280–283, 285, 295, 301.

[96] Chaumeix (1758): Vol. 1, 178.

52 ROUSSEAU'S POLITICS OF TASTE

As I discuss in Chapter 5, Rousseau would similarly link this controversy directly to the modern reception of Epicureanism in his (tempered) criticisms of Helvétius.

Conclusion

In exploring the complex and contested reception of Epicureanism in eighteenth-century France, this chapter has advanced two interrelated claims. First, it has shown that accusations of Epicureanism could refer in the first instance to a denial either of sociability, or of the immaterial soul and God's providence. This should serve as a salutary caution to approach with scepticism any identification of eighteenth-century moral and political thought as somehow *essentially* Epicurean. But it has also shown, second, that the very recognition of this polyvalence itself allows us to see more clearly to what use particular authors put Epicureanism in particular texts. Diderot's *Encyclopédie* entry demonstrates that he both intended and was understood to intervene directly in contemporary theological controversy surrounding the existence of an immaterial soul.

Today, historiographical discussion of eighteenth-century or Enlightenment Epicureanism is dominated by two rival traditions of the history of political thought. Contextualist historians interpret Epicureanism as a denial of sociability in their studies of the rise of political economy, seeking to gain insights into the tenuous balance between economic inequality and political equality. Conversely, historians and political theorists indebted to the work of Leo Strauss interpret Epicureanism as an atheistic denial of transcendent moral values, tracing the decline of the 'tradition' of political philosophy in terms of what they sometimes call the 'political theological problem'.[97] As we have seen, both interpretations of modern Epicureanism capture some aspects of the historical picture. We have also seen that the decision of eighteenth-century authors to interpret Epicureanism in terms of either atheism or sociability was a polemical one, intended to intervene in contemporary political controversy. We might therefore ask: When contextualists and Straussians diverge in the presentations of modern Epicureanism, do they also do so on the basis of a polemical or political decision? It is undoubtedly the case that the accounts of modern politics that emerge from these rival traditions have significant differences. However, the intimate connection between sociability and political

---

[97] See Heinrich Meier, *Leo Strauss and the Theologico-Political Problem* (Cambridge: Cambridge University Press, 2006) and Stephen Benjamin Smith, 'Leo Strauss's Discovery of the Theologico-Political Problem', *European Journal of Political Theory* 12 (2013): 388–408.

theology, seen throughout this chapter, suggests that the two traditions might be more closely aligned than they are typically taken to be.

Both schools have produced important interpretations of Rousseau's relationship to modern Epicureanism, and I engage them throughout this book. But before doing so directly, the next chapter extends my historical-contextual approach to Rousseau. For, in order to clarify the implications of how our contemporaries read his Epicureanism, it helps to examine how Rousseau was initially received as an Epicurean by his contemporaries. As we will see, that reception was characterised by the same dynamic at play in this chapter: some readers emphasised Rousseau's Epicurean atheism, others emphasised his Epicurean denial of sociability, some brought them together. Yet others linked Epicurean hedonism closely to the spread of luxury in commercial society, or applied a distinction between 'vulgar' and 'refined' Epicureanism to Rousseau. Noting this shift in emphasis helpfully alerts us to a growing interest in Epicureanism's potential contribution to accounts of aesthetic judgement, as seen in both Rousseau's contemporary reception and in his reception of Alexander Pope as an Epicurean. Taken together, the historical evidence in these two chapters suggests a new narrative of the eighteenth-century reception of Epicureanism – in which a topic of investigation situated somewhere between sociability and atheism undergoes an important but neglected shift from atheism to aesthetics.

3

Rousseau's Epicureanism: From Atheism to Aesthetics

Introduction

This chapter is about Rousseau's reception as an Epicurean. Today, that reception is informed by a revisionist emphasis on the importance of Epicurean ideas to the development of several foundational premises of modern political thought. Epicurus' materialist denial of providence and the immortal soul provided argumentative support for modern theories of secular political authority, just as hedonist arguments against natural sociability informed modern theories of sovereignty and political economy. Rousseau's position in this historiography is complicated: for some, he was an Epicurean because he followed Hobbes' denial of natural sociability and providence; for others, he rejected Epicureanism when he modified Mandeville's account of pity.[1] Perhaps this ambiguity is to be expected, especially in light of the previous chapter. For if Epicureanism had variable meanings in eighteenth-century moral and political thought and, therefore, essentialising claims about an Epicurean tradition or its revival must be rejected, then so must we approach Rousseau's Epicureanism with an appropriate degree of scepticism.

My approach in this chapter mirrors that of the previous one. I begin by reconstructing Rousseau's contemporary reception as an Epicurean. As we will see, the first readers of the second *Discourse* identified Rousseau as an Epicurean primarily because they read him as a vulgar materialist. That is, they saw his denial of natural sociability and his account of justice as an artificial virtue as implications of his natural-philosophical atheism. Because Rousseau's earliest

---

[1] Cp. Tuck (1999) with Pierre Force, *Self-interest before Adam Smith: A Genealogy of Economic Science* (Cambridge: Cambridge University Press, 2003).

critics have never been addressed comparatively, reconstructing this context is necessary and valuable in itself. As in the previous chapter, this reconstruction cautions against applying essentialist claims to Rousseau's reception as an Epicurean. But it also allows us to preserve the sceptical impulse without embracing its most radical conclusion. While the initial aspects of Rousseau's reception as an Epicurean are broadly continuous with earlier discussions in biblical criticism, natural jurisprudence, and the history of science, Rousseau eventually came to describe his own ideas as amounting to a sort of refined Epicureanism. To understand what he meant in doing so, we must understand why those contemporaries who first received him as an Epicurean saw him, instead, as a vulgar one. Once again, then, understanding Epicureanism's historical variability increases rather than diminishes its value as an interpretive tool and historiographical category.

One central aim of this chapter is to enable us to see Rousseau as part of a broader shift in the modern reception of Epicureanism. My story takes place in different contexts. Adam Smith was one of the first to translate sections of the second *Discourse* to English. In addition to a suggestive emphasis on Rousseau's style, he linked what we can call the Epicurean foundations of the text to Scottish debates about sociability in specifically commercial societies. Rousseau's friend Jacob Vernet similarly saw Rousseau as contributing to the luxury debates occurring in Geneva. But he read the account of pleasure and the theatre in *d'Alembert* as a critique of a specifically 'fashionable' form of Epicureanism. Unbeknownst to any of these readers, Rousseau defended Alexander Pope from accusations of Epicureanism, intervening in French debates with a focus on the relationship between literary form and philosophical content. As my story unfolds, we will see that the reception of Epicureanism had different contours in different contexts. But while I am attentive to contextual specificity, I am centrally concerned to highlight a crucial but neglected continuity – namely, that interest in Epicureanism was increasingly broached with issues of sentiment, imagination, and beauty.

There was, in short, a shift from atheism to aesthetics in the modern reception of Epicureanism. Recognising Rousseau as part of this broader shift reciprocally elucidates the most distinctive aspects of his reception of Epicureanism. Just as today, Rousseau's contemporary reception as an Epicurean was quickly complicated. But if readers have grown more sensitive to this complexity, his critique of Pope's reception as an Epicurean remains neglected. Recovering it reveals Rousseau's engagement with a range of ideas that would inform his subsequent self-identification as a refined Epicurean. He argued that the potentially vicious implications of hedonism could be overcome by an appropriate sentimental awareness of beauty. In doing so, he articulated a critical ethos that

56   ROUSSEAU'S POLITICS OF TASTE

emphasised the combination of reason and sentiment involved in judgements of taste. Precisely this combination of reason and sentiment is the common element behind each of Rousseau's terms for something like good taste – that is, it highlights why and how refined Epicureanism involves a kind of temperate sensuality that facilitates the taste for virtue. Excavating Rousseau's earliest articulation of that idea not only demonstrates how reconstructing his reception *as* an Epicurean allows us better to appreciate his reception *of* Epicureanism. It also, thereby, further prepares the ground for the analytical reconstruction of Rousseau's account of the politics of taste that follows. For it is in his application of these aesthetic concerns to an understanding of modern politics that Rousseau truly breaks new ground.

A Reputation Gained

Of the many critical responses to Rousseau's second *Discourse*, there were two that his contemporaries considered most 'worthy of consideration': the Jesuit priest Louis Bertrand Castel's *L'homme moral opposé à l'homme physique* (1756) and the Prussian Astronomer Royal Jean de Castillon's own *Discours sur l'inégalité* (1756).[2] Both authors identified Rousseau as an Epicurean to emphasise that his denial of natural sociability and account of justice as an artificial virtue were grounded on his apparent materialist natural philosophy. While Castillon and Castel are known to some of Rousseau's historically sensitive interpreters, a third, Hermann Samuel Reimarus, is generally neglected.[3] A Prussian heterodox follower of Christian Wolff, Reimarus used the label 'Epicurean' to bring together Rousseau's denial of sociability with that of divine providence to a greater extent even than Castel. His 1755 critique of Rousseau received seven printings by 1798. Castel's was appended to the Geneva edition of Rousseau's collected works in 1784. Together, they ensured that the second *Discourse* was read as an Epicurean pamphlet well into the nineteenth century.

---

[2] Anonymous, *Lettres relatives à divers ouvrages de Jean-Jacques Rousseau, dont son Discours sur l'origine de l'inégalité* (Paris, 1763). Cf. Henry Fuseli, *Remarks on the Writings and Conduct of J. J. Rousseau* (London: T. Cadel, 1767).

[3] Jean Morel, 'Recherches sur les sources du Discours de l'inégalité', *Annales de la Société J.-J. Rousseau* V (1909): 119–198. John T. Scott, 'The Theodicy of the Second Discourse: The "Pure State of Nature" and Rousseau's Political Thought', *American Political Science Review* 86:3 (1992): 696–711. Strauss (1953).

Louis-Bertrand Castel

Castel's critique of Rousseau's Epicureanism was part of his general concern with the theological implications of materialism.[4] His engagement with the second *Discourse* was not his first encounter with Rousseau. They met briefly in 1742 and Castel subsequently published two volumes of letters attacking Rousseau's first *Discourse* and *Letter on French Music* (1754). In these, he deployed a bifurcated history of philosophy classifying all physical theories in essentialist terms as either Aristotelian or Epicurean according to whether they understood the universe to be governed by either providential design or random chance.[5] He saw his attack on the second *Discourse* as a defence of orthodox belief and absolute royal authority, following Rousseau from the arts to the political terrain. This entailed a refutation of Rousseau's account of human nature, which, he wrote, reduced human beings to 'pure physicality and pure animality, which is purely deist, and perhaps Epicurean'.[6]

Castel began his attack by claiming that Rousseau was Epicurean because he had denied providence. He distinguished Spinoza's mechanism from Epicureanism's 'purely physical nature of chance', noting that, whatever 'nature' meant in the second *Discourse*, it was completely devoid of spirituality and divine direction. He then focused on Rousseau's description of the random process by which the solitary individual transitioned to family life, the essential component and fundamental unit of society. He complained that Rousseau offered no adequate account of how the initial union of male and female could have occurred, so that the purpose of nature would seem logically unfulfilled if based on his principles. Here, Castel remarked, Rousseau could simply deny the existence of any purpose in nature, and likewise providential design. But he could not account for why similar human beings had then

---

[4] Donald S. Louis-Bertrand Castel Schier, *Anti-Newtonian Scientist* (Cedar Rapids, IA: Torch Press, 1941).

[5] Louis-Bertrand Castel, *Lettres d'un académicien de Bordeaux sur le fonds de la musique: à l'occasion de la lettre de M. R*** contre la musique françoise*, 2 vols (Paris: Bibliothèque de l'Arsenal; Brussels: Bibliothèque Royale de Belgique). Cf. *Seconde lettre philosophique pour rassurer l'univers contre les critiques de la première. En réponse à MM. Les auteurs des Réflexions sur les ouvrages de littérature* (Paris: Prault père, 1737); *Amusements du cour et de l'esprit, Géométrie naturelle en dialogues, Dissertation philosophique et littéraire* (Paris, 1738).

[6] Louis-Bertrand Castel, *L'homme moral opposé a l'homme physique de Monsieur R***: Où l'on réfute le Déisme du jour* (Toulouse, 1756): 7–8, 5, 31. Cf. Louis-Bertrand Castel, 'Lettre sur la politique dans ses rapports avec la physique', *Journal de Trévoux* (1725): xxi, 698–729 and 'Lettres a M. l'abbé de Saint-Pierre sur la véritable cause primitive et insensible de la pesanteur en général et de la chute des corps en particulier', *Journal de Trévoux* (1731): xxii, 2084–2095; 1732.i, 57–59; 1732.ii, 221–240.

58 ROUSSEAU'S POLITICS OF TASTE

come into existence: deformed monstrosities were as likely to result as were mushrooms or mullets. Even if such union could occur by chance, the couple would have 'all of Cynical or Epicurean society' to decline without providential design to direct their natural inclinations to procreate. Castel argued that Rousseau had effectively allowed bestiality into his system, for his Epicurean denial of providence could not explain human procreation.[7]

The centrepiece of Castel's critique was his treatment of Rousseau's denial of natural sociability. Because he was primarily concerned with Rousseau's apparently materialist ontology, he focused his attention on the account of pity as a substitute for the principle of sociability. Against Rousseau's claims of pity's ability to temper *amour-propre*, Castel insisted that it would always remain practically ineffective on Rousseau's terms. Precisely because it was 'purely brutal, physical and sensitive', Rousseau's pity could not possibly motivate moral behaviour on any consistent basis. Rather, Rousseau's humans could only consult pity momentarily, while otherwise being driven by a self-interest which made them run fiercely after their own good 'without concern for the interest of others'.[8] On Castel's reading, Rousseau's Epicurean materialism excluded even the possibility of humankind ever becoming sociable.

Castel introduced this critique of the physical basis of pity by comparing Rousseau to Hobbes. Hobbes was impious to the extent that he supposed humans prone to impiety. Rousseau's view of humans as nothing more than organised matter meant that they were utterly incapable even of impiety. With space for neither virtues nor vices, neither moral relations nor moral duties, Rousseau's reductive theory of human nature rendered the very categories of piety and impiety meaningless. Thus, in addition to marking him as even more radical than Hobbes, the apparently Epicurean ontology that supported Rousseau's denial of sociability was inseparable from what Castel elsewhere termed his 'full atheism'. The rhetorical strategy of the second *Discourse*, Castel wrote, was simply to 'argue against the good' by emphasising 'the evil' that comes from man's failure to observe the former. For Castel,

> the strength of [Rousseau's] reasoning consists in the fact that there would be no evil if there were no good; and it is the good which is to blame for all the evil that arrives in this world. That is to say, that if all would be evil there would be no evil, and evil would on the contrary be the cause of good.

[7] Castel (1756): 205, 206, 208.
[8] Ibid.: 119–120.

In seeking to expose Rousseau's denial of providence by way of a critique of his conception of pity and *amour-propre* in moral agency, Castel was thus one of the first of many commentators to read the second *Discourse* as a theodicy.[9]

Castel concluded his critique of Rousseau's Epicureanism by attacking his apparent materialist rejection of an immortal soul. While he recognised that Rousseau presented his vision of natural man as a hypothesis, he nevertheless chastised him for ignoring the 'nature of the soul'. As a consequence, his natural man was seen to lack any moral capacity whatsoever. Moreover, Rousseau did not merely exclude morality from his natural man, he excluded any morality whatsoever in his attempt to surpass his atheist, materialist, forebears – Hobbes and Locke. As Castel made clear in his concluding remarks, the essence of Rousseau's Epicureanism was his 'pure materialism'. It had to be ruthlessly attacked because it demonstrated his 'complete atheism'.[10]

Castel branded Rousseau an Epicurean because he thought he detected an atheistic materialism that denied both providence and the existence of an immortal soul. While he was concerned with Rousseau's denial of sociability and vision of justice as an artificial virtue, he did not identify these as evidence of Epicureanism. Instead, it was the denial of theological orthodoxy that was the essence of Rousseau's Epicureanism. Castel's distinctions between, first, Hobbesian and Epicurean materialism and, second, Epicurean chance and Spinozist mechanism are underdeveloped, and could be questioned. For my purposes, however, it suffices merely to note that Castel positioned Rousseau as the most radical of the atheist *philosophes*. 'Only Epicurus', he wrote, could excuse Rousseau's declamation 'against the Universe, France, and all of Paris'. Castel thus considered it an almost holy duty to attack Rousseau and expose him as 'an example and lesson of evil'.[11] Rousseau's criticism of modern French society and politics compounded Castel's distress. But the Jesuit priest saw his attack on the Epicureanism of the second *Discourse* as, above all, a defence against atheism.

Jean de Castillon

A literary review of the period celebrated Jean de Castillon for engaging the second *Discourse* 'as a philosopher' rather than transporting it to the 'absolutely

---

[9] Ibid.: 117, 221, 122. Cf. Victor Gourevitch, 'Rousseau on Providence', *Review of Metaphysics* 53 (2000): 565–611.

[10] Castel (1756): 209, 217, 213.

[11] Ibid.: 208.

foreign terrain' of theology.[12] Unlike Castel, Castillon was a natural lawyer familiar with the classical tradition.[13] So, while he often had 'recourse to Divinity', he contextualised his critique as following the examples of Grotius, Pufendorf, Cumberland, and Burlamaqui.[14] Castillon was the most forceful and philosophically able of Rousseau's contemporaries to label him an Epicurean. Commenting on the critical scholarship aroused by Rousseau's first *Discourse*, he lamented the lack of a similar response to the second *Discourse* and branded it an Epicurean pamphlet:

> It has been almost one year since [Rousseau] raised the delusions of the Epicureans about our origin; since he reduced our forefathers to the rank of the most stupid beasts; since he accused us of being the most wicked and ferocious of all the animals: and these accusations have still not been rejected? We should expect that others going further in the same direction will rob us . . . I know not what they can take from us after we have been deprived of all humanity.[15]

Castillon aimed to combat these Epicurean delusions and return man to his rightful 'honour and well-being'. He took exception to Rousseau's claims that 'it is by accident that we are what we are' – that nature had endowed humans with faculties only in potential, and that the social interaction that conditioned their actualisation was the product of chance. For Castillon, this was a rejection of the very 'foundation of all philosophy' – the principle that nature does nothing in vain.[16]

The foundation of Castillon's critique of Rousseau is a reaffirmation of natural sociability. 'Natural man' was endowed with principles of conduct in all of his natural relations, including with his fellows. Reason, the moral sense, and imagination constituted man's eternal nature, and the principles which they revealed were 'incontestable'. As he went on to explicate them, the most basic principle was that 'men have never been dispersed; the present and perceptible advantages of society are sufficient to retain them in this state; and they can easily obey the natural law' – the definition of the latter being 'engraved on their soul, though . . . not written in their minds'. Castillon reduced his engagement with Rousseau and the entire natural law discourse to two fundamental hypotheses:

---

[12] *Journal Encyclopedic, par une societé de gens de lettres* 2:2 (Leige, 1757): 3–25, 8.
[13] See John Aikin and William Enfield, *General Biography; or Lives, Critical and Historical, of the Most Eminent Persons of All Ages, Countries, Conditions, and Professions* (London, 1799): 280–281.
[14] Castillon (1756): xxx, vii.
[15] Ibid.: vi–vii.
[16] Ibid.: viii, ix–xi, xv–xvi, xvii–xviii.

ROUSSEAU'S EPICUREANISM

Either men formerly lived in dispersion, or they have always been in society: these are the only two available hypotheses. The one is no more novel than the other. The first is a dream of the Epicureans, which Rousseau has adopted and adorned in the most seductive appearances. The second is a truth seen by the other philosophers and that I described in the simplest manner. Nothing new in his book any more than in mine. But what I say is true, though common; what he says is false, though more rare.[17]

The denial of natural sociability cannot neatly be separated from the natural-philosophical assumptions that underpin Lucretius' account of the natural condition. My point here is that Castillon branded Rousseau an Epicurean in order to emphasise his denial of natural sociability, not his apparent atheism or ontological commitments.

Castillon's reception of Rousseau's Epicureanism was firmly grounded in the classics. Suggesting comparisons between the second *Discourse* and lengthy excerpts from Book V of Lucretius' *De rerum natura*, he quoted the original Latin and provided his own French translations to highlight the striking parallels between the imagery in both texts. Lucretius' first humans were 'far hardier' than civilised men and not 'as prone to being overwhelmed by heat or cold'.[18] Rousseau's natural men were 'accustomed from childhood to the inclemencies of weather . . . [with] a robust and almost unalterable temperament'. In Lucretius' state of nature 'no one knew how to work the land with iron tools . . . or cut the barren branches down from the tall trees with pruning hooks'.[19] Rousseau wondered whether, if his natural man 'had had an axe, could his wrists have cracked such solid branches'. Finally, for Lucretius, 'mostly they would take a mess of acorns for their mat amongst the groves of oak . . . and springs and rivers beckoned them to slake their dry throats'.[20] Rousseau famously saw his natural man 'sating his hunger beneath an oak, slaking his thirst at the first stream, finding his bed at the foot of the same tree that supplied his meal, and with that his needs are satisfied' (*DI*:134–135/3:135). The array of examples he provides buttresses Castillon's argument that Lucretius' description of the first humans 'accords with that of our *philosophe*'.[21]

---

[17] Ibid.: xx–xxi, xxi, xxiii, xxv, xxx.

[18] *DRN*:V.927; 931–933.

[19] Ibid.: V.937.

[20] Ibid.: V.939–946.

[21] Castillon (1756): 261. These and other intertextual parallels are discussed in Moishe Black, 'De rerum natura and the second Discourse', in *Rousseau and the Ancients*, ed. Ruth Grant and Phillip Stewart (Montreal: Pensée Libre, 2001): 300–309.

62   ROUSSEAU'S POLITICS OF TASTE

Castillon saw Rousseau's account of justice as the most radical element of his Epicureanism. If intertextuality demonstrated that 'Lucretius enters first in the ideas of Rousseau', this was simply evidence of his adopting a standard, if mistaken, position on the matter of sociability. What most alarmed Castillon was Rousseau's pessimistic treatment of modern society. He next cited Lucretius' vivid description of the death of a single man, with which the Roman poet contrasted the increased death toll enabled by technological and social progress. As Castillon remarked, this account can indeed appear restrained relative to Rousseau's rhetorical flourishes.[22] While Rousseau and Lucretius broadly agreed in their conception of human nature, there was an essential difference: whereas Rousseau attributed 'jealousy, pride, and the love of vengeance' to civilised humans, 'Lucretius gives, at least the greater part of mankind, the commitment to justice'.[23] For Castillon, Rousseau was an Epicurean because he derived his account of the state of nature from Book V of *De rerum natura*. But his apparent denial of justice rendered his Epicureanism even more radical than that of Lucretius.

Castillon also argued that Rousseau's sceptical account of the origin of languages was drawn from Lucretius. It was widely acknowledged that Lucretius' robust naturalistic description – his claim that 'it was nature that gave the tongue its different sounds to say, and expedience that formed the names of things' – was designed to oppose the account offered in Plato's *Cratylus*.[24] Castillon suggested that Rousseau used this Epicurean argument to ground his famous claim that it is clear from 'how little care nature has taken to bring men together through mutual needs and to facilitate their use of speech, how little it prepared their sociability' (*DI*:149/3:151). He refuted it by insisting that man was an innately rational and social animal: 'man reasons, speaks, and lives in society; man isolated by nature could never reason, speak, nor form society. Thus, men have never been without reason, without language, without society.'[25] For Castillon, Rousseau's Epicureanism was evident in his use of a sceptical account of the origin of languages to underpin his denial of natural sociability.

Whereas Castel distinguished Rousseau's Epicureanism by way of a contrast with Hobbes and Spinoza, Castillon's engagement points rather to

---

[22] Cp. *DRN*:V.999–1010; *DI*:137–138/*OC*3:138.

[23] Castillon (1756): 266; *DRN*:V.1026–1027.

[24] Lucretius, *DRN*:V.1027–1028. Cf. *DRN*:V.1029–1037, 1053–1082. Plato, *The Cratylus, Phaedo, Parmenides and Timaeus of Plato*, trans. Thomas Taylor (London: Benjamin and John White, 1793): 389a–d; *DRN*:V.1038–1052.

[25] Castillon (1756): 84–85. See Avi S. Lifschitz, 'The Revival of the Epicurean History of Language and Civilization', in Leddy and Lifschitz (2009): 207–226.

Pufendorf and Locke. The 166 lines from Lucretius that Castillon marshalled as evidence of Rousseau's Epicureanism correspond *exactly* to the Lucretius excerpts in two of the most important books of Pufendorf's highly influential *Law of Nature and Nations*.[26] Rousseau's depiction of the physical side of natural man can be read as responding to considerations raised by Pufendorf.[27] In that sense, attacking Rousseau as an Epicurean allowed Castillon to distance Pufendorf from similar charges. But Castillon also addressed the controversy surrounding Locke's 'thinking matter' hypothesis that, we have seen, exercised great influence on the reception of Epicureanism in mid-century France. He sympathetically reconstructed Rousseau's claim that mechanical causes could explain neither the formation of ideas nor the related faculties of the mind, including 'adopting, rejecting, and suspending judgment'. Castillon then questioned if the soul is indeed more active in choosing between objects than it is in recalling, comparing, or combining ideas: 'are the determinations of the will always dependent on motives? Are they never uniquely the effect of our activity? Is the soul any less the author of its choice because the motives direct it?'[28] Castillon's critique thus differs from Castel's in important respects: his defence of natural sociability is not grounded in appeals to revelation but focuses instead on Rousseau's Epicurean account of the origin of language and ambiguous treatment of judgement; and his primary intellectual interlocutors were not Hobbes and Spinoza but, rather, Pufendorf, Locke, and indeed Lucretius.

Hermann Samuel Reimarus

Hermann Samuel Reimarus attacked Rousseau from the German principality Hanover. *The Principal Truths of Natural Religion* (1766; originally published in 1755 as *Abhandlungen von den vornehmsten Wahrheiten der natürlichen Religion*) grouped Rousseau with Buffon, Maupertuis, and La Mettrie as modern Epicureans who had suggested that life originated from matter by spontaneous generation, a process governed by chance. His direct engagement with Rousseau is not as sustained as either Castel's or Castillon's. But it is noteworthy for the way that it combines a theological perspective with considerations of natural law and sociability. Reimarus was a biblical scholar who considered Rousseau's second *Discourse* to embody the same materialist, anti-providential

---

[26] Pufendorf (1729): 315. Cp. Castillon (1756): 255–266 with Pufendorf (1729): 100 and *DRN*:V.923–1029; Castillon (1756): 287–293 with Pufendorf (1729): 315 and *DRN*:V.1027–1089.

[27] Douglass (2015): 70–71.

[28] Castillon (1756): 44.

64 ROUSSEAU'S POLITICS OF TASTE

natural philosophy that so upset Castel. And like Castel, what concerned Reimarus most about those he attacked, and what he intended to critique by branding them Epicureans, was their denial of spiritual substance and providential design. But unlike Castel and like Castillon, Reimarus also drew attention to the political-philosophical implications of this Epicurean materialism.

His critique of Rousseau was the centrepiece of a rationalist philosophical system Reimarus developed in dialogue with Christian Wolff.[29] Distinguishing human rationality from animal instinct, he acknowledged that Rousseau, too, had adopted the appropriate philosophical procedure. But Rousseau, he wrote, had abused this methodological necessity by following his 'brutish inclinations':

> It is well known that Mr. Rousseau, of Geneva, has lately exerted his imagination, in representing to us, among other animals in a desert, an original man in his natural state, as a brute, or something worse. This is not done, with the view of other authors on the Law of Nature, to show, under a fiction, that such a state is rather unnatural and extremely miserable; and by that consideration to induce us to a social and friendly life with other men: but to maintain, that nature has formed man only for a brutal state, and that he would be most happy in such a state; that, on the other hand, reflection, society, dominion, property, and the difference of states, are unnatural; and that all the improvements supposed to result from them, tend only to render mankind more wretched and depraved.[30]

Reimarus began by taking aim at Rousseau's contention that it is 'not so much the understanding that constitutes the specific difference between man and the other animals, as it is his property of being a free agent' (*DI*:141/3:141).[31] After a hurried summary of Rousseau's description of the foundation of civil society on the unequal distribution of property, he moved quickly to a criticism of the political implications of this account of human nature. Reimarus argued that human liberty requires for its exercise the conditions provided by the 'social

---

[29] For Reimarus' background and context, see Julian Jaynes and William Woodward, 'In the Shadow of the Enlightenment: I. Reimarus Against the Epicureans', *Journal of the History of the Behavioural Sciences* 10:1 (1974): 3–15. Ian Hunter, *Rival Enlightenments: Civil and Metaphysical Philosophy in Early-Modern Germany* (Cambridge: Cambridge University Press, 2001): 265–273.

[30] Hermann Samuel Reimarus, *The Principal Truths of Natural Religion, Defended and Illustrated, in Nine Dissertations: Wherein the Objections of Lucretius, Buffon, Maupertuis, Rousseau, La Mettrie, and Other Antient and Modern Followers of Epicurus Are Considered, and Their Doctrines Refuted*, trans. R. Wynne (London: B. Law, 1766): 315–353, 316–317.

[31] Cp. Reimarus (1766): 317.

and conversable state'. As such, it would have been more logical if Rousseau had argued that, because 'the powers naturally innate to man can be exercised only in a social life, therefore a social life must be natural to man'. Rousseau's failure in reasoning here stemmed from his misunderstanding of nature itself. According to Reimarus, whereas Rousseauian nature is nothing but a spontaneous manifestation of power outside of the social state, nature rightly understood is a power or innate faculty that 'is and ever resides in a thing'. That the exercise of such a power might be inhibited by internal defect or external impediment was irrelevant. For Reimarus, because the use of reason is natural to man, the social and conversable state conditioning its exercise is the natural state of man.[32]

Having defended natural sociability from this rationalist teleological position, Reimarus attacked Rousseau's pessimistic account of social inequality and suffering. He complained that Rousseau's misunderstanding of nature led him to mistake these social evils as essential rather than merely accidental. This critique was the immediate foundation for Reimarus' comparison between man and animal. Both were sensitive creatures motivated by pleasure and pain and both were governed by self-love, the first natural law. As such, sensual enjoyment did contribute to human happiness. But fleeting sensory pleasures could not satisfy rational humans. Moreover, though honour and wealth were goods made possible by reason, they could not secure the 'inward contentment' that human beings ultimately seek – only the 'consciousness of wisdom and virtue' by which they are acquired could do so. With the further awareness of 'futurity' and the attendant complications of psychological 'concern' and an infinite increase of desires, humans achieved happiness with the greatest difficulty relative to animals. It was only through deploying their reason in such a way as to facilitate the 'acknowledgment of an all-wise, benign, and powerful Creator and governor of the world' – and through recognising providential design – that they could achieve the inward 'quietude' secured by wisdom and virtue.[33]

Reimarus concluded his dissertation with an alternative narrative of the transition from the state of nature to civil society that was meant to illustrate the particular advantages that man's rational capacity conferred on him over brute creation. Men came into the world in a 'destitute state'. Absent the 'instinct and innate skill' possessed by animals, they deployed their 'peculiar gift' of reason to institute language and develop the arts and sciences. 'Societies were founded, laws instituted, and magistrates appointed' so that men could live in safety while enjoying the conveniences of communal life. Chief among these

[32] Ibid.: 381, 320, 321, 323–324.
[33] Ibid.: 327–311, 330–332, 333, 335–337, 337.

conveniences was knowledge, which, unlike sensual pleasure, could not be carried to excess and led to a rational comprehension of God and an awareness of the spiritual dimensions of the universe and the individual soul. Reimarus held humans to be the only created beings capable of perfecting their capacities and predictably attributed this to the unique character of reason: unlike animals, man 'has an unlimited understanding, a will ever desirous of higher perfection, and a rational freedom to choose the best means in order to attain his ends'. Man's rational capacity meant that a state of pure happiness was potentially achievable, though not in the temporal realm. Because unassisted reason could not secure happiness without the love and reverence of God, the basis of human contentment was found in the rational comprehension of providential design and the immortal soul.[34]

As had Castel, Reimarus branded Rousseau an Epicurean for his apparent denial of these theological tenets. Though he cited the *Discourse* only once and offered no textual excerpts, he seems to have had in mind Rousseau's faculty of *perfectibilité*, through which the individual and species adapted to the 'fortuitous concatenation of several foreign causes' to arrive quite accidentally at the present state, as a denial of providence (*DI*:159/3:162). Moreover, Rousseau had introduced *perfectibilité* as a sceptical means of deferring judgement on the ultimate nature of the soul, which led to his description of liberty as the soul's essential faculty being read as entailing a composite soul, part spiritual and part corporeal. Reimarus' critique is valuable because it combines Castel's theological perspective with Castillon's natural law approach to sociability. For Reimarus, liberty was dependent upon God's gift of reason, both required social interaction for their actualisation, and so demonstrated natural sociability. Rousseau's inversion of the priority of reason over liberty implied a materialist account of the soul, denying its immortality and denying natural sociability. And the random irrational events described by Rousseau in terms of perfectibility similarly denied a natural sociability that, Reimarus emphasised, was providentially endowed.

A Reputation Complicated

As the above reconstruction shows, Rousseau's initial reception as an Epicurean took on similar contours to the debates over Epicureanism surveyed in Chapter 2. This is perhaps unsurprising, insofar as his early critics were intervening in the same practical and discursive context. Their attention to Epicureanism helpfully directs us to the convergence of some of the

---

[34] Ibid.: 338, 339–347, 348, 353.

fundamental philosophical premises of the second *Discourse*. They also remind us that the first accounts of Rousseau's Epicureanism were intended primarily to emphasise his materialism. This is a useful insight in conceptual terms, for it invites us to return to Rousseau's underexplored relationship to materialism (as I do in the conclusion of this chapter). But it is especially valuable in historiographical terms – for it demonstrates that, as in the case of Diderot, so were the points of emphasis in Rousseau's initial reception as an Epicurean broadly continuous with earlier discussions of Epicureanism in biblical criticism, natural jurisprudence, and the history of science. But we must be careful not to see modern Epicureanism through a nationalist lens. Narrowly Franco-centric interpretations of eighteenth-century Epicureanism, for instance, once supported narratives of 'secularisation' that obscured our view of the importance of earlier English debates with a decidedly theological character.[35] There is an analogy here with Rousseau's reception as an Epicurean. In mid-century France, the emphasis in receptions of both Epicureanism and Rousseau's relationship to it tended to fall somewhere between 'atheism' and 'sociability'. However, if we expand our field of vision to include different contexts, then we will encounter different concepts and different points of emphasis.

The following discussion contextualises Rousseau as part of a broader shift in the modern reception of Epicureanism. His early critics were notably silent about his approach to pleasure. Reimarus, for his part, distinguished between transient sensory pleasures and the stable contentment provided by the consciousness of wisdom and virtue. As the latter type of pleasure was ultimately theologically grounded in one's recognition of providential design, he implied that Rousseau's Epicurean materialism extended to a vulgar celebration of sensual pleasure. But the lack of any direct and substantial engagement with Rousseau on pleasure is even more surprising when we consider other contemporary receptions of his Epicureanism. Adam Smith in Scotland and Jacob Vernet in Geneva emphasised Rousseau's contribution to debates over luxury and moral agency in modern commercial societies. In doing so, their receptions of Rousseau can be seen as part of an increasing interest in the importance of sentiment, beauty, imagination, or aesthetics, which suggests a shift from atheism to aesthetics in the modern reception of Epicureanism.

Rousseau's Epicureanism and the Luxury Debates, via Adam Smith

Adam Smith is certainly the best known of the first reviewers of the second *Discourse*. After a long period of scholarly neglect, his 1756 letter to the editors

---

[35] Thomson (2008).

of the short-lived *Edinburgh Review* has emerged as a touchstone in Smith studies and, more recently, in revisionist accounts of Rousseau as a theorist of politics in commercial society.[36] These accounts typically focus on Smith's insight that Rousseau's arguments had much in common with those presented in the second volume of Bernard Mandeville's *Fable of the Bees* (1728). For Smith, the authors shared 'principles' that, while he never identified them as Epicurean, can readily be seen as such: they denied natural sociability, offered a developmental account of society, and held justice to be an artificial virtue that served to entrench inequality in favour of the rich and powerful.[37] But he also identified three differences between them. First, whereas for Mandeville the 'primitive state of mankind' is 'wretched and miserable', Rousseau 'paints it as the happiest and most suitable to his nature'. Second, where Rousseau sees socialisation as an accident, for Mandeville society emerges out of the first humans' recognition of their indigence and concomitant need for cooperation. Third, and most important for Smith, Rousseau argues against Mandeville that the natural sentiment of pity is 'capable of producing all those virtues, whose realities Dr. Mandeville denies'.[38]

One of the more intriguing elements of the letter is Smith's attention to Rousseau's style. At least since Francis Hutcheson's *Inquiry into the Original of our Idea of Beauty and Virtue* (1725), Scottish thinkers saw aesthetics as an important part of the philosophical investigation of human nature.[39] Smith was no exception. His early 'History of Astronomy' assessed the adequacy of philosophical systems by their capacity not simply to explain the material world

---

[36] Jeffrey Lomonaco, 'Adam Smith's "Letter to the Authors of the Edinburgh Review"', *Journal of the History of Ideas* 63:4 (2002): 659–676. Ryan Patrick Hanley, 'Commerce and Corruption: Rousseau's Diagnosis and Adam Smith's Cure', *European Journal of Political Theory* 7:2 (2008): 137–158. Dennis Carl Rasmussen, *The Problems and Promise of Commercial Society: Adam Smith's Response to Rousseau* (Philadelphia: Penn State University Press, 2010): 59–71. Paul Sagar, 'Smith and Rousseau, after Hume and Mandeville', *Political Theory* 46:1 (2018): 29–58. Charles L. Griswold, *Jean-Jacques Rousseau and Adam Smith: A Philosophical Encounter* (London: Routledge, 2017).

[37] That Smith did not explicitly identify these positions as Epicurean may be related to his treatment of Mandeville's 'licentious system' and Epicureanism as distinct moral theories in *The Theory of Moral Sentiments*, ed. D. D. Raphael and A. L. Macfie (Oxford: Oxford University Press, 2014).

[38] Adam Smith, 'A Letter to the Authors of the Edinburgh Review', in *The Glasgow Edition of the Works and Correspondence of Adam Smith: Essays on Philosophical Subjects*, ed. W. P. D. Wightman (Oxford: Oxford University Press, 1980): 250.

[39] For an overview of the Scottish context, see Gordon Graham, 'Beauty, Taste, Rhetoric, and Language', in *Scottish Philosophy in the Eighteenth Century Volume 1: Morals, Politics, Art, Religion*, ed. Aaron Garret and James A. Harris (Oxford: Oxford University Press, 2015): 131–162.

but also to soothe and satisfy the imagination.[40] And his *Lectures on Rhetoric and Belles-Lettres* (1762) attend to the linguistic dimensions of the shift from ancient to modern societies – he argued that political language needed to be updated to satisfy the new sorts of moral needs that accompanied commercial society.[41] He wrote the 'Letter' when he was delivering these lectures at Glasgow, and his aesthetic concerns are apparent throughout the review. That most readers overlook this concern may be partly explained by the tendency either to assume or seek explanations of how far (or not) Smith's moral theory was influenced by Rousseau.[42]

My interest here lies rather in Smith's contextualising Rousseau as part of a wider stylistic shift in modern moral philosophy. The writers most concerned with questions of moral philosophy were now French, not English. What interested Smith in this shift was not that it had produced genuine philosophical advances – the French in any case lacked 'the original and inventive genius of the English'. Instead, Smith emphasised aesthetic developments, with the 'taste, judgment, propriety, and order' characteristic of the French language allowing for familiar ideas to be presented in new ways. He explained that descriptions of early humans are 'agreeable to the imagination' because we tend to imagine their lives as ones of either 'profound indolence' or 'astonishing adventures'. Our 'natural taste' for both indolence and adventure accounts for our youthful passion for 'pastoral poetry' and 'books of chivalry and romance'. It also explains why state of nature stories so 'excite the public curiosity'. As Smith summarised,

> Mr. Rousseau, intending to paint the savage life as the happiest of any, presents only the indolent side of it, which he exhibits indeed with the most beautiful and agreeable colours, in a style, which, though laboured and studiously elegant, is everywhere sufficiently nervous, and sometimes even sublime and pathetic. It is by help of this style, together with a little philosophical chemistry, that the principles and ideas of the profligate Mandeville seem in him to have all the purity and sublimity of the morals of Plato.[43]

---

[40] Adam Smith, 'The History of Astronomy', in *Essays on Philosophical Subjects*, ed. D. D. Raphael (Indianapolis, IN: Liberty Fund, 1980): 33–105.

[41] Adam Smith, *Lectures on Rhetoric and Belles Lettres*, ed. J. C. Bryce (Oxford: Oxford University Press: 2014): 148, 223.

[42] For a notable exception, see E. G. West, 'Adam Smith and Rousseau's *Discourse on Inequality*: Inspiration or Provocation?', *Journal of Economic Issues* 5:2 (1971): 56–70 (69). Cp. Paul Sagar, *Adam Smith Reconsidered: History, Liberty and the Foundations of Modern Politics* (Princeton, NJ: Princeton University Press, 2022): 113–142.

[43] Smith, 'A Letter to the Authors': 251.

Given that Smith wrote that Rousseau's text 'consists almost entirely of rhetoric and description', this reference to pastoral poetry is typically seen as sarcastic or, at best, an attempt to unmask a disguised satire.[44] But with Rousseau's refined Epicureanism in mind, Smith's discussion of Rousseau's style in the context of his divergence from Mandeville is rather astute. For it suggests that a concern with taste and aesthetic judgement are also present in Rousseau's account of self-love or *amour-propre* and its relationship to pity in the second *Discourse*.

One way of grasping the substance of Rousseau's style is to note that Smith likely borrowed this idea of 'philosophical chemistry' from his friend David Hume. In his *Enquiry* (1748), Hume used the phrase to describe systems of moral philosophy that, like Mandeville's, sought to 'resolve the elements' of apparently other-regarding sentiments – such as benevolence, friendship, public spirit, or fidelity – into the basic element of 'self-love'. By means of this philosophical chemistry, according to Hume, 'an Epicurean or a Hobbist' could argue that self-love was an 'original passion' that issued in behaviours that were then deemed either virtuous or vicious. This required a sort of chemical reaction, through which self-love was 'twisted and moulded' 'by a turn of imagination, by a refinement of reflection, by an enthusiasm of passion'.[45] Hume of course saw the imagination as central to all areas of philosophical enquiry; and he identified a hedonistic tendency in its productive power to combine ideas and create new ones.[46] As we will see, Rousseau developed precisely this kind of moral psychology: lacking any principle of natural sociability, and with our natural capacity for pity suppressed in society, sentiment and the imagination could nevertheless be activated to moderate or refine an original, Epicurean concern for self-interest or self-love.

That Smith referred to the second volume of the *Fable* in particular alerts us to similarities between Mandeville and Rousseau's views of self-love.[47] In the first volume (1714), Mandeville's account of self-love is broadly consistent with that of Pierre Nicole: human pride stimulates our search for pleasure, contributing to state flourishing by spurring emulation and a striving to increase one's

[44] Ibid. Cf. Hont (2015): 21.
[45] David Hume, *An Enquiry Concerning The Principles of Morals*, ed. Tom L. Beauchamp (Oxford: Clarendon, 1998): 90–91.
[46] See Timothy M. Costelloe, *The Imagination in Hume's Philosophy: The Canvas of the Mind* (Edinburgh: Edinburgh University Press, 2018) and, more widely, *The British Aesthetic Tradition: From Shaftesbury to Wittgenstein* (Cambridge: Cambridge University Press, 2013).
[47] For discussion of this distinction, and the view that most scholarship on the Rousseau and Smith connection has failed to take it seriously, see Robin Douglass, 'Morality and Sociability in Commercial Society: Smith, Rousseau – and Mandeville', *The Review of Politics* 79:4 (2017): 597–620 (600–606).

social standing through consumption and trade.[48] The second volume (1723) introduced a distinction between 'self-love' and 'self-liking', which was further developed in his 'Inquiry into the Origin of Honour' (1732). Both were instincts common to all animals. But where self-love leads us to care for our self-preservation, self-liking leads us to value ourselves above our 'real worth'. When 'excessive, or ill-turned', self-liking generated behaviours that were judged prideful because of the offence they caused to others. But self-liking could also be 'moderate and well-regulated', in which case it could motivate behaviours that caused others to think well of us. In this way, sociability was an effect of refined or well-regulated natural selfishness.[49]

One immediate target of Mandeville's distinction was Shaftesbury. In his *Inquiry* (1711), Shaftesbury offered an anti-Hobbesian defence of natural sociability grounded in the pleasure that humans naturally derive from liking and being liked by others. Most importantly – or, for Mandeville, egregiously – Shaftesbury took this as evidence of a 'natural affection for the whole' that, in turn, provided a motivation to act 'with regard to the public good'. While virtue, on Shaftesbury's account, did not require self-denial, any action devoid of this other regard was a vice to be avoided. Mandeville characteristically responded by insisting that liking and being liked by others was in reality motivated by a more fundamental self-liking.[50] And while Smith did not draw the connection, the distinction foreshadows Rousseau's account of *amour de soi* and *amour-propre*.[51]

Historians of political thought more often read Mandeville's *Fable* not as a response to Shaftesbury but as occupying the extreme pole on a spectrum opposite the Archbishop Fénelon.[52] Within this framework, Smith's 'Letter' is then taken to signal Rousseau's position in the eighteenth-century luxury debates. In broad terms, the debates concerned the related problems of both excessive economic inequality and over-centralised political authority at home and international competition and war abroad. Fénelon's *Adventures of Telemachus* (1699) presents a comprehensive vision of reform in which the threat of warfare abroad would be minimised by first rebalancing the relationship between agriculture and industry at home. It was a radical proposal that

---

[48] Mandeville (1924): 1:77, 79.

[49] Ibid.: 2:129–132. For discussion of Mandeville's distinction, and the argument that 'it is important not to overstate the extent to which it separates his later and earlier writings', see Robin Douglass *Mandeville's Fable: Pride, Hypocrisy, and Sociability* (Princeton, NJ: Princeton University Press, 2023): 35–38.

[50] Mandeville (1924): 2:131; 1:371–428. Cf. Douglass (2023): 94–105.

[51] Brooke (2012): 181–183.

[52] I.e., Sonenscher (2020): 26–50 and Hont (2006).

involved the suppression of luxury and its associated arts, forced population movement from the cities to the countryside, and involved the restriction of individual desires to 'the true necessities of nature'.[53] Mandeville famously argued that the problem was more apparent than real. He adopted a rigorous definition of 'necessity', arguing that civilisation itself was coterminous with an equally rigorous definition of 'superfluity' and 'luxury'. On his terms, to abstain from luxury in the way Fénelon advised would thus be to undermine the very basis of society.[54] Mandeville also argued that, while the inequality that accompanied luxury was indeed highly problematic in an absolute monarchy such as Fénelon's France, it was significantly less so in a 'free' state like Holland or Britain. For in such a state, the divisive effects of inequality could be mitigated by the unique combination of centralised authority and political representation. Mandeville's notorious conclusion about the public benefits of private vices rests on this foundation of moral rigorism and distinctively modern republicanism.[55]

I am not concerned here with whether we should see Mandeville's *Fable* primarily as a response to Shaftesbury or to Fénelon. As Robin Douglass rightly notes, this context is illuminating mostly 'because Fénelon's ideas were in the air, so to speak, for Mandeville never responded explicitly to *Télémaque* (and he was usually happy to name his targets)'.[56] Nor am I concerned with why, exactly, Smith decided to discuss and translate Rousseau for his Scottish audience. But noting his aesthetic concerns suggests that the view that 'we simply do not know why' he did so overstates the case; and the view that he was drawing 'attention to the one French work, above all others, that had taken up the branch of modern philosophy lately neglected in England' is only part of the story.[57] For Smith seems to have taken Rousseau's text to exemplify the central contribution of the French discussions – namely, its rhetorical and stylistic advances. Whatever the case, we have good grounds to see Mandeville's *Fable* as a more-or-less self-conscious alternative to the most prominent modern versions of the sort of Platonism that Smith sarcastically derided as sublime in his review of the second *Discourse*. And whether it was his intention or not, we can see his review as a signal that, whatever

---

[53] Francois de Fénelon, *Telemachus, Son of Ulysses*, ed. Patrick Riley (Cambridge: Cambridge University Press, 1994): 160–169.

[54] I.e., Mandeville (1924): 1:109–125.

[55] See Hont (2006) and Hans W. Blom, 'The Idea of Europe: From Antiquity to the European Union', in *The Republican Mirror: The Dutch Idea of Europe*, ed. A. Pagden (Cambridge: Cambridge University Press, 2002): 91–117.

[56] Douglass (2023): 96.

[57] Sagar (2022): 126; Douglass (2017): 604, n. 18.

ROUSSEAU'S EPICUREANISM

73

similarities to the Platonic position of someone like Shaftesbury we might discern in Rousseau, they are refinements of a more fundamental Epicureanism.

Jacob Vernet on Rousseau and Fashionable Epicureanism

Shortly after the second *Discourse* was received as an Epicurean text, his Genevan compatriot Jacob Vernet hailed Rousseau for offering 'the best defence against' what he called 'fashionable Epicureanism'.[58] Like Smith, Vernet's interest in modern Epicureanism stemmed from his concern with luxury and the role of pleasure in moral agency rather than a denial of the immortal soul, providence, or even sociability. Unlike Smith, he applied the Epicurean label directly to Rousseau. He was referring to the account of personal taste and public morality that Rousseau outlined in his *Letter to d'Alembert on the Theatre*. A brief consideration of Vernet's work helps to clarify both what he meant by fashionable Epicureanism and Rousseau's critical engagement with Epicureanism. For as we will see, Vernet anticipated Rousseau's subsequent contrast, in *Julie* (1761), between vulgar and refined Epicureanism.

That the two Genevans shared some common ground on such matters is evident in Rousseau's two references in *d'Alembert* to Vernet's 1752 *Instruction chrétienne*. He first cited Vernet's discussion of toleration to support his defence of the Genevan clergy's role as moral censors (*LD*:260/5:13). He then quoted from Vernet's anticipation of his own argument that the moral evaluation of theatrical performances was dependent on their variable effects in particular contexts. While some performances provided 'agreeable and useful' moral lessons, others corrupted audiences by depicting a 'relaxed morality' that served to justify 'vanity, idleness, luxury, and immodesty' (262–263/5:16–17).[59] Fashionable Epicureanism was simply Vernet's later specification of this relaxed morality: it induced Genevans to pursue the 'three idols' of 'money, vainglory, and sensual pleasure', distracting them from the truly 'great objects of God, virtue, and the Fatherland'. Vernet and Rousseau agreed on the hedonic basis of human agency: each, Rousseau quoted Virgil, is 'led by his pleasures'.[60] For that reason, they also agreed that the theatre could provide salutary support for moral education by leading spectators to take pleasure in the objects appropriate to their local *moeurs*. Rousseau's *d'Alembert*, Vernet wrote, might help to change private taste and public opinion regarding objects of pleasure

---

[58] 'Vernet à Rousseau, le 24 novembre 1758', *CC*5:239–241.

[59] Jacob Vernet, *Instruction chrétienne*, Vol. 1/5 (Geneva: Gosse, 1756): 362–363.

[60] Cf. Abbé Du Bos, *Critical Reflections on Poetry, Painting and Music*, trans. Thomas Nugent (London: J. Nourse, 1748): I.2: 20–21.

74 ROUSSEAU'S POLITICS OF TASTE

and, thereby, 'revive in the hearts of our citizens what remains of the manly virtues of our fathers'.[61] In response, Rousseau agreed that Vernet had grasped the 'essence of the problem' facing their compatriots 'clearly and distinctly'.[62]

Vernet and Rousseau thus saw fashionable Epicureanism as an ideological justification for luxury and commercial society. In the chapter following his account of the theatre from which Rousseau quoted, Vernet labelled luxury a 'secret poison' that led agents to pursue 'worldly' rather than 'spiritual goods' by accustoming them to 'superfluous commodities and delicacies' and all that 'flatters their senses'.[63] Several years later, he clarified this view of luxury's connection with Epicureanism in his analysis of Rousseau's exchange with d'Alembert. To Vernet, d'Alembert was propounding a '*philosophism*' that was best understood as a revival of 'Epicureanism and atheism'. He and the *philosophes* were in fact *philosophists*: 'Epicureans ... materialists ... men who sought to revive the most irreligious opinions of certain pagan philosophers'.[64] A theatre in Geneva would be no more than a 'school of Pagan philosophy' precisely because its citizens' tastes had already been infected by this degenerate 'Epicurean philosophism'. To support this conclusion, Vernet paraphrased Rousseau approvingly: 'the deprivation of taste is always due to the deprivation of morals'.[65]

In denominating Epicureanism 'fashionable' in his letter to Rousseau, Vernet was already operating with a distinction he later drew in his *Réflexions* (1769) between a 'speculative' and a 'practical Epicureanism'. Speculative Epicureanism corresponded to d'Alembert's *philosophism* – an 'abuse of the mind' that emerged in Athens, was revived in Rome, and spread throughout modern and contemporary Europe. This 'atheist' and 'materialist' philosophy 'excuses and authorises' the relaxed morality of practical Epicureanism, the worldly pursuit of 'gold and pleasures', 'self-interest, and personal vanity'. Theory and practice were thus reciprocally dependent: each supported the other in a vicious circle, wherein creeping libertinism demanded further ideological justification that, in turn, produced a credulous people, a hypocritical clergy, and irreligious philosophers. In this way, for Vernet, the 'evil of luxury' always accompanied 'the spirit of irreligion', and impiety caused the 'deprivation of *moeurs*' just as great wealth led to luxury consumption. It was to this

---

[61] 'Vernet à Rousseau, le 24 novembre 1758', CC5:240.
[62] 'Rousseau à Vernet, le 18 décembre 1758', CC5:256–258.
[63] Vernet (1756): 3.17, 368–369.
[64] Jacob Vernet, *Lettres critiques d'un votageur anglois sur l'article Geneve du Dictionnaire encyclopédique, et sur la Lettre de M. d'Alembert à Rousseau touchant les spectacles* (Copenhagen: Claude Philibert, 1766): 97, 124.
[65] Ibid.: 207; Rousseau, *LD*:264/*OC*5:18.

ROUSSEAU'S EPICUREANISM

interaction between speculative and practical Epicureanism that Vernet referred in claiming that 'every century of luxury is a century of Epicureanism'.[66]

Vernet's praise significantly complicates our understanding of Rousseau's reception of Epicureanism. What are we to make of this situation? None of Castel, Castillon, or Reimarus were simply mistaken in their view that Rousseau's second *Discourse* was constructed on Epicurean premises – he explicitly denies natural sociability, is sceptical about the immortal soul and the origin of languages, and offers both a purposely anti-providential natural philosophy and an ambiguous account of judgement. But neither was Vernet simply wrong that Rousseau's remarks on pleasure in the *Letter to d'Alembert* distinguished him from at least one kind of contemporary Epicurean. While he never responded to his early critics, Rousseau concurred with Vernet's account of the problem he intended to address in the *Letter* – namely, that Genevan citizens were increasingly mistaken in their judgements of pleasure and this threatened to undermine their republican constitution. Indeed, as I discuss in Chapter 4, the *Letter* can helpfully be understood as attempting to correct those judgements and, thereby, enable Genevans to find 'agreeable' those objects that would be truly 'useful' to them, individually and collectively.[67] Perhaps Rousseau simply changed his mind? As I explored in Chapter 1, both the logical and historical consistency of his 'system' is a perennial theme in the literature, and his reception of Epicureanism has also been read as evolving in at least certain respects.[68] I return to this possibility below. Prior to that, however, I turn in the next section to Rousseau's analysis of the critical controversy surrounding the reception of Epicureanism in Alexander Pope's *Essay on Man*. This neglected source helpfully widens the perspective Vernet's discussion opens up on Rousseau's reception of Epicurean hedonism.

Rousseau on Pope's Epicureanism

In a letter dated 17 January 1742, Rousseau addressed the controversy surrounding the early French reception of Alexander Pope's *Essay on Man*. The recipient of the letter was François Joseph de Conzié, a Savoyard nobleman

---

[66] Jacob Vernet, *Réflexions sur les moeurs, sur la religion, et sur le culte* (Paris: Claude Philibert, 1769): 113, 12, 32–33, 34, 68, 33.

[67] Sonenscher (2008): 148–163. Cf. Vickie Sullivan and Katherine Balch, 'Spectacles and Sociability: Rousseau's Response in His Letter to d'Alembert to Montesquieu's Treatment of the Theatre and of French and English Society', *History of European Ideas* 41:3 (2015): 357–374.

[68] Christopher Brooke, 'Rousseau's Second Discourse, between Epicureanism and Stoicism', in *Rousseau and Freedom*, ed. Christie McDonald and Stanley Hoffmann (Cambridge: Cambridge University Press, 2010): 44–57.

76

and friend of Rousseau's patron and lover Mme de Warens, with whom he developed a philosophical friendship around 1734. The amateur bibliophile had earlier sent Rousseau a copy of J. Seré Rieux's 1739 translation of Pope's *Essay*, the third to appear in French in just three years.[69] He also included a manuscript, which is no longer extant but referred to by Rousseau as the *Critical Sentiments*.

That Rousseau engaged with Pope is unsurprising, for the *Essay* was a touchstone for anyone thinking about human nature in the mid-eighteenth century. Especially in the Anglophone world – and only slightly less in France – Pope's account of self-love attracted great critical attention from moralists and theologians. For him, human agency is rooted entirely in the passions, which are but varieties of self-love. Our passions are ineliminable and drive us in different, often contradictory directions. Every individual is dominated by a 'master passion' that can absorb all the rest. We employ our reason simply to judge the appropriate means by which to satisfy our passions – it is like a compass telling us where to direct the ship propelled by the winds of self-love. Pope's account is sometimes seen as a verse translation of Mandeville's *Fable*.[70] And like both Mandeville and Pierre Nicole, Pope argued that, while our passions tend generally to disorder, they could be mixed or combined to produce order – our desire to be praised by others could be leveraged by skilful legislators to generate sociability in the state.

Rousseau's primary aim in the letter was to defend Pope against two accusations to which this account of self-love gave rise. The first was that he was impious; the second was that he was a kind of Epicurean. In the context of Rousseau's reception by Castel and Reimarus, it is noteworthy that he separated rather than connected these two accusations. Most intriguingly, he grounded their separation on a distinction between two different types or modes of criticism. A *philosophic* critic assessed a work's logical coherence and was best suited to address the accusation of impiety. A *poetic* critic assessed a work's beauty and was best suited to address the accusation of Epicureanism.[71] Ultimately, Rousseau implied, the best critics were those who operated in

---

[69] For the contents of Conzié's library, see Claudius Bouvier, 'La biliotheque des Charmettes', *Memoires et Documents de la Societe Savoisienne d'Histoire et d'Archeologie* 55 (1914): 133–176. The reception of Pope's *Essay* has been exhaustively treated in Émile Audra, *L'influence francaise dans l'oeuvre de Pope* (Paris: Champion, 1931).

[70] For discussion of Pope's account of self-love in the wider context of eighteenth-century imaginative literature, including Mandeville, see Arthur Lovejoy, *Reflections on Human Nature* (Baltimore, MD: Johns Hopkins University Press, 1961): 42–46, 169–178.

[71] Jean-Jacques Rousseau, 'Letter to François Joseph de Conzié', in *Rousseau: Lettres philosophiques*, ed. Jean-Francois Perrin (Paris: Librarie Générale Français, 2003 [1743]): 45–58 (45).

both modes – the synthesis of reason and sentiment characteristic of good taste. Indeed, the letter can be read as performing precisely this synthesis and, thereby, establishing what I will call Rousseau's ethos of critique.

Rousseau began his defence of Pope by adopting the philosophic mode of criticism. The unknown critic's accusation of impiety was evidently based on one of logical incoherence, itself stemming from an unsympathetic interpretation of a notorious line early in Pope's Epistle III: '*Tout est lié. Qui sait où la chaîne se perd?* (The chain holds on, and where it ends, unknown)'.[72] For Rousseau, Pope's account of the Great Chain of Being was indeed ambiguous, and this exposed him to critical scrutiny. But good criticism also demanded charitable interpretation: the ambiguity did not imply the impiety that the critic had illegitimately assumed, rather than proved. Rousseau sought to untie this 'Gordian knot of Pope's system' by sympathetically reconstructing the argument of Epistle I – that there are many possible worlds, that the world of God's creation must be one in which 'all that rise, rise in due degree', and that, therefore, there is a Great Chain of Being.[73] He accepted the conclusion of a hierarchical organisation of terrestrial life forms in a system of proportional gradation. Whatever was impious in Pope's system resided in the further supposition that this proportionality extended beyond creation, and that the Chain 'leads immediately to God'. Rousseau emphasised that the argument was logically coherent, or valid on 'formal terms'. The problem was that it was unsound – or 'absurd' – because it supposed a regular interval between finite creatures and their infinite creator.[74] That Rousseau here anticipates his later agreement with Voltaire's 'correction' of 'Pope's system' suggests consistency on this position over at least fourteen years.[75]

It is significant that Rousseau shifted to the poetic mode of criticism when it came to assessing Pope's Epicureanism. On his account, while it was certainly fair to interrogate Pope's equivocation over God's relationship to the Great Chain of Being, branding him an Epicurean could only be done in bad faith. 'Are you not shocked', he wrote, 'to see Pope accused of Epicureanism precisely in the places where his morality is elevated nearly to the heights of the

---

[72] Ibid. This translation is from Alexander Pope, *Essai sur l'homme de M. Pope*, trans. Jean de Seré Rieux (London, 1739), which Rousseau claims not to have had before him and which he likely cites from the author of the *Critical Sentiments*.

[73] Rousseau (1743): 49–51. Cf. Pope, *Essay on Man* I.43–44; 1.45–46; 1.237–240. See, classically, Arthur O. Lovejoy, *The Great Chain of Being: A Study in the History of an Idea* (Cambridge, MA: Harvard University Press, 1964).

[74] Rousseau (1743): 47.

[75] *Letter to Voltaire*, CW3:114/OC4:1067.

Gospels?'[76] Because he was commenting on the verses added by the unknown critic, we cannot know the content of the particular accusation to which he referred. But many of Pope's early critics seized on his accounts of both the relation between reason and passion and the role of pleasure and self-interest in moral virtue. As Jean-Pierre de Crousaz, the most widely read of these critics, glossed part of Epistle III in 1742: 'The passions are corrected, restrained, and first inclined toward virtue by a sense of interest. But from these prospects, which first excite their attention, men rise to more pure desires, and more exalted views; which, when they have once found the value of them, they never forsake.'[77] Rousseau agreed with the critical consensus when he noted that such discussions 'contain the seeds of extremely dangerous errors'. But he disputed the accusation of Epicureanism by appealing to the moral beauty of Pope's poem. Turning instead to Epistle IV, he claimed that 'no man the least bit sensitive to beauty would not feel his heart warmed by the sublime maxims' found there.[78] Rousseau's appeal to sentiment as an aesthetic standard of judgement was thus inseparable from his insistence on contextualising individual lines of the poem within the work as a whole. As we will see, he later insisted that his readers approach his own work with precisely this ethos of interpretation or critique.

We can better appreciate Rousseau's defence of Pope on this score by turning to other contemporary critics. None of the contemporary French translations and none of the French commentaries refer to Pope as an Epicurean *directly*. But that is not to say that Pope's early readers and critics were unaware of or unconcerned with his relation to Epicureanism.[79] The author of the earliest French translation of the *Essay*, Etienne de Silhouette, noted that Pope's discussion of pleasure early in Epistle IV was designed to express, respectively, the Epicurean, Sceptic, and Stoic accounts of pleasure: 'one grants his pleasure is but rest from pain / one doubts of all, one owns even virtue vain'.[80]

---

[76] Rousseau, (1743): 54.

[77] Jean-Pierre de Crousaz, *A Commentary on Mr Pope's Principles of Morality, or Essay on Man*, trans. anonymous (London, 1742): 177.

[78] Rousseau (1743): 54.

[79] Alexander Pope, *Essai sur l'homme*, prose trans. Silhouette (Paris, 1736). Alexander Pope, *Les principes de la morale et du goût: en deux poems*, trans. Jean-François Bellay (Paris, 1737). Alexander Pope, *Maximes et réflexions morales*, trans. Jean Rieux (Paris, 1739). Anonymous, 'Reflexions sur le livre de M. Pope, intitule: Essai sur l'Homme', *Journal de Trévoux* III (March 1737): 401–425. Anonymous, 'Essai sur l'Homme, par M. Pope, traduit de l'Anglois en François par M d[e] S[s] ilhouette', *Journal des Scavans*, April 1736, 235–240. Anonymous, 'Les Principes de la Morale et du Gout, en deux Poëmes graduates de l'Anglois de M. Pope, par M. du Resnel', *Journal des Scavans*, July 1737, 402–413.

[80] Pope, *Essai*, trans. Silhouette, 82; Pope, *Essay on Man*, IV. 25–26.

ROUSSEAU'S EPICUREANISM

Crousaz, for his part, employed a typical strategy when he likened Pope to Horace, a well-known but eclectic source of Epicurean tenets whom Crousaz said often 'treats morality with much juster notions than the Stoics, and seems to write from his heart; but, in other places, appears a very vulgar Epicurean, a mere sensualist'.[81] Immediately following this description of Horace's vulgar Epicureanism, Crousaz cited Epistle III: 'Interest, assisted by reflections / Brings for the virtues from the womb of the passions'.[82] Crousaz never directly accused Pope of Epicureanism as Rousseau suggested that the author of the *Critical Sentiments* had done. But the gloss quoted above follows immediately from his quotation of these lines and reference to Horace. Thus, we can take them together as providing an indirect accusation that identifies as 'vulgar Epicureanism' Pope's acceptance of one or all of ethical egoism, the priority of passion over reason, and the celebration of sensual pleasure.

One line of defence against the accusation of vulgar Epicureanism thus understood was to insist that Pope's intention had merely been to refute radical asceticism, in both its Augustinian and Stoic varieties. His friend William Warburton presented two arguments to this effect in his 1740 vindication of the *Essay*. While Warburton is largely neglected in modern scholarship, Rousseau names him in his discussions of the 'Lawgiver' and 'Civil Religion' (*SC*:72, 146/3:384, 464). Rousseau could have been thinking of Warburton's *Alliance between Church and State* (1736) but these are typically seen as references to his *Divine Legation of Moses* (1737–1741), which has been reconsidered as one of the central works of England's distinctively conservative and clerical or 'Arminian Enlightenment'.[83] As the foremost apologist for the Anglican settlement, Warburton denounced what he saw as the modern revival of Epicurean ideas by, especially, Hobbes and La Rochefoucauld. But it is not entirely surprising that he embraced and defended what others saw as the Epicurean elements of Pope's account of the passions. For in both the *Divine Legation* and his earlier *Critical and Philosophical Enquiry into the Causes of Prodigies and Miracles* (1727), Warburton generally uses 'Epicurean' as an epithet to refer to materialism and the denial of providence, rather than hedonism or self-love.[84] In this sense, his defence of Pope from charges of Epicureanism is part of his

---

[81] See Frank Stack, *Pope and Horace: Studies in Imitation* (Cambridge University Press. 1985).

[82] Crousaz (1742): 177.

[83] Along with Edward Gibbon's *Decline and Fall* (1776–1789): J. G. A. Pocock, 'Clergy and Commerce: The Conservative Enlightenment in England', in Rodolfo Ajello et al (eds), *L'Età dei Lumi: studi storici sul settecento Europeo in onore di Franco Venturi* (Naples, 1985). 1, 523–62.

[84] William Warburton, *A Critical and Philosophical Enquiry Into the Causes of Prodigies and Miracles, as Related by Historians: With an Essay Towards Restoring a Method and Purity in History*, 2 vols (London: Thomas Corbett, 1727): 1:9, 10, 36, 109.

80 ROUSSEAU'S POLITICS OF TASTE

long-standing efforts to distance the poet from his association with the radical anti-clericalism of Pope's erstwhile teacher Lord Bolingbroke.[85]

Warburton's first approach was to claim that Crousaz was guilty of a misreading that 'made an Epicurean god the master of the universe'.[86] For Warburton, Pope's insistence that 'partial Ill is Universal good' was intended to reject the 'extravagant' Stoic idea that moral virtue required the total extirpation of the passions – it allowed Pope to argue that passionate stress is itself a 'salutary agitation' that preserves our 'life and vigour'. On Warburton's account, any accusation of vulgar Epicureanism failed utterly to grasp Pope's intended meaning. Rather than arguing how the passions ought to be treated, he was simply illustrating that the passions were natural. Moreover, Warburton pointed out, Pope argued that because God's providence ensured that the passions 'are turned, from their natural bias, to promote the happiness of mankind', they 'should not be quite uprooted and destroyed, as the Stoics and their Followers in all Religions foolishly attempted'.[87] For Warburton, Pope's acceptance of divine providence meant that his rejection of Stoic asceticism could remain very far indeed from vulgar Epicureanism.

Warburton's second argumentative strategy was to note the role of 'temperance' in Pope's moral system. This was the positive dimension of Pope's rejection of radical asceticism. On the one hand, Pope clearly defended the passions' positive role in cultivating virtue insofar as they could be tempered by reason.[88] But, on the other hand, it was equally clear that Pope's was not a reductive rationalist position. Were reason unable to temper the passions, Pope famously suggested that individuals could still pursue pleasures virtuously because each had a 'master passion' that would temper their behaviour by absorbing all the rest.[89] In this way, Warburton's defence of Pope from the indirect attribution of vulgar Epicureanism invokes and elucidates a spectrum

[85] B. W. Young, *Religion and Enlightenment in Eighteenth-Century England* (Oxford: Clarendon, 1998): 166–212.

[86] Warburton argued that the misreading stemmed from a mistranslation of the *Essay* by the Abbé du Resnel. To Rousseau, Silhouette's translation had 'more grace and poetry' but du Resnel's was 'closer to the English'. While this had become the consensus view among French critics, it is tempting to see this opinion as a further sign that Rousseau had a better grasp of English than has long been believed. See Marian Hobson, 'Jean-Jacques Rousseau and Diderot in the Late 1740s: Satire, Friendship, and Freedom', in *Rousseau and Freedom*, ed. Christie McDonald and Stanley Hoffmann (Cambridge: Cambridge University Press, 2010): 58–76.

[87] William Warburton, *A Vindication of Mr. Pope's Essay on Man, from the Misrepresentations of M. de Crousaz. By the Author of The Divine Legation of Moses Demonstrated. In Six Letters* (London: J. Robinson, 1740): 69–70.

[88] Ibid.: 70, citing Pope, *Essay*, II.115–120.

[89] Ibid.: 71, citing Pope, *Essay*, II.127–132.

of views on the relationship of pleasure and the passions to virtue. It is not unlike the spectrum that, as we saw in Chapter 1, Rousseau encountered in his reading of Plato's *Republic* and *Phaedo*. At one end, there is radical Stoic or Augustinian asceticism, the extirpation of passion or wholesale rejection of pleasure. At the other, there is vulgar Epicureanism, any or all of radical egoism, hedonism, or sensualism. Pope's critics claimed that a rejection of the former necessarily implied an acceptance of the latter. In rejecting that conclusion, Warburton distinguished a view of temperance that has evident similarities with the position Rousseau would eventually describe as his own 'Epicureanism of reason'.

This reconstruction of Warburton's defence allows us to see what was unique in Rousseau's critique of Pope's reception as an Epicurean. He addressed Pope's moral teaching: unlike Warburton, he drew no substantial connections between Epicureanism and impiety, and he focused entirely on the relationship between pleasure and virtue. And while Warburton was also concerned with the relationship between literary form and philosophical content, he was vastly inferior to Rousseau as a literary critic – his 1747 edition of Shakespeare was much derided, but it evinces his desire to contribute to contemporary discussions of literary style and aesthetics.[90] Thus Rousseau launched his defence only after an emphatic pronouncement of his critical ethos:

> The great defect of critics is that of attaching themselves to some particular thoughts which, open to ambiguity when taken separately, can only be determined in their true meaning when examined in their relations with the body of the work, and with the place where they should be. It is especially the regular abuse of all those who judge things superficially, and it is, unquestionably, that of our critic.[91]

On this interpretive principle, Pope's discussion of self-love and self-interest in Epistle III ought to have been contextualised within the work as a whole.

Where Warburton turned to Epistle II, Rousseau insisted that Pope's ethical system had to be understood as culminating in the account of happiness in Epistle IV. It was there that one could find Pope's most important moral principles – namely, that 'virtue alone is happiness below' and that 'God in externals could not place content'.[92] For his part, Crousaz had quoted lines from Epistle III that,

---

[90] See Arthur Sherbo, 'Warburton and the 1745 "Shakespeare"', *The Journal cf English and Germanic Philology* 51:1 (1952): 71–82.

[91] Rousseau (1743): 55.

[92] Pope, *Essay*, IV, 308, 66.

Rousseau again acknowledged, contained dangerous concessions to egoism.[93] But Rousseau took Pope to have overcome their vicious potential with his subsequent account of happiness: 'Reason's true pleasures, all the joys of sense / Lie in three words, Health, Peace, and Competence'.[94] Rousseau provided his own gloss on Pope's developed moral system on this basis. Sympathetically seen and appropriately felt, Rousseau wrote, Pope taught:

> That whoever is endowed with good sense and a good heart has the source of happiness within himself. That happiness does not consist in external goods. That this happiness cannot exist without virtue and without the sweet peace of the heart that he calls *le digne fille du ciel*. That, therefore, vice can never be happy. That virtue delivered with pain enjoys still more contentment than vice in the midst of pleasures.[95]

Such were the principles of Pope's fundamental teaching on happiness. They were, Rousseau emphasised, repeated 'at least twenty times' in Epistle IV.[96]

Rousseau's defence of Pope hinges on a distinction between vulgar and refined Epicureanism that he saw himself as introducing to the critical reception of the *Essay*. On his reading, Pope was not a radical Stoic who held that virtue alone rendered man content. Like Warburton, he thought that this was only sensible, for to put 'the height of man's felicity' in physical health and simplicity was to acknowledge that self-interest and pleasure could be compatible with virtue and happiness, provided that each was properly understood. To be sure, this was not the way that 'the lessons of Epicurus . . . are *ordinarily presented*'.[97] But if they were 'the true principles of Epicurus', he continued, 'then all honest men should have the glory of being his follower'. There was thus some truth to the ascetic critique of vulgar Epicureans racing after 'honours and chimerical goods'. But it was equally true that radical Stoics were ignorant of true pleasure. For Rousseau, Pope's moral system was intended precisely to return them both to 'the real source of happiness' within.[98] Only a vulgar critic could see this as vulgar Epicureanism. A critic who combined a rational appreciation of argument with a sentimental awareness for beauty – that is, a critic with taste – would both see and, perhaps most importantly, *feel*, that Pope's was a refined Epicureanism.

---

[93] Crousaz, Commentary, 177–178. Citing Pope III.137–146 in Du Resnel trans., 194.
[94] Rousseau (1743): 54–55. Citing Pope, IV.77–80 in Du Resnel trans., 210.
[95] Rousseau (1743): 55.
[96] Ibid. Citing Pope, *Essay*, IV, v.307–308, 315–316.
[97] Rousseau (1743): 54–55 (my emphasis).
[98] Ibid.: 56.

Conclusion

Rousseau's critical ethos and his appeal to the beauty of Pope's poem direct our attention to the aesthetic dimension of his reception of Epicureanism. While this connection is entirely overlooked in the literature, a final contemporary critic of his Epicureanism suggests how it can be explored. Stéphanie Félicité, Comtesse de Genlis was a novelist and theorist of 'sensitive education' (1806). Two generations younger than Rousseau, she revealed concerns similar to his older critics when she accused him of having joined 'the materialists, the atheists, the Epicureans'.[99] Her ire was directed not at the second *Discourse* but at Rousseau's account in *Confessions* of his plan to compose a work entitled *The Wise Man's Materialism*. Though never completed, it would have described how one might control physical stimuli to support virtuous self-command through what he called an 'external regimen' (*C*:343/1:408). On Genlis' reading, it would have been little more than a kind of 'medicine book', reducing virtue to 'good digestion' on the assumption that morality could be generated 'like tea, through infusion'. Such a procedure might preserve the morally vicious from '*some* excesses', she conceded. But it could never 'restore them to virtue', for it granted 'absolute power of the physical over the moral' world.[100] Once more, it was his apparent vulgar materialism that marked Rousseau as an Epicurean.

The critical ethos that Rousseau deployed in his letter about Pope can, in turn, be applied to Genlis' accusation of his Epicurean materialism. Put most generally, his concern in the *Wise Materialism* was with the way our values and desires change over time. He emphasised that these variations depend 'in large part' upon prior sensations. But a sympathetic critic will note that Rousseau also explained that they 'depend on us' as well. His key insight, he suggested, had something to do with our active mental ability to interrupt the stream of sense impressions. The 'external regimen' that would 'force the animal economy to support the moral order' was itself a result of human memory, judgement, and imagination. As we will see in the following chapters, these mental faculties enabled us to compare our sensations across time and space, to form judgements about them, and to derive principles from them. His version of materialism was 'wise', then, because it grounded morality in the activity of our minds, first, and the body, second (*C*:343/1:409). Seen from this perspective, Rousseau's plan to write the *Wise Materialism* is the clearest indication of his intention to write a

---

[99] Stéphanie Félicité de Genlis, *Alphonsine, ou la tendresse maternelle*, Vol. 1/4 (Paris: H. Nicolle, 1806): 9.

[100] Genlis (1806): 8.

treatise on what was then coming to be called aesthetics: 'the science of what is sensed or imagined'.[101] While Rousseau never used the term aesthetics, the core of the underlying mental activity he described was precisely the imagination's ability to mediate between mental and physical experience.

Such a reading may seem overly sympathetic. But we will see in Chapter 5 that it fits with the account of judgement in *Emile*. And it can be supported by drawing once more on Rousseau's critical ethos and contextualising the *Wise Materialism* as a part within *Confessions* as a whole. Three books after he introduced it, he subsequently cautioned his readers not to be 'deceived by the title' into thinking that it would have been a 'true treatise in materialism'. He suspected that just such a mistaken impression had led to d'Alembert's stealing his plans for the project; he even worried that it would lead to accusations perhaps not unlike those later launched by Genlis (*C*:509/1:608). Moreover, the imagination is fundamental to what he identified as the central passage of *Confessions*: his account of his meeting in Venice with the prostitute Zulietta. There, he provides a detailed description of the imagination's ability to associate physical impressions with general ideas and moral qualities, and to turn general ideas into particular sensations with rather intense emotions. This is how he came to view the same woman as an embodiment of divine beauty, at one moment, and 'a sort of monster, the outcast of nature, men, and love', the next. In this sense, his imagination was the 'poison' that nature implanted in his head to spoil the appetite for happiness it implanted in his heart. (*C*:270/1:321–322; *E*:210–212/4:303–306). But it also enabled what he considered his unique awareness of the contradiction between natural merit and social station, both in the particular case of Zulietta, and in the more general sense he famously described as his 'illumination' on the road to Vincennes (*LM*:575/1:1135–1136). The imagination's ability to generate something moral out of something physical might well have been Rousseau's fundamental insight.[102] It certainly differentiated his materialism from the vulgar determinism that Genlis and Rousseau's earlier critics accused him of when they branded him an Epicurean.[103]

If such a reading is at all persuasive, then it raises the question noted in Chapter 1 about the consistency of Rousseau's thought. He abandoned the *Wise Materialism*, after all, and he developed his plans for it only after the second *Discourse* had been received as an Epicurean text. This was around the time

---

[101] Alexander Gottlieb Baumgarten, *Aesthetica*, Vol. 2 (Frankfurt/Oder: Kleyb, 1758). Cf. Simon Grote, *The Emergence of Modern Aesthetic Theory: Religion and Morality in Enlightenment Germany and Scotland* (Cambridge: Cambridge University Press, 2017).

[102] Sonenscher (2020).

[103] As noted in V. D. Musset-Pathay, 'Introduction', in Musset-Pathay ed., *Oeuvres complètes de Jean-Jacques Rousseau*, Vol. 2/7 (Paris: Perronneau, 1818): 569–570.

of the publication of Helvétius' *De L'Ésprit*, which, as we will see, he read as advancing a vulgar Epicurean materialism. Would it have clarified his materialism, or perhaps marked an evolution in his reception of Epicureanism? The following chapters go some way to answering this question. But to conclude this discussion, I will simply take Rousseau's critical ethos one step further. When he suggested that good criticism enabled access to the author's intention in writing, he anticipated the hermeneutic principle he would later ask his readers to adopt in interpreting his own work. His account of Zulietta fulfilled his intention in writing *Confessions* because, he wrote, it was the best depiction of his 'natural disposition' (*C*:269/1:320). As we have seen, he repeatedly insisted that his works constituted a coherent system. He also suggested that, in order to understand it, one had to read his works in reverse order – starting with his autobiographical *Dialogues* and contextualising each work as a part of the greater whole. This method would reveal the 'dispositions', 'affections', or 'internal sentiment' behind his work, which was the 'surest way to bring an equitable judgment to bear' on the matter of his consistency (*D*:30, 212–213/1:697, 933–934). That Rousseau had been applying this same critical ethos to other authors since at least 1742 is one reason to take seriously his instructions for how to understand his system. By opening up a new perspective on what is perhaps the perennial issue in Rousseau scholarship, the foregoing reconstruction shows definitively that the question of Rousseau's reception of Epicureanism is of more than merely historical or antiquarian interest.

Beyond intramural debates in Rousseau studies, this chapter points to more general conclusions for historians of political thought. Following Castillon's example, the best analysts of Rousseau's Epicureanism have focused on the subtle ways in which Rousseau diverged from Lucretius in the second *Discourse*. We will see in what follows that this approach helps to clarify Rousseau's method of conjectural history and the political-economic dimensions of his thought. But considering the aesthetic dimensions of his reception of Epicureanism helpfully alerts us to his more positive debts to Lucretius. As the epigraph of his *Dissertation on Modern Music*, for instance, he chose a citation from Lucretius' account of how civilisation had 'spoiled our taste' for 'ancient' forms of melody and rhythm.[104] This concern with the historical variability of moral values informed both Rousseau's plans for the *Wise Materialism* and Vernet's account of fashionable Epicureanism.

In this way, finally, the chapter's reconstruction provides a foundation on which more fully to appreciate the distinctiveness of Rousseau's modern

---

[104] *CW*7:27/*OC*5:155. Lucretius, *DRN*:V.1415.

Epicureanism. His engagement with Epicureanism was part of a broader shift underway in the middle of the eighteenth century. As we have seen, Scottish, English, and French discussions of Epicureanism were increasingly driven less by concerns with atheism and more by an interest in aesthetics. Mandeville's Epicurean emphasis on utility (the *honestum et utilitas*) was part of his refutation of Shaftesbury's Platonic assertion of objective moral beauty (the *pulchrum et honestum*).[105] Considering Rousseau's reception *as* an Epicurean usefully reminds us that his reception *of* Epicureanism exhibits a similar combination of interest in both utility and beauty. Bringing the *pulchrum* back into view, as it were, helpfully shifts our attention from thinking about modern Epicureanism in the more familiar terms of sociability, conventional justice, or atheism, and invites us to think, somewhat differently, about Epicureanism and sentiment, beauty, imagination, or aesthetics in modern political thought. This new perspective allows us to see the originality of Rousseau's particular version of Epicureanism as lying in his application of these aesthetic concerns to an understanding of modern politics. The remaining chapters of this book are written from this new perspective.

---

[105] Mandeville (1924): 2:325, 331, 343. Cf. Douglass (2023): 101–103.

Part II

4

The Problem of Modern Liberty: Sociability, Taste, Commerce

Introduction

What happens to our usual ways of seeing Rousseau once we see him as contributing to the complex and contested modern reception of Epicureanism? The discussion up to now has advanced several closely related historical claims. The variability of eighteenth-century uses of Epicureanism is sufficient to reject essentialist understandings of a modern Epicurean tradition or revival. Taking this sceptical insight seriously allows us better to appreciate the ways that eighteenth-century thinkers engaged with Epicurean ideas. By elucidating the range of possible positions on Epicureanism, we were alerted to the sometimes subtle rhetorical and polemical choices made in texts like Diderot's article on Epicureanism and Rousseau's letter on Pope's *Essay*. And by surveying thinkers in different contexts, we were able to identify both continuities and differences in the modern reception of Epicureanism. As my story expanded beyond mid-century Paris, we saw that Rousseau was part of a broader shift in the modern reception of Epicureanism – what I have called a shift from atheism to aesthetics.

My aim in the next two chapters is to clarify Rousseau's status as a theorist of the modern state from the perspective of his refined Epicurean politics of taste. The connection is not entirely obvious. Accounts of what makes a modern state theory 'modern' tend to diverge along the related lines of periodisation and conceptualisation. Quentin Skinner showed that the modern concept of the state gradually emerged throughout the sixteenth and early seventeenth centuries to describe an idea of public power as 'abstract' against the feudal notion of 'personal and charismatic' authority. For Skinner, the modern state is 'an omnipotent yet impersonal power' and a state theory is modern if it

90 ROUSSEAU'S POLITICS OF TASTE

understands public powers to derive not from a ruler's person but from their holding what Hobbes called 'the office of the sovereign'.[1] For Istvan Hont, on the other hand, specifically modern state theories must also be grounded in an account of 'commercial society'. With the rise of public credit to finance foreign wars, the Hobbesian state became modern when it came in the eighteenth century to be understood as a fiscal state. Consequently, state theories had to account for a new form of moveable (rather than landed) property and social relations characterised by increased mutual dependence and a highly developed division of labour.[2] For Hont, because Hobbes lacks an account of commercial society, he is better considered the last of the pre-modern or medieval state theorists.

There is a familiar view of the state theory of the *Social Contract* as articulating a sort of modern Epicureanism in the Hobbesian sense.[3] We saw that Rousseau adopted the Epicurean foundations of modern state theory – the denial of natural sociability. And as one of his early critics put it, whoever 'says that the law is the expression of the general will is the follower of Epicurus, of Thomas Hobbes, and of Jean-Jacques Rousseau'.[4] On this view, Rousseau agreed with both Epicurus and Hobbes that justice is grounded in a conventional agreement among self-interested agents; and the legal standard of justice, the general will, flows from each citizen's consideration of their own self-interest in casting their votes in the assembly. We saw Pufendorf attribute to Hobbes the Epicurean view of justice as a pledge of reciprocal utility, a pact neither to do nor suffer harm rather than a 'thing in its own right'.[5] Many of Rousseau's contemporaries saw him as continuing this aspect of modern Epicureanism.

If Rousseau's adoption of modern sovereignty theory is uncontroversial, his status as a theorist of politics in commercial society is contested. This is

---

[1] Quentin Skinner, *The Foundations of Modern Political Thought: Volume 2, The Age of Reformation* (Cambridge: Cambridge University Press, 1978): 2, 358; Quentin Skinner, 'The State', in *Political Innovation and Conceptual Change*, ed. Terence Ball, James Farr, and Russell L. Hanson (Cambridge: Cambridge University Press, 1989): 90–131.

[2] Hont (2005) and Istvan Hont and Michael Ignatieff, *Wealth and Virtue: The Shaping of Political Economy in the Scottish Enlightenment* (Cambridge: Cambridge University Press, 1986). Hont's account critically develops that in John Pocock, *The Machiavellian Moment: Florentine Political Thought and the Atlantic Republican Tradition* (Princeton, NJ: Princeton University Press, 2016); John Pocock, *Virtue, Commerce, and History: Essays on Political Thought and History, Chiefly in the Eighteenth Century*, Vol. 2 (Cambridge: Cambridge University Press, 1985).

[3] Strauss (1953). Tuck (2017). Douglass (2015).

[4] Achille Nicolas Isnard, *Observations Sur Le Principe Qui a Produit Les Révolutions de France, de Genève et d'Amérique, dans les Dix-Huitieme Siecle* (Evreux: Veuve Malassis, 1789): 22.

[5] Epicurus, 'Sovereign Maxims': 673–675 (§31, 33).

THE PROBLEM OF MODERN LIBERTY

91

partly because he never used the concept himself. Hont used it to express two related ideas. First, a commercial society is one with relatively well-developed manufacturing industries and foreign trade. In this sense, a commercial society is distinguished from an agricultural society. Second, a commercial society is one in which the ruling moral psychology is that of commercial sociability – it is a 'society that lacks primary human sociability but builds everything (both good and bad, by definition) out of the needs of selfish individuals having to live together'. In this sense, a commercial society is distinguished from societies held together by other-regarding moral-psychological bonds, like 'mutual love or affection'.[6] Hont used a reading of Adam Smith to capture both ideas.[7] But if they can be disaggregated, then one can be a theorist of commercial *sociability* without being a theorist of commercial *society*. And if Rousseau is not the latter, then, on one reading, his cannot be a theory of the specifically modern state.[8]

Rousseau's realistic sense of the economic limits of modern politics is clear in the *Social Contract*. As I noted in Chapter 1, there are two ways that modern states differ from the Roman Republic and Greek *polis*. First, moderns are more concerned with private interest and gain than with freedom, partly because the greater material effort required to meet individual survival needs in severe northern climates necessitates a developed division of labour, and partly because of a moral condemnation of slavery. The second side of Rousseau's ancient/modern periodisation is aesthetic: moderns speak muted and indistinct languages, incapable of eloquence, and lacking the persuasive power to stir patriotic affection for the common good. While it tends to be overlooked, Rousseau was not alone in recognising the aesthetic dimensions of the shift from ancient to modern societies – both Smith and Hume offered similar reflections.[9] Its inclusion at the heart of the *Social Contract* is crucial because it introduces the problem that Rousseau set himself in his political theory – how to preserve freedom in the uniquely modern situation of economic necessity and aesthetic impoverishment. 'No longer having the same advantages', he asks, 'how are we to preserve the same rights' (*SC*:115/3:430–431; cf. *CW*9:292–293/3:880–881).

Seeing Rousseau as an Epicurean supports the Hobbesian reading of the *Social Contract*. But we must see him as a refined Epicurean, specifically, in

---

[6] Hont (2015): 42, 9.

[7] Ibid.: *passim*, and Hont (2005): 159–184. For criticism, see Sagar (2022): 12, n. 2.

[8] See Robin Douglass, 'Theorising Commercial Society: Rousseau, Smith and Hont', *European Journal of Political Theory* 17:4 (2018): 501–511. Cf. Sagar 2022: 113–142.

[9] Smith (2014): 148, 223. David Hume, *Essays, Moral, Political, and Literary, Vol. 1*, ed. Tom L. Beauchamp and Mark A. Box (Oxford: Clarendon, 2021): 91–118.

order fully to appreciate his answer to his problem of modern liberty. If originally Hobbesian individuals always remain selfish, then one way they can live together is to pursue and exchange personal 'utilities', building durable social relations through the 'utilitarian bonds created by commercial reciprocity'.[10] Another way is by seeking something more like self-approval, making social relations durable by providing avenues for recognition. Both approaches to moral theory are applicable to modern commercial societies for the same reason that they are Epicurean: they both begin and end with the self. Rousseau's state theory is grounded in the idea that self-interest is irreducibly given by the physical side of human nature. But much of what is most interesting in his political thought stems from his reflections on the desire for self-approval given by the moral side of human nature. And insofar as these reflections centre on questions of sentiment, beauty, and especially the imagination, then seeing Rousseau as a refined Epicurean helps to clarify his understanding of the complicated interplay between self-interest and self-approval in modern politics.

This chapter begins to make these arguments by revisiting some of Rousseau's most enduring texts in light of the foregoing historical reconstruction. With issues of pleasure and taste firmly in view, I now switch from a primarily historical to a primarily exegetical mode of presentation. First, I argue that the critique of commerce in Rousseau's first *Discourse* reveals his fundamental concern with the relationship between 'utility' and 'agreeableness' as criteria of judgement. In these terms, a myopic focus on self-interest (or utility) can be balanced by pursuing pleasure (or agreeableness), but only if pleasure is pursued appropriately. Then, I argue that Rousseau's engagement with Lucretius in the second *Discourse* similarly clarifies his view of the modern necessity of a developed division of labour between town and country. As we will see, Rousseau theorises a kind of structural analogy between the individual and society, wherein commercial society enforces an imbalance both between judgements of utility and agreeableness and between agriculture and industry. This reading of the *Discourses* supports my argument that Rousseau saw refined Epicureanism as one way of redressing these imbalances. In *Julie*, he critiques vulgar Epicureanism and celebrates refined Epicureanism as a model of good taste that can establish an equilibrium between utility and agreeableness in the household. That discussion, in turn, elucidates his attempt in *d'Alembert* to correct Genevans' judgements of pleasure and, thereby, enable them to find agreeable those objects that are truly useful to them, both individually as citizens and collectively as a people. For if good taste can be cultivated in the household, then citizens of modern states might be able to balance the

---

[10] Hont (2015): 7.

THE PROBLEM OF MODERN LIBERTY   93

necessary pursuit of self-interest with an enjoyment of pleasure. Bringing these texts together in this way has the further benefit of clarifying Rousseau's attentiveness to literary form – from novels, to operas, and even comedies.

Broadly, this second part of the book demonstrates that reading Rousseau through the lens of refined Epicureanism illuminates aspects of his thought that are too often neglected, precisely by providing a new way of seeing the relationship between works that are too often seen as characterised by some inherent contradictions. The central argument of this chapter is that we should see Rousseau as an internal critic of modern commercial society. This sets the scene for my reconstruction of the aesthetic dimensions of *amour-propre* and a democratic account of the general will in Chapter 5. These arguments are in many ways the culmination of my reconstruction of the modern reception of Epicureanism in Part I. I begin Part II, then, by outlining Rousseau's account of refined Epicureanism.

Refined Epicureanism

The early readers of the second *Discourse* were correct: Rousseau is an Epicurean insofar as it is a foundational premise of his political thought that human beings are not naturally sociable. Some readers have found his Epicurean position on sociability difficult to grasp. One source of confusion is his use of the commonplace vulgar understanding of Hobbes to articulate it. We saw that he presented the sociability debate as a choice between Pufendorf's view of humans as naturally weak and fearful and the view that humans were naturally intrepid and aggressive, a position which neither Hobbes nor Epicurus actually held but which is consistently attributed to them. Confusion also arises from the radical scepticism of his intervention in the debate. With Hobbes and Epicurus, he held that sociability was not natural but an artefact of history: sociability is 'natural' insofar as society follows directly from an attribute of human nature; but sociability is 'unnatural' in the sense that society is only indirectly sociable, not intentionally or directly. But Rousseau went against both Hobbes and Epicurus when he historicised reason and the passions along with the state. In this sense, his critics were right to note that he radicalised Hobbes' Epicurean account of sociability. But he also rejected Pufendorf's *imbecillitas*, which was similarly taken to be an Epicurean position: in making sociability an effect of individual considerations of utility, it accorded with Epicurus' account of justice as a pledge of reciprocal usefulness, an agreement not to harm one another. Rousseau insisted that the first humans were self-sufficient and hence had no need to establish relationships of reciprocal utility beyond sporadic alliances like hunting parties. But as Castillon noted, and as we will see further

94 ROUSSEAU'S POLITICS OF TASTE

in what follows, his anti-Pufendorfian image of the physical harmony of the first human and its habitat was another piece of what he considered his more authentic Epicureanism.

Rousseau's position was the great ideological threat to orthodox readers. The vulgar Hobbesian radical lack of sociability, or its eventual collapse into asociality, could always be overcome by religious conversion or state coercion. But the position that Rousseau, Smith, and Hume all held was that the predominance of utility and self-interest in moral psychology was a constant dynamic. It was not to be overcome by the state but mitigated or neutralised by its own force. What Kant would later name unsocial sociability both preceded and ran alongside the state after its formation. As such, political stability was seen to require a state that could coexist with a society based on this continually unsociable dynamic. In the modern condition, in other words, the state had to be consistent with and grounded in commercial society.

Rousseau's view of Epicureanism both marked his distance from Hobbes on sociability and bridged the gap with Stoicism regarding the relationship between virtue and pleasure. Another reason for confusion about his position is that the names of the Hellenistic sects functioned as ideal types, extreme poles of a spectrum of diverse opinions; the most frequently cited source for their content was Cicero's *de Finibus*, the whole point of which was the dialectical interplay between the two doctrines.[11] Precisely because they were ideal types, Rousseau could intriguingly describe the psychological state of savage peoples in the second *Discourse* as a synthesis of Stoic *apatheia* and Epicurean *ataraxia* (*DI*:187/3:192).[12] Indeed, Rousseau's engagement with the doctrine shows that he recognised the internal complexity of the Epicurean position and had a surprisingly self-conscious and sophisticated set of views on what Epicureanism could and should involve. And although he shared the commonplace negative view of vulgar Epicureanism, he still insisted on differentiating this from a refined Epicureanism that he claimed as his own.

Rousseau's clearest account of the distinction between vulgar and refined Epicureanism comes in a posthumously published fragment surviving from the drafting of *Emile* and *Julie*. Epicureanism, he wrote,

> . . . is good at the very most to grasp the piece that falls into our mouth, but it is sophistic and false when it makes us move our mouth forward to

---

[11] Ibid.: 14. For more detailed discussion, focusing on the British context, see Tim Stuart-Buttle, *From Moral Theology to Moral Philosophy: Cicero and Visions of Humanity from Locke to Hume* (Oxford: Oxford University Press, 2019).

[12] Cp. Brooke (2010): 54. Jimmy Casas Klausen, *Fugitive Rousseau: Slavery, Primitivism, and Political Freedom* (New York: Fordham University Press, 2014): 17–21.

THE PROBLEM OF MODERN LIBERTY 95

receive it ~~when it makes us take one step in order to go seek it~~. The ~~only~~ true conclusion of Epicurus' doctrine is always to keep ourselves to the good ~~to prefer the good~~ that is closest to us. Every Epicurean who runs after pleasures is a madman who does not know what he wants and does not understand anything in his master's system ~~every consistent Epicurean is necessarily a Stoic~~ (*E*:681–682/4:874).[13]

The resonances between this fragment on Epicureanism and Rousseau's defence of Alexander Pope are obvious. Just as Pope's teaching that the real source of happiness is internal followed the 'true principles of Epicurus', so here is Epicurus' 'true conclusion' that we should pursue those goods that are 'closest to us'. And just as Rousseau distanced Pope from the 'ordinary' presentation of Epicureanism, so here he contrasts the refined Epicurean with the 'false' Epicurean 'madman'.

In fact, Rousseau was concerned with the Epicurean approach to pleasure and happiness even prior to his intervention in the critical reception of Pope's *Essay*. In an unpublished 'Memorandum' on education from 1740, he explored two paths to happiness. The first was always to satisfy one's passions and ceaselessly enjoy pleasure and voluptuousness. The second was to eliminate one's passions altogether and neither possess nor desire pleasures. But the conventional choice between these positions was a false one, for both were unrealistic 'chimeras'. True happiness consisted in the 'continuous, slight agitation' of the soul, which could only be achieved through a balance of 'honour and delicacy'. The only 'reasonable' approach in practice was thus to seek temperance through taste: 'to temper the ardour of our passions by means of the multiplicity of tastes that weaken them by dividing them'.[14] Shortly thereafter, he explained that learning 'the practice of innocent pleasures' allowed one to abandon the 'sad austerity of the Stoa'.[15]

When he wrote the fragment on Epicureanism, Rousseau was more consistently presenting the different philosophical approaches to pleasure in explicitly Hellenistic terms. As he explained in a letter that he evidently intended as a public statement, human agency is always rooted in self-interest. As such, one should

> never confuse, as the Stoics did, happiness with virtue. It is certain that to do good for the sake of good is to do it for one's own sake, out of

---

[13] Strikethrough indicates Rousseau's own edits.
[14] *CW*12:99–103/*OC*4:13–16.
[15] *CW*12:18/*OC*2:1140.

96 ROUSSEAU'S POLITICS OF TASTE

self-interest, since it gives the soul an internal satisfaction, a contentment with itself without which there is no true happiness . . . virtue does not bestow happiness, but it alone teaches one to enjoy it when one has it.[16]

Rousseau accepted the hedonic basis of moral agency. And if he sometimes avoided Hellenistic terminology, he consistently rejected libertine hedonism and advocated this refined Epicureanism.

From this perspective, Jacob Vernet was also correct in his assessment of Rousseau as a critic of vulgar or 'fashionable' Epicureanism. But it is significant that Rousseau only agreed with his compatriot that they were confronting the same problem. For they disagreed fundamentally in their respective analyses of the political causes and consequences of Epicureanism in their native Geneva. Vernet advocated a political-theological solution: vulgar Epicureanism stemmed from weakness of will, which could be combated by practising the revised Calvinism of the Genevan state Church.[17] Rousseau agreed that vulgar Epicureans lacked self-command but his civil religion notoriously ruled out any such solution (SC:149–151/3:467–469). Consistent with his refined materialism, moreover, he always emphasised that the severity of the problem was inseparable from the same material conditions that separated ancient from modern politics. *D'Alembert* intervened directly in Genevan debates surrounding the demographic and political-economic effects of feminine taste.[18] His was a remarkably realistic – or 'optimist' – assessment that distanced him considerably from Vernet's moralism.[19]

Rousseau's analysis of political economy and aesthetics in Geneva mirrored his formulation of the problem of modern liberty. As he saw it, gradual participation in international trade had led Swiss people from all cantons to imitate cultural practices imported from France, and women such as the patrician *demoiselles* of Geneva's upper town began to adopt modes of urban sociability inimical to the sumptuary laws that supported their republican constitution. As a result, the Swiss in general began to seek the vain pleasures of luxury while losing the natural taste for rural isolation. Agricultural production therefore flagged, and depopulation resulted from the lack of an

---

[16] 'Rousseau à d'Offreville, le 4 octobre 1761', CC9:143–149.

[17] Jacob Vernet, *Instruction chrétienne*, Vol. 1/5 (Geneva: Gosse, 1756). Richard Whatmore, *Against War and Empire: Geneva, Britain, and France in the Eighteenth* (New Haven, CT: Yale University Press, 2012): 47–50, 63.

[18] Helena Rosenblatt, 'On the "Misogyny" of Jean-Jacques Rousseau: The Letter to d'Alembert in Historical Context', *French Historical Studies* 25:1 (2002): 91–114.

[19] Hont (2014): 74.

THE PROBLEM OF MODERN LIBERTY 97

increase in production proportionate to the increase in consumption.[20] His critique of vulgar Epicureanism and the *demoiselles* of taste went hand in hand: the immoderate pursuit of the pleasures of vanity, luxury, and intemperate sensuality combined in a vicious circle with economic imbalance between town and country, and demographic crisis. This analysis of the interaction between international trade, domestic production and consumption, and the cultural determination of taste is repeated across Rousseau's major theoretical works, including the second *Discourse* and *Julie*.

He first introduced the opposition between vulgar and refined Epicureanism in order to elucidate the political-economic distinction that frames *Julie*. This was between the urban 'man of the world' and the 'country-dweller'. Men of the world are 'vulgar Epicureans' who lack self-command and operate with a mistaken criterion of sensual pleasure. As such, enjoyment of true pleasure remains beyond their continuous grasping. The emergence of the novel as a uniquely modern aesthetic form provided ideological justification for this licentiousness by celebrating the 'refinements of city taste . . . the paraphernalia of luxury, Epicurean morality'. Upon consuming these artistic representations, country-dwellers become averse to their 'station' and 'leave the village [for] the capital', depopulating the countryside (*J*:13–14/2:18–20). As we will see, the salutary morality that Julie inculcates at Clarens is based on the 'Epicureanism of reason' (444), a temperate sensuality that demonstrates her refined appreciation of Epicurus' system. Rousseau's response to his diagnosis of the vicious circle of vulgar Epicureanism at the heart of the culture of modern commercial society was thus to provide an alternative image that might generate a virtuous circle of refined Epicureanism. Clarifying at least one of his intentions in writing it, he addressed *Julie* to women in the countryside, so that they might exercise their natural moral authority in the household and 'restore their taste for true pleasures'. The protreptic purpose of his notion of refined Epicureanism is evident: imitation of his heroine's refined Epicureanism would attach country-dwellers to their station, addressing economic imbalance and counteracting the scourge of depopulation by inspiring in them what Rousseau termed here 'the taste for virtue' (15–19/2:21–26).

Rousseau described his opposite, positive ideal of refined Epicureanism in more detail later in *Julie*. The above fragment on Epicureanism was likely a first draft of that description. But before exploring it further, the next section relates Rousseau's rejection of vulgar Epicureanism more directly to his critique of commercial society. Vulgar Epicureans lack self-command in part because they operate with a mistaken criterion of pleasure. Refined Epicureans are able to

---

[20] 'Rousseau à duc de Luxembourg, le 20 janvier 1763', *CC*15:48–69.

98 ROUSSEAU'S POLITICS OF TASTE

enjoy those goods already within their grasp because a true understanding of Epicurus' doctrine allows them to regulate their judgements regarding objects of pleasure. In these terms, the distinction between vulgar and refined Epicureanism alerts us to a fundamental feature of Rousseau's first *Discourse* – namely, his ruthless critique of the ways that modern commerce introduces and reinforces mistaken criteria of judgement.

The Politics of Taste in Commercial Society: The First *Discourse*

Rousseau's account of taste clarifies his critique of politics in commercial society in the first *Discourse*. In one sense, his argument is well known. Originating in the vices of vanity and pride, the flourishing of the arts and sciences during the Renaissance had not perfected but corrupted modern morality (*DSA*:9/3:9–10). But the centrality of judgements of taste to that argument is frequently overlooked. My claim that he found some virtue in taste might be surprising in light of his analysis: 'the dissolution of morals, the necessary consequence of luxury, in turn leads to the corruption of taste' (20/3:21). This analysis informs the familiar view of Rousseau's 'passionate protest against the easy-going and somewhat rotten civilization of the century of taste'.[21] But here the adjectives are more important than the noun. When the Abbé Raynal accused him of preferring 'rusticity to politeness', Rousseau was indignant, insisting that his critics had ignored what was for him an 'essential distinction'. He preferred rusticity not to politeness per se but only to the 'prideful and false politeness' of his century. He applied the same distinction to taste. For, as he clarified in the 'Final Reply' (1751) to his critics, taste, too, stemmed from the cultivation of letters:

> Since public approval is the first reward of literary labours, it is natural that those who pursue such labours should reflect on the means to please; and these reflections eventually shape style, purify taste, and disseminate graciousness and urbanity everywhere. All these things may, perhaps, be regarded as supplements to virtue; but they can never be said to *be* virtue, and they will rarely be combined with it. There will always be this difference, that he who makes himself useful works for others, whereas he who seeks only to make himself agreeable works solely for himself.[22]

---

[21] Leo Strauss, 'German Nihilism', ed. David Janssens and Daniel Tanguay, *Interpretation* 26: 3 (1999): 353–378 (359).
[22] 'Final Reply', *CW*2:112/*OC*3:74.

THE PROBLEM OF MODERN LIBERTY   99

Part of Rousseau's critique of commercial society was thus a critique of a commercial culture that encouraged and rewarded the separation of the 'agreeable' from the 'useful' in matters of taste.

The distinction between the useful and the agreeable is part of a well-established classical discourse concerning the appropriate 'criterion' of moral judgement. Associated above all with Cicero, Rousseau's contemporaries used it to discuss what they called 'the foundation of morality'.[23] In this context, it became central to the modern idea of 'fine art' as a kind of consumption that, while superfluous, was nevertheless safe from the charge of moral corruption.[24] For Rousseau, it was the basis of his further distinction between good and bad taste: while useful men cultivated what he called here 'the taste for the solid virtues' and, later, simply 'the taste for virtue', agreeable men cultivated the 'taste for inconsequential speech (*niaseries*)', the 'taste for letters', or, simply, 'the taste for luxury'.[25] On his terms, the central issue in 'this question of luxury' was political – whether it was better for a state to be 'brilliant and short-lived, or virtuous and long-lasting' (*DSA*:19/3:20). His ideological target was the general view that 'luxury makes for the splendour of states', and, in particular, what he saw as the emerging consensus that it was 'sound policy' to prohibit luxury in small states and promote it in large ones (18/3:19).[26] He recognised that economic strength had become a central concern of modern states. But he challenged his contemporaries to reflect on the appropriate criterion of political success.

As in the classical tradition on which he drew, Rousseau reduced the problem to one of judgement. It was a matter of 'by what lustre' a state should be judged; or, as he also put it, 'what shall be our criterion' (17/3:18). In conditions of luxury and inequality, he argued, what 'corrupts our judgment' about politics is a 'senseless education' generally and, specifically, the 'preference for the agreeable over the useful talents' it introduces (22, 24/3:24, 26). Modern education and culture had thereby naturalised the false view that 'commerce and money' were the only relevant markers of state success (18–19/3:19–20). Crucially, however, Rousseau did not advocate simply reasserting utility over

---

[23] James Moore, 'Utility and Humanity: The Quest for the Honestum in Cicero, Hutcheson, and Hume', *Utilitas* 14:3 (2002): 365–386.

[24] Cp. Guyer (2014) with Larry Shiner, *The Invention of Art: A Cultural History* (Chicago: University of Chicago Press, 2003) and Paul Oskar Kristeller, 'The Modern System of the Arts: A Study in the History of Aesthetics Part I', *Journal of the History of Ideas* 12:4 (1951): 496–527 and 'The Modern System of the Arts: A Study in the History of Aesthetics (II)', *Journal of the History of Ideas* 13:1 (1952): 17–46.

[25] 'Final Reply', *CW*2:111–112/*OC*3:73–74.

[26] 'Letter to Raynal', *CW*2:26/*OC*3:32.

agreeableness. His vigorous defence of 'morals and virtue' as the appropriate criterion stemmed instead from his refusal to 'maintain the pretence' that luxury could be treated 'independently of the sciences and arts'.[27] In short, he was both insisting that political success could not be reduced to considerations of either utility or agreeableness alone, and critiquing the philosophy and culture that mistakenly framed the problem of political judgement as an either/or dilemma.

Rousseau's aim to re-establish a balance between the useful and the agreeable lies behind his claim in the above passage that taste could provide a 'supplement' to virtue. Aesthetic objects like 'music and theatre' had to be agreeable to be successful. They could also be useful – but only if they were conducive to 'public order'. In modern commercial society, artistic productions had become a 'necessary' varnish on morally corrupt behaviour: they helped 'prevent a greater corruption' by preventing 'vice' from turning into 'crime'. This was possible because, while taste, politeness, and propriety always threatened to 'destroy virtue', they could nevertheless preserve what Rousseau called a 'public simulacrum' of virtue. This simulacrum – or image – he explained, 'consists in a certain mildness of morals which sometimes compensates for their lack of purity, a certain appearance of order which averts terrible confusion, a certain admiration for beautiful things [*les belles choses*] which keeps good things [*les bonnes choses*] from being entirely forgotten'.[28] He used similar language in a passage about the relationship between simulacra and beauty in *Julie*. Julie advises St. Preux to forget the 'vain moralists' and search his soul: 'it is there you will rediscover the source of that sacred fire that so often kindled in us the love of sublime virtues; it is there that you will find that eternal simulacra of the truly beautiful the sight of which inspires us with a holy enthusiasm, and which our passions constantly sully but can never destroy' (*J*:183/2:223). Taste could never *be* virtue. But if cultural artefacts promoted morals, order, and beauty, then they could offer a reminder of goodness and supplement virtue.

We can better grasp Rousseau's idea of the simulacrum of virtue by contrasting it with what he called 'vain simulacrum'. The latter concept grounds his essential distinction between the 'taste for *niaseries*' and 'the taste for the solid virtues' in the 'Final Reply'. There, Rousseau excoriates all of philosophy as useless, the 'vain simulacra conjured by men's pride' that are not 'good for anything'.[29] While more obscure than the debate about the criterion, Rousseau

---

[27] 'Final Reply', *CW*2:116/*OC*3:79.
[28] 'Preface to Narcissus', *CW*2:196/*OC*2:972.
[29] 'Final Reply', *CW*2:111/*OC*3:73.

THE PROBLEM OF MODERN LIBERTY   101

also drew this concept of the simulacrum from its roots in the classical tradition. In the passage from *Julie*, for instance, Rousseau cites Plato's *Symposium* as the 'genuine philosophy of lovers' and the source of Julie's advice to St. Preux (*J*:183/2:223). Perhaps his most revealing use of the idea comes from the free translation of Plato's *Republic* he composed while drafting *d'Alembert*. Just as political revolution destroys the city, so imitative poetry destroys the soul by 'confounding through vain simulacra true beauty with the lying attraction which pleases the multitude, and apparent grandeur with genuine grandeur'.[30] And, finally, in the *Political Economy*, he alluded to Plato's cave to explain the observable 'contradiction' in 'corrupt men' who are in some respects honourable but deceptive in others – thus the 'enemies of virtue in society adore its simulacrum in their caves' (*PE*:145/3:247).[31] In a modern commercial culture that instils a senseless preference for the agreeable over the useful, the arts and sciences are but vain simulacra. Grounded in nothing other than the pride of their creators, they lead spectators to judge false but pleasing attractions mistakenly as true beauty. This, in turn, leads them to value and praise what is only apparently but not genuinely valuable and praiseworthy. But if the useful and the agreeable could be combined and rebalanced, then the arts and sciences could serve as a public simulacrum of virtue corresponding to the eternal simulacra of the truly beautiful within each private individual. Taste would still not *be* virtue. But it would then be possible to cultivate the taste *for* virtue.

The deeply critical approach of the first *Discourse* is often seen as incompatible with Rousseau's insistence that he intended all of his works to be useful. He claimed to have 'seen the evil' of contemporary corruption while leaving others to 'seek the cure'. But he also argued that being useful did not require him to provide such a cure. For he had also tried to discover the 'causes' of corruption, and this causal knowledge was useful in itself. The two parts of the *Discourse* correspond to the methodological division of labour we saw in his account of useful political theory. In Part I, a survey of examples grounds the 'historical inference' that vanity engenders moral corruption via the intermediary of the arts and sciences, a trans-historical truth 'observed at all times and in all places' (*DSA*:9/3:10). Part II, he subsequently clarified, 'confirms' this inference with causal 'reasoning' presented as a 'genealogy': 'the first source of evil is inequality; from inequality arose riches . . . from riches are born luxury and idleness; from luxury arose the fine arts, and from idleness the sciences'.[32] While he acknowledged that this genealogy is somewhat obscure in

---

[30] 'On Theatrical Imitation', *CW*7:347/*OC*5:1208.
[31] Rousseau is paraphrasing from Diderot's *Encyclopédie* article 'Natural Right': *CW*3:138.
[32] *CW*2:48/*OC*3:49–50.

the *Discourse*, he elaborated it throughout his replies to his critics. Ultimately, he clarified, the modern taste for the arts and sciences stemmed from two morally disreputable sources rooted in inequality: 'idleness and a craving for distinction'.[33] While the term *amour-propre* does not appear in the first *Discourse*, it does figure in his clarification: 'anyone who cultivates the agreeable talents wants to please, to be admired, and indeed wants to be admired more than anyone else is. Public applause is to be his alone'.[34] By clarifying both the material and psychological dimensions of inequality, Rousseau was moving towards the concerns that he would fully elaborate in the second *Discourse*.

In his replies to his critics, Rousseau argued that this causal account was useful because it distinguished his critique from the moralising approach of his contemporaries. Against these 'sermonizers', he clarified causes and revealed reasons to support the conclusion that contemporary vices 'belong not so much to man as man, as to man badly governed'.[35] This rejection of original sin was a 'consoling' truth because it rescued individuals from condemnation and recovered the possibility of clear or good conscience; it was a 'useful' truth because it facilitated a realistic assessment of contemporary corruption that was free of the temptation to fatalism. On this basis, his contemporaries could finally acknowledge that they were in fact 'wicked'. But the knowledge that their moral failings were contingent could, in turn, motivate them to 'wish to become as good as they could be'.[36]

While critique did not have to be constructive to be useful, the *Discourse* nevertheless clears a path to moral improvement. The text begins with Rousseau adopting the rhetorical posture of a 'good' man and ends with him adopting that of a 'vulgar' man. As a good man, he seeks only self-approval, a 'prize' to be found 'in the depths of my heart' (*DSA*:5/3:5). As a vulgar man, he advises his readers not to seek their happiness in 'reputation' or 'someone else's opinion' but, rather, to 'return into oneself and listen to the voice of one's conscience in the silence of the passions'. Individuals of all stations were thus able to follow this 'genuine philosophy', to know that it is more important to 'act well' than to achieve 'glory' or 'distinction', better to be a good man who was useful than an agreeable man who was merely pleasing (27–28/3:30). Crucially, both the good and vulgar practise a version of the refined Epicurean position we saw in his review of Pope – that the true sources of pleasure and happiness are internal rather than external goods.

---

[33] 'Preface to Narcissus', *CW*2:191/*OC*2:965.
[34] Ibid. *CW*2:193/*OC*2:967.
[35] Ibid. *CW*2:194/*OC*2:969.
[36] 'Letter to Bordes', *CW*2:182/*OC*3:104.

THE PROBLEM OF MODERN LIBERTY   103

This analysis also informs Rousseau's defence of his continued public activity as an artist. The publication of the *Discourse* generated the first iteration of the consistency dilemma: If his moral teaching was to retreat into one's conscience, and if the quest for reputation was so thoroughly corrupting of morals, then how could he compose music and drama for public consumption? His response relied on his distinction between good and bad taste. He conceded that his writings for the theatre and his music were incapable of generating moral reform. But he insisted that there simply is no contradiction in critiquing the corruption of contemporary taste and cultivating those 'tastes whose progress I approve'.[37] The idea of a cure for contemporary corruption was unrealistic.[38] And while artistic or cultural productions could not transform bad men into good ones, they could still be useful. In part, they were useful to the extent that they were agreeable. As pleasing 'trifles', they would distract morally corrupt individuals from doing evil. This, in turn, was useful to the small number of genuinely good people, because it protected them from being taken advantage of. Moreover, it remained possible that these few good people would still be 'edified' by his public works. In conditions of moral corruption, he wrote, this was 'all the good it was in my power to do'. From this perspective, trying to do more than merely please one's audience nevertheless required that one know how to please them.

Rousseau's position in the first *Discourse* is that of an internal critic of commercial society. One reason that we are not accustomed to viewing Rousseau this way is that the extreme nature of his critique has always led his readers to view him as a sort of radical Cynic who, like Diogenes before him, ostentatiously upheld the value of 'nature' and rejected all trappings of 'culture' out of hand. But when Raynal wrote that 'it is impossible to be too emphatic about truths that clash head-on with the general taste', Rousseau disagreed, insisting that 'children should be left some baubles'.[39] Working for others entailed both a realistic assessment of the economic limits of moral reform and an aesthetic awareness of how to please them — being useful meant being agreeable, but being merely agreeable was useless. His reference to baubles recalls his dismissal of the 'baubles of the fashionable little philosophy' in the passage about microscopes and telescopes with which this book began. It also anticipates the famous discussion of commercial society in Book III of the *Wealth of Nations*, where Smith argued that the persistence of luxury after the fall of Rome had

---

[37] 'Preface to Narcissus', *CW*2:196/*OC*2:972.

[38] 'Rousseau à Vernes, le 2 avril, 1755', *CC*3:115–117.

[39] 'Letter to Raynal', *CW*2:26/*OC*3:33. Baubles translates Fr. *osselets*, a children's game known since Homer, and recurrent in literature.

been responsible for the collapse of feudalism in modern Europe: like the Roman elite before them, so had feudal landlords destroyed their social and economic power by pursuing luxury products, or 'trinkets and baubles, fitter to be the playthings of children than the serious pursuits of men'.[40] For Smith, luxury was the engine that powered the rise of modern Europe; for Rousseau, it was more of an economic poison. But as his disagreement with Raynal suggests, Rousseau's refined Epicureanism extends to his recognition that some luxury had become necessary in modern commercial society – even if only, and perhaps especially, for children.

Utility and Commercial Sociability: Rousseau's Second *Discourse*

. . . and with that, his needs are satisfied (*DI*:134/3:135)

The concern with depopulation and the tension between town and country that frames *Julie* is most familiar from the second *Discourse*. Many later commentators have joined Rousseau's contemporaries in noting the abundant intertextual borrowings between the second *Discourse* and Lucretius' *De rerum natura*.[41] The most interesting of them, however, recognise that it is rather Rousseau's divergences from his Epicurean model that, while subtle and easy to miss, reveal much of what is most peculiar about the second *Discourse*.[42] This section follows the lead of these commentators to explore two of Rousseau's most illuminating divergences from Lucretius.[43] As we will see, Rousseau articulated his view of the economic dimensions of the problem of modern liberty

---

[40] Adam Smith, *An Inquiry into the Nature and Causes of the Wealth of Nations* (Indianapolis, IN: Liberty Fund, 1982): 421. See Hont (2005): 106–107, 354–388. For the French reception of Smith, see Kenneth E. Carpenter, *The Dissemination of the Wealth of Nations in French and in France 1776–1843* (New York: Bibliographical Society of America, 2002) and Gilbert Faccarello and Philippe Steiner, 'The Diffusion of the Work of Adam Smith in the French Language: An Outline History', in *A Critical Bibliography of Adam Smith*, ed. Keith Tribe (London: Pickering and Chatto, 2002).

[41] Classically, Morel (1909), Strauss (1953), Black (2001).

[42] See Leo Strauss, *Seminar in Political Philosophy: Rousseau*, ed. J Marks (Estate of Leo Strauss, 2014), (online) https://leostrausscenter.uchicago.edu/. I discuss Strauss' reading in detail in Jared Holley, 'Theory, Practice, and Modernity: Leo Strauss on Rousseau's Epicureanism', *Journal of the History of Ideas* 78:4 (2017): 621–644.

[43] Istvan Hont, 'Luxury and the Route to Revolution in Rousseau's Discourse on Inequality', in *University of Cambridge Political Thought and Intellectual History Research Seminar*, 2010. Victor Gourevitch, 'The "First Times" in Rousseau's Essay on the Origin of Languages', *Graduate Philosophy Journal* 11 (1986): 123–146. Victor Gourevitch, 'Rousseau on Providence', *Review of Metaphysics* 53 (2000): 565–611. Victor Gourevitch, 'Rousseau's Pure State of Nature', *Interpretation* 16 (1988): 23–59.

THE PROBLEM OF MODERN LIBERTY 105

by refining the accounts of both the earliest humans and the origins of the division of labour in society from the fifth book of Lucretius' Epicurean poem.

While the similarities must not be overstated, we can note that Rousseau's understanding of nature as an equitable proportion indeed shares significant affinities with Epicurean *isonomia*. The typical translation of this concept as *isonomy* or 'equality before the law' explains its use in political theory. But there is also a long history of its use in cosmological, psychological, and biological discussions to denote a system of natural justice preserved by the 'internal equipoise of its components', as opposed to relying on 'the intervention of any higher, external power'.[44] For Epicurus and Lucretius, the concept is importantly one of *equity* rather than *equality* – Cicero's rendering of the Greek concept as *aequabilis tributio* is best translated as 'equitable apportionment' or 'just proportionality' rather than 'equilibrium' or 'equal division'.[45] Epicurus argued that the numbers of mortal and immortal beings were equitably proportioned such that there were no fewer Gods than there were men.[46] By the same principles, Lucretius described an equitable proportion between the forces of preservation and destruction in the universe at large, and between the forces of creation and destruction in each of the innumerable particular worlds therein.[47] Crucially, the balance of these forces is not strictly equal: preservation prevails at all times over destruction in the universe, destruction ultimately prevails over creation in each world, and this natural proportionality is equitable or just.

The state of nature in the first part of the second *Discourse* describes a proto-human being whose physical forces are equitably proportioned to the natural obstacles to its self-preservation. Rousseau referred to this proportion as the 'pure' or 'genuine' state of nature. He distinguished it sharply from what he called the 'genuine youth of the world' (*DI*:167/3:171). The latter phrase is a direct allusion to the Latin *novitas mundi*, which Lucretius used to describe the condition of the earliest humans: 'Amidst the acorn-laden oaks they refreshed themselves' and 'many another kind of food besides the flowering *youth of the world* then produced'.[48] Castillon was the first to register

[44] Gregory Vlastos, 'Isonomia', *The American Journal of Philology* 74:4 (1953): 337–366 (361–363).

[45] Norman DeWitt, *Epicurus and his Philosophy* (Minneapolis: University of Minnesota Press, 1964): 271–272.

[46] Cicero, *On the Nature of the Gods*, trans. H. Rackham (Cambridge, MA: Harvard University Press, 1933): 51, 107.

[47] Lucretius, *DRN*:II.300–302, 526–533, 569–576. Cf. Epicurus, 'Letter to Herodotus': 571, 573, 591 (§41, 42, 60).

[48] Lucretius, *DRN*:V.937–945, 780, 818. Rousseau was most likely consulting the original Latin text, with guidance from one or both of Barbeyrac's translations of Pufendorf (where the phrase does not appear, 1740:183) or Titus Lucretius Carus, *Lucrece, De la nature des choses; avec*

widespread recognition of this Lucretian inspiration for Rousseau's famous image of the natural physical harmony of creature and habitat in the pure state of nature: 'I see an animal . . . the most advantageously physically organized of all . . . satisfying his hunger beneath an oak, quenching his thirst at the first stream, finding his bed at the foot of the same tree that had furnished his meal, and with that his needs are satisfied' (134/3:133).

This is Rousseau's 'natural goodness', the balance of (merely) physical needs and faculties in humanity's 'original constitution'. Rousseau's 'youth of the world', on the other hand, describes the moral needs of the 'nascent society' of family units, social esteem, and limited property that follows in his conjectural history. He labels his youth of the world 'genuine' precisely to mark this fundamental contrast with Lucretius: psychologically, it is the 'golden mean' between the 'indolence' of the pure state of nature and 'petulant' *amour-propre*, a balance of not merely physical but also moral or imaginative needs and faculties. It describes a state of nature that is Hobbesian in the sense of lacking common political laws, whereas the pure state of nature is that of humanity 'abandoned to ourselves' with no moral relations whatsoever. As the state reached by 'most of the savage peoples known to us', the genuine youth of the world is a fact 'given as real', a balance or equitable proportion of nature and artifice. The genuine state of nature is a 'conjecture' from which all artifice is radically bracketed (*DI*:159, 132/3:162, 132–133).[49] Recognising this refinement of Lucretius thus helps to clarify that both Rousseau's pure state of nature and the radical nature/culture binary it underpins are indeed hypothetical rather than in some sense factual or properly historical.[50] Indeed, a return to a state that could be described as 'pre-cultural' was both impossible *and* undesirable: the point of Rousseau's critique was to show that not all cultural expression was irredeemably

---

des remarques sur les endroits les plus difficiles de Lucrece. Traduction nouvelle, trans. Jacques Parrain des Coutures, 2 vols (Paris: Thomas Guillian, 1685). His translation – '*la véritable jeunesse du monde*' – may be unique. Fusil (1928) asserts that Rousseau was following Parrain (171). But cp. Parrain uses 'l'âge du monde se perfectionnant' (II:269). Castillon (1756) uses 'le monde, encore nouveau et plein de vigueur' (258). Cf. Parrain, II:251, which has <u>mundi novitatem</u> as 'cet age nouveau' and II:255, where <u>novitas mundi</u> is 'cette nouveauté du Monde'.

[49] Cf. Rousseau, 'Idea of the Method in the Composition of a Book', *CW*12:240/*OC*2:1244.

[50] My reading thus supports Gourevitch (1988): 34 and Frederick Neuhouser, *Rousseau's Critique of Inequality: Reconstructing the Second Discourse* (Cambridge: Cambridge University Press, 2014): 33–37. *Contra* Strauss (1953), Roger D. Masters, *The Political Philosophy of Rousseau* (Princeton, NJ: Princeton University Press, 1976): 115–118 and Mark F. Plattner, *Rousseau's State of Nature: An Interpretation of the Discourse on Inequality* (Dekalb: Northern Illinois University Press, 1979): 17–25. Christopher Kelly, 'Rousseau's "Peut-etre": Reflections on the Status of the State of Nature', *Modern Intellectual History* 3:1 (2006): 75–83.

THE PROBLEM OF MODERN LIBERTY 107

corrupt and to defend the possibility that human social interaction might come to approximate the natural balance of needs and faculties.

Noting the importance to Rousseau of proportionality or equilibrium clarifies the argumentative structure of the second *Discourse*. The main text begins with a distinction between two kinds of inequality. Those inequalities are 'natural' which consist in 'physical' differences of 'age, health, strength of body, qualities of the mind, or of the soul'. Those inequalities are 'moral or political' which consist in positional 'privileges' such as wealth, honour, power, and authority (131/3:131–132). Rousseau undertook to 'defend the cause of humanity' by demonstrating that modern states are founded on and reinforce an unjust proportion between natural and moral inequality. All moral inequality that is not 'exactly proportioned' to physical inequality is 'contrary to natural right'. As such, the inequality that 'prevails among all civilized people' is unjust – the few are 'glutted with superfluities while the starving multitude lacks in necessities' (188/3:194). By contrast, Rousseau's alternative image of the balance between needs and faculties in the 'youth of the world' parallels his idealised account of Geneva in the *Discourse*'s dedication, which describes how both 'public order and private happiness' can be maintained together if and when the two types of inequality are in just proportion. As the condition of one's being both a 'good man' and an 'honourable and virtuous patriot', the theoretical possibility of a just proportionality of natural and moral inequality proves the possible convergence of man and citizen (114–118/3:111–116).

The economic dimension of Rousseau's problem of modern liberty is further clarified by his refinement of Lucretius' account of the origin of the division of labour. Lucretius suggests that metallurgy developed when humans discovered that accidental fires had melted metals that were buried underground.[51] Rousseau agreed that humans likely began to use iron by imitating the operations of nature. But he preferred to explain its discovery as following a volcanic eruption rather than Lucretius' 'accidental fire'. He also followed Lucretius to explain the development of human knowledge of agriculture through the imitation of natural processes (168/3:171–172).[52] But he rejected Lucretius' subsequently connecting this imitation to the development of agriculture as an organising principle of society.[53] For both, humanity's knowledge of both metallurgy and agriculture came through imitating natural processes. But Rousseau rejected as implausible Lucretius' view that this knowledge

[51] Lucretius, *De rerum natura* V: 1252–1261, in *On the Nature of Things*, trans. W. H. D. Rouse, revised by Martin F. Smith (Loeb, 1992): 475–477.

[52] *DRN*:V:1361–1369.

[53] *DRN*:V:1370–1379.

could have been immediately applied to productive processes. For him, while early humans indeed possessed a basic mimetic capacity, it was unreasonable to assume that they would have possessed the foresight required to extrapolate the use of iron to forge tools. Crucially, this meant that there was a fundamental paradox in any theoretical account of the development of agricultural production as an organising principle of society. 'Large-scale cultivation', he insisted, would have required the implements that only metallurgy could have provided (169/3:173).

This refinement of his classical model distances Rousseau's account from the sequencing that would later become conventional in the four-stages theory of economic development. Just as large-scale agriculture required metallurgy, so metallurgy required sufficient demand for its implements. Given that the earliest humans had no need of one another, this demand could only arise 'the moment one man needed the help of another' and 'it became useful for one to have provisions for two' (167/3:171). *De rerum natura* was likely an important source in the development of the four-stages theory.[54] But Lucretius placed far less emphasis than his modern heirs on both chronology and the dependence of social structures on the mode of subsistence.[55] As regards the former, Rousseau's sequence was in the first instance logical rather than strictly historical. I have noted his scepticism of ideas of historical facts and truth: for him, the practice of conjectural history was 'the art of choosing among several lies the one best resembling truth' (*E*:393–396/4:527–531). In this methodological sense, his account was more like that of Lucretius or Plato than Smith or Turgot.[56] The point of this part of his history was that civilisation was a function of the complicated interaction between the underlying logics of agriculture and industry; his primary concern was not to specify either historical or logical priority but to reveal the sequencing question as a paradoxical chicken-and-egg scenario much like the relationship between language and society. Thus, rather than proceeding in distinct stages from agriculture to industry, Rousseau insisted on their logical interdependence, arguing that agricultural society required metallurgy and exchange. A solution to the problem of modern liberty could therefore not avoid commercial society. For modern agriculture was impossible without cities, markets, and some luxuries, and a radical imbalance between them was as dangerous as intentional attempts to redress it were likely to be.

---

[54] Catherine Wilson, 'Political Philosophy in a Lucretian Mode', in *Lucretius and the Early Modern*, ed. D. Norbrook, S. Harrison, and P. Hardie (Oxford: Oxford University Press, 2016): 259–282 (273).

[55] Ronald L. Meek, *Social Science and the Ignoble Savage* (Cambridge: Cambridge University, 1976): 9–10.

[56] Cf. Hont (2005): 354–388, (2014): 74–76.

THE PROBLEM OF MODERN LIBERTY   109

It was dangerous because, in addition to being necessary, economic exchange between town and country was, for Rousseau, by definition unequal. As he went on to explain, agricultural production is 'less lucrative' because its products – subsistence goods – satisfy physical needs that are limited by humanity's natural consumption capacity. And because agricultural foodstuffs are 'indispensable' to all, they can be priced no higher than 'the capacities of the poorest' to pay for them. Conversely, industrial manufacturing is more lucrative because its products – luxury goods – satisfy moral or psychological desires that are largely 'useless'. As a result, they can be priced according to the whims of humanity's imaginative capacity, which is by definition unlimited (*DI*:202/3:206; *E*:333–334/4:456–457). Because Rousseau held more strongly than Lucretius that psychological dispositions and social structures were related 'in principle to the ways in which men provide for their subsistence', he also held that the necessarily unequal socio-economic structure of modern commercial society produces the two different kinds of people he introduced in *Julie*. This division of the population into 'the farmer and the citizen' generates a fundamental economic limit and tension for modern politics (*DI*:202/3:206). The great danger was that the tension would resolve itself upon the establishment of a military dictatorship: when, in a modern repetition of Caeser's crossing the Rubicon, a disastrous taxation regime caused hordes of dispossessed farmers to move to the city and take employment in the standing army (184–186/3:189–191). Rousseau's portrayal of Julie's refined Epicureanism was part of his attempt to forestall the depopulation of the countryside. Thus understood, it was equally an attempt to prevent the cycle of despotism and radical egalitarianism he famously predicted at the close of the second *Discourse*.

Rousseau's critical engagement with Lucretius' Epicurean poem elucidates his assessment of the problem of modern liberty by revealing him to be a theorist of politics in commercial society. His first refinement of his model, concerning the youth of the world, clarifies that his conception of nature is opposed not to culture per se but to vain or corrupt culture. This allows us to see the aim of his constructive political theory as being the establishment of a paradoxically 'natural culture': an artificial approximation of the natural balance of needs and faculties. The second refinement, concerning the division of labour, shows that such an approximation had to take account of the underlying logic of commerce, for market exchange and economic inequality were ineliminable structural features of modern politics. The first humans were unsociable and self-sufficient. But it was still reasonable to conjecture that society formed when, through random historical events, one man found it useful to have provisions for two – the foundations of society are mutual interdependence and reciprocal utility. Rather than indulging in pure-agrarian back-to-the land fantasies, then, striking a balance between town and country, or agriculture and industry, meant establishing an equitable proportion between not simply physical but also moral or imaginative needs and faculties. And because it was grounded in sense and imagination, the problem of modern liberty was both economic and aesthetic.

While the second *Discourse* is helpfully read as setting the problem to be solved in Rousseau's later works, it can also be read as deepening the first *Discourse*'s question about the criterion of political judgement. Rousseau accepted the reality of commercial society because a developed division of labour, luxury production, and commercial exchange are necessary structural features of modern politics which a political theorist needed to address as such. But alongside economic inequality, he also emphasised that 'civil' or social inequality is likewise inevitable among private individuals in modern conditions of reciprocal need and mutual interdependence. While 'the foundations of society' are 'the needs of the body', the 'needs of the mind' make it 'agreeable' (*DSA*:6/3:6). Once society is founded to satisfy physical needs, the tendency to 'compare' ourselves with and make 'use' of each other always leads us to distinguish between good and bad men. This distinction, in turn, grounds the distribution of social goods like 'prestige and authority'. Rousseau's analysis of the inevitability of these distinctions gives rise to his identification of a new criterion of political judgement, which he calls here 'the surest indication of a well or badly constituted state': namely, the 'agreement or conflict' between virtue or 'personal merit', on the one hand, and social goods like 'wealth, nobility or rank, [and] power', on the other. These types of social inequality ultimately reduce to wealth, which can be used to purchase rank and power. The central problem confronting any theorist of politics in commercial society is therefore the criterion of political judgement – the balance between wealth and virtue (*DI*:183–184/3:188–189). My discussion of the second *Discourse* in this section demonstrates how deeply this problem is interlinked with that of depopulation. In that sense, it has also shown that Rousseau was merely being consistent in claiming that the 'number and population' of citizens is the 'surest sign' of 'whether a given people is well or badly governed' (*SC*:105/3:419–420).

Rousseau only gestured at the means of achieving the balance between utility and agreeableness in the second *Discourse*. But he was clear that it would require a new understanding of pleasure. For mistaken notions of pleasure interact with the competitive psychological dynamics of *amour-propre*, each fuelling the other. The 'frenzy to achieve distinction' leads the rich and powerful to seek pleasure solely through their possession of scarce positional goods, to 'value those things they enjoy only to the extent that others are

THE PROBLEM OF MODERN LIBERTY   111

deprived of them' (*DI*:184/3:189). But the problem was not restricted to the dominant class, for the 'blind ambition' of *amour-propre* leads all citizens to pursue the pleasure of self-approval, mistakenly, according to their relative position in the social hierarchy: 'looking below more than above', they 'come to hold domination dearer than independence, and consent to bear chains so that they might impose chains on others in turn' (183/3:188). In short, it was impossible to be free in modern commercial society without establishing sources of pleasure and self-approval other than these positional goods rooted in nothing but vanity. He hinted at the solution he later described in the *Social Contract*: establishing a legal hierarchy of rank to recognise and distinguish citizens in proportion to their 'real services' to the state; and allowing public opinion to set the criterion of personal merit, for 'the people is the genuine judge of morals' (222/3:222–223). I explore the details of both *amour-propre*'s relationship to pleasure and what Rousseau here called simply a more 'substantial work' in the next chapter. To conclude this section, I note a final parallel with Lucretius' poem that serves to introduce my discussion of Julie's refined Epicureanism in the household of Clarens.

Alongside the economic decline discussed above, the second *Discourse* also charts a perhaps more familiar story of modernity as the gradual separation of mankind from natural sentiments, such as pity, through increasing rationalisation. We have seen that Rousseau's account of pity is sometimes taken as evidence of his rejecting Epicureanism. But we should note that the Epicurean tradition is not silent about pity. Indeed, Lucretius gives pity an important but under-appreciated role in his description of the phase of communal life in which male household heads begin to associate as neighbours:

> Then also neighbours began to join in friendship amongst themselves in their eagerness to do no harm and suffer no violence, and asked protection for their children and womankind, signifying by voice and gesture with stammering tongue that it was fair (*aequum*) for all to pity the weak. Nevertheless, concord could not altogether be produced, but a good part, indeed the most, kept the compacts (*foedera*) unblemished, or else the race of mankind would have been even then wholly destroyed, nor would birth and begetting have been able to prolong their posterity to the present day.[57]

This account is entirely unique in ancient philosophy for presenting pity as a motivation for the first compacts: in Lucretius' narrative, justice, language,

---

[57] Lucretius, *DRN*:V.1019–1027.

and friendship originate at this moment when men, motivated by pity for their wives and children, agree to extend pity to the wives and children of others in order to protect their own families.[58]

Whether or not Rousseau appreciated Lucretius' novelty in this respect, it is instructive to note how his own account of pity diverges from this model. It is generally agreed that Lucretius' appeal to sentiment here 'softens' Epicurus's utilitarian emphasis on the rational calculation of self-interest. Rousseau similarly notes that pity 'softens' and 'tempers' the desire for self-preservation and *amour-propre*. But where for Lucretius men make women the objects of their pity, for Rousseau it is women who are the paradigmatic subjects of pity. Motivated by pity to protect their children and to stop altercations in the marketplace, women rather than men prevent the spiral of violence that threatens to destroy the human race. Moreover, whereas Lucretius' account combines a concern for others with an element of self-interest, Rousseau argues against Mandeville that the 'force of natural pity' involves 'no personal interest whatsoever'. Finally, whereas in Lucretius pity motivates the first compacts of association – and, debatably, justice – Rousseau emphasises that it is the weakening of pity that makes conventions of justice necessary.[59] Instead of the 'sublime maxim of reasoned justice *Do unto others as you would have them do unto you*', pity is the ground of the 'maxim of natural goodness . . . *do your good with the least possible harm to others*' (*DI*:152–154/3:153–157).

As his treatment of pity suggests, Rousseau looked to women to solve the psychic imbalance of reason and sentiment by optimising their mutual interaction through taste. We saw above that he made the same appeal for women to address economic imbalance. But on this side of the story, what we need from each other matters less than how we feel about each other – and, perhaps especially, how we feel about what we need from each other. It is a crucial but frequently overlooked feature of the second *Discourse* that Rousseau appealed to Genevan women to temper the imagination and correct the taste of both male household-heads and their children. In the Epistle Dedicatory, he called on women to defend their city against 'vain luxury' by using their 'simple and modest attire' to create the conditions most favourable to 'beauty'. Their 'persuasive' sweetness would disabuse especially young men of their corrupt taste for French culture; instead of the 'easy pleasures' of a puerile and 'fatal taste', they would reinstate the taste for 'useful things' and 'august freedom'.

---

[58] Elizabeth Asmis, 'Can an Epicurean Live His Epicureanism? Pity and Self-Interest' (unpublished ms): 8, 12. I am grateful to Liz for sharing her paper and for discussion of this point.

[59] Ibid.: 10. Cp. Phillip Mitsis, *Epicurus' Ethical Theory: The Pleasures of Invulnerability* (Ithaca, NY: Cornell University Press, 1988): 84, n. 56.

THE PROBLEM OF MODERN LIBERTY 113

And while their 'amiable and innocent dominion' was restricted to 'conjugal union' in the household, it served the political imperative of maintaining the 'love of laws in the state and concord among the citizens'. That is, by exercising good taste in the household, Geneva's 'citizen-women' would cultivate the habits of good taste necessary to prepare male citizens for making the kind of sound political judgements involved in articulating the general will (*DI*:121–122/3:119–120).

Julie's Taste as Refined Epicureanism

The distinction between refined and vulgar Epicureanism is drawn according to the particular types and sources of pleasures pursued by modern hedonists. Refined Epicureans understand the difference between the pleasures of 'nature' they pursue and those of 'fashion' and 'vanity' pursued by vulgar Epicureans (*J*:15–19/2:21–26). This distinction constitutes the theoretical or rational core of refined Epicureanism. But it is importantly grounded in and supported by the sentimental core or affective disposition of 'temperate sensuality' (451, 544/2:552, 662). Temperance is habitual moderation of natural pleasures and, thus, the virtue most needed in conditions of luxury (*D*:114/1:807).[60] That refined Epicureanism is a variety of temperance or moderation is crucial, for, as I noted in Chapter 1, Rousseau took moderation as self-command to be the virtue responsible for securing freedom (*SC*:53, 78, 124/3:364, 392, 444; *E*:390, 633/4:524, 817). Finally, by terming the refined Epicureans' temperance 'sensual', Rousseau meant that virtue could be secured by the 'mixture' of pleasurable sensations or the 'multiplication of tastes' (*D*:114/1:807).[61] The hedonic basis of virtue distinguishes Rousseau's refined Epicurean theory of self-command from the sober avoidance of pleasure associated with Christian or Stoic asceticism. Moreover, it grounds Rousseau's claim that 'in order to eschew splendour and luxury, one requires not so much moderation as taste' (*J*:447/2:546). In this way, I argue, refined Epicureanism is precisely the taste for modern liberty.

Rousseau's refined Epicureans prefer the goods of nature. In *Emile*, he defined nature as an individual's disposition to pursue pleasure according to various standards or criteria. First, physical sensation; then, the awareness of the relation between the inner world of the self and objects of pleasure in the external world; and, ultimately, judgements regulated by the criterion or 'idea of happiness or perfection given us by reason'. This progression from

---

[60] Rousseau, 'Discourse on the Virtue Most Necessary for a Hero', *CW*4:8/*OC*2:1270.
[61] Cf. 'Memorandum on Education', *CW*12:100/*OC*4:14.

sensation to reason mirrors the progression in the second *Discourse*. The dictates of physical nature are always necessarily refracted through prevailing fashion and opinion, such that nature can only be 'more or less corrupted' by culture (*E*:163/4:248). And just as Rousseau followed Epicurean hedonism, so does his ideal of happiness rest on a basic Epicurean foundation: the 'continual flux' between pleasure and pain meant that the height of human happiness is a 'negative condition' consisting in the least amount of pain. Attaining happiness thus meant rebalancing the necessary 'disproportion between our desires and faculties', also familiar from the second *Discourse*: 'the road of true happiness . . . consists in diminishing the excess of the desires over the faculties and putting power and the will in perfect equality'. This 'absolute happiness' is humanity's 'natural condition' insofar as it characterises the moral psychology of infants. Like the natural goodness of the pure state of nature, it is 'impossible' to regain. For just as in the second *Discourse*, so here in *Emile* is the physical harmony of needs and faculties upset by the imagination, a 'superfluous' faculty tending endlessly to increase our desires. The imagination could not, of course, be eliminated; in this sense, superfluity was natural and necessary for happiness. Achieving happiness thus required tempering the imagination in order to approximate the natural equality of need and ability in an unequal but equitable proportion (*E*:210–214/4:303–308).

As we have seen, Rousseau liked to use the metaphor of a microscope to describe the distinctive combination of reason and sentiment involved in judgements of taste. He first used it in the following passage from Julie, which ought to be more widely appreciated:

> How many things are there which one perceives only through sentiment and which one cannot account for? How many of those *je-ne-sais-quoi* that so frequently recur and about which taste alone decides? Taste is in a way the microscope of judgment; it is taste which brings small objects within our reach, and its operations begin where those of the latter end. What then is required to cultivate taste? To practice seeing as well as feeling, and to judge the beautiful by inspection as well as the good by sentiment.

Julie's education is designed to cultivate her ability both 'to feel and to see' the 'very good and the very beautiful'. Rather than examining rational 'principles and rules', she studies 'books of good taste and morality' to facilitate her awareness of natural goodness and beauty through the synthesis of reason and sentiment (*J*:47–48/2:58–59). Taste is not so much a distinct faculty, then, but a way of optimising the mutual interaction of reason and sentiment.

THE PROBLEM OF MODERN LIBERTY

This education cultivates Julie's natural taste and prepares her to adopt refined Epicureanism as a 'philosophy'. As mentioned, the rational core of refined Epicureanism is the distinction between the true pleasures of nature and the pleasures of 'fashion' or 'vanity' pursued by vulgar Epicureans. This distinction will be explored in more detail in the next chapter. Here, it suffices to note that Rousseau explained that judgements of taste concern 'the agreeable': amusements and pleasures that are 'not connected with our needs' (*E*:512–513/4:671–672). The idea of natural beauty as a balance provides a criterion of aesthetic judgement. But it is always only more or less corrupted by culture and fashion – what Rousseau called in his *Dictionary of Music* (1766) the 'arbitrary conventions' and 'prejudices of custom or education'.[62] This distinction between natural and fashion-based taste grounds a subsequent redefinition of superfluity and luxury. We saw that Rousseau considered superfluity to be natural insofar as the imagination is a superfluous faculty that cannot be eliminated. Julie's refined Epicureanism, he explains, allows her uniquely to indulge in superfluous imaginary pleasures: 'she counts nothing as superfluous that can contribute to the well-being of a reasonable person; but she calls superfluous everything that serves merely to shine in others' eyes'. By redefining superfluity in this way, refined Epicureanism allows the natural 'luxury of pleasure and sensuality' to replace the corrupt 'luxury of magnificence and vanity' (*J*:435/2:530–531).

The sentimental core of refined Epicureanism that Rousseau called 'temperate sensuality' was both a theory and practice of deferred gratification. Julie is a voluptuary, 'made to know and taste all pleasures'. But her sensuality is that of a refined Epicurean: because she tastes virtue as the 'supreme' sensual pleasure, she can indulge all other pleasures whilst still savouring them in a manner resembling the 'austerity' of the Stoic who would 'abstain' from them. Superfluous sensual pleasure is not problematic per se. What worries Rousseau is that it 'changes in nature' once enjoyment of its sensation becomes habitual, for it 'ceases to be a pleasure when it becomes a need'. Julie avoids dependence on these luxuries not through asceticism but through 'passing and moderate privations'. That is, by deferring sensual gratification, she 'gives value' to those 'slight' pleasures with which judgements of taste are concerned. Her enjoyment of sensual pleasure thus becomes precisely the means through which she achieves self-command, enjoying the pleasure of remaining 'mistress of herself' (*J*:544, 443, 451/2:662, 541–541, 552).

This account of self-command is Epicurean because it presents virtue as the means to the end of greater pleasure. Julie's 'moderate privations' are

---

[62] Rousseau (1779): 428–429/*OC*5:842–843.

116 ROUSSEAU'S POLITICS OF TASTE

themselves simply a 'new means of pleasure'. Giving up the daily habit of taking coffee, for instance, serves to 'heighten her taste for it': disciplining her craving makes it more acute and increases the sensual gratification of finally taking coffee as a 'token of festivity'. While Julie is temperate for 'the same reasons that carry voluptuaries to excess', her hedonism is nevertheless 'praiseworthy and honest'. The unpublished fragment on Epicureanism cited above was almost certainly an early draft of Julie's summary of her hedonism:

> I can see that those vulgar Epicureans, for never wanting to miss an opportunity, miss them all, and, always bored in the lap of pleasures, never know how to experience a single one. They squander the time they think they are saving up, and ruin themselves like misers because they do not know how to lose anything peacefully. I do very well by the opposite maxim, and I believe that I would yet prefer on this point too much severity to too much leniency. Sometimes I break off an outing for the sole reason that I enjoy it too much; by resuming it later, I enjoy it twice. However, I work at maintaining the control of my will over myself, and I would rather be accused of capriciousness than allow myself to be governed by my fancies. (*J*:451–452, 443–444/2:552, 542)

Rousseau later identifies this opposite maxim explicitly as refined Epicureanism, the principle on which 'the good things of life, and those that are purely for pleasure' are enjoyed at Clarens (544, 444/2:662, 542).

Julie's refined Epicureanism solves the problem of the senseless imbalance between utility and agreeableness identified in the first *Discourse*. Part of Rousseau's solution to the aesthetic dimension of the problem of modern liberty was to maintain a strict separation of private and public, morality and politics. Like the women of Geneva, Julie exercises moral authority with a 'persuasive sweetness' by speaking what Rousseau calls 'the language of signs'.[63] Her refined Epicureanism is concerned with 'physical things' like clothing, food, and furniture. For Rousseau, the appropriate domain of women's taste is 'the judgement of the senses', whereas one should 'consult the taste of men in moral things that depend more on the understanding'. But as the microscope of judgement, taste is the means by which 'the mind is imperceptibly opened to ideas of the beautiful of every sort, and finally to the moral notions related to them'. Julie's taste in furniture, for example, generates moral pleasure because through it, like her modest clothing, she speaks the language of signs 'to the

---

[63] See Etienne Gilson, 'La méthode de M. Wolmar', in *Les idées et les lettres*, ed. Etienne Gilson (Paris: Vrin, 1932): 275–298.

THE PROBLEM OF MODERN LIBERTY   117

heart through the eyes' (*J*:446/2:545). This is because the symmetry, regularity, and proportion in her organisation of physical space is both known and felt to be imitative of the beauty and goodness of well-ordered nature. Sensory experience of this physical space has the moral effect of enabling the inhabitants of Clarens both to see and to feel the coincidence of the public good with their private good in their imagination – that is, Julie cultivates their taste for virtue because 'everything one sees in this house joins together the agreeable and the useful' (384, 455, 386/2:466, 556, 469–470).

Julie demonstrates how a refined Epicurean practice of taste contributes to the harmony of utility and agreeableness in the household. But Rousseau's novel does not fully consider the public, political role of judgements of pleasure in the modern state. Shklar influentially insisted that Clarens could not serve as a political model. As an independent and self-sufficient household, it belongs not to modern commercial society but to what Rousseau called elsewhere humanity's 'second state', with 'less opposition of interests than convergence of understanding'.[64] But Rousseau envisioned a crucial, albeit indirect, political role for households.[65] Julie's duties extend beyond the confines of the home to the wider village. Her example instils a patriotic 'love of the fatherland and that of liberty' amongst the peasantry. Her 'great maxim' is a calibrated response to Rousseau's stated goal in writing the novel: she strives for each villager 'to take pride in himself', to be happy in his own station, and 'above all to make sure that the happiest of all, which is that of a villager in a free state, is not depopulated in favour of the others' (*J*:439/2:536). Her marriage to Wolmar is thus an example of the 'civil effects' of marriage without which, Rousseau wrote in the *Social Contract*, it is 'impossible for society to endure' (306/2:372; *SC*:151/3:469). In this way, Rousseau's theory of erotically reinforced patriotism responds to both the aesthetic and economic dimensions of the problem of modern liberty. If taste is the microscope of judgement, then each citizen receives his microscope in the laboratory of the household. Thus, the harmony of justice and utility that Rousseau identified as the goal of the state was possible only if refined Epicureanism combined utility and agreeableness in the household.

---

[64] Rousseau, 'Letter to Christophe de Beaumont', *CW*9:28/*OC*4:937.

[65] Cp. Nicole Fermon, *Domesticating Passions: Rousseau, Woman, and Nation* (Hanover: Wesleyan University Press, 1997), Penny Weiss, *Gendered Community: Rousseau, Sex, and Politics* (New York: New York University Press, 1993), and Joel Schwartz, *The Sexual Politics of Jean-Jacques Rousseau* (Chicago: Chicago University Press, 1984) with Rosenblatt (2002) and Eileen Hunt Botting, *Family Feuds: Wollstonecraft, Burke, and Rousseau on the Transformation of the Family* (Albany: SUNY Press, 2006): 15–68.

The Public Harmony of Utility and Agreeableness: The *Letter to d'Alembert*

Just as the early readers of the second *Discourse* were right about Rousseau's Epicurean denial of sociability, so was Vernet correct to read *d'Alembert* as a defence against the spread of vulgar Epicureanism. This section draws the chapter to a close by returning to the problem with which it began. Rousseau's *d'Alembert*, I argue, responds to his problem of modern liberty by describing how a refined Epicurean understanding of pleasure can play a positive role in the politics of a modern commercial state. While Epicureanism is not mentioned in the letter, Rousseau composed it during a temporary hiatus from his work on *Julie*, to which he does refer. As we will see, he carried over his refined Epicurean account of taste and pleasure from the novel's treatment of Clarens to the letter's account of the civil effects of aesthetic judgement. In this way, he also deepened and clarified his consideration of the politics of taste in the first *Discourse*. For just as *Julie* demonstrates how refined Epicureanism combined the useful and agreeable in the household, so *d'Alembert* attempts to correct Genevans' judgements of pleasure and, thereby, enable them to find agreeable those objects that are truly useful to them, both individually as citizens and collectively as a people.

Rousseau's refined Epicurean approach to pleasure is central to his arguments in the letter. As a form of 'amusement' the principal object of which is to please its audience, the theatre must be evaluated in the first instance by the pleasure it provides rather than its potential utility. *D'Alembert* distinguishes amusements as providing either 'natural' pleasures, which derive from 'labours, relations, and needs', or 'frivolous' pleasures, which derive from idleness, a lack of self-approval, and the 'neglect of simple and natural tastes'. This distinction clearly parallels the two sets of distinctions we have seen above – between fashion-based vanity and natural voluptuousness, and between vulgar and refined Epicureanism. Again accepting the basic hedonist premise that 'each is led by his pleasures', Rousseau worries that Genevan youth will become vulgar Epicureans, 'men of the world' running after frivolous pleasures that will undermine their republican constitution (*LD*:261–263/5:15–17). And, once more, he responds to the threat of vulgar Epicureanism by attempting to persuade Genevans to become refined Epicureans.

Rousseau links this distinction between types of pleasure with his critique of the rationalist view of moderation discussed in Chapter 1. *D'Alembert* is often taken as evidence of his 'Platonic' aesthetics: while contemporaries like Kant argued that aesthetic judgement operated according to independent criteria, Rousseau followed Plato to argue that, because all entertainment is

THE PROBLEM OF MODERN LIBERTY 119

'made for the people', it must be judged according to its moral and political 'effects on the people' (262–263/5:16–17).[66] D'Alembert's initial promotion of the theatre was grounded in his own brand of Platonism.[67] Genevans need not worry about moderation, he wrote, because the theatre would bring 'a fineness of tact' without libertinism, providing an additional sentimental support for good morals by forming their taste. This required 'laws that are severe and well administered'. But once established within the bounds of rational legislation, a theatre would transform Geneva from a 'dull' city into 'the seat of decent pleasures'.[68] Rousseau responded by paraphrasing the critique of vulgar temperance which we have seen he annotated in the *Phaedo*: 'is it possible that in order to become temperate and prudent we must begin by being intemperate and mad?' This reference reveals the premise he and d'Alembert shared – that humans necessarily pursue pleasure but lack an 'immediate disposition' to regulate their passions or moderate their sentiments. D'Alembert's solution was simply unrealistic, for neither reason nor law could ground moderation: reason 'is good for nothing on the stage' and 'the laws have no access to the theatre'. Rejecting this legalistic solution left Rousseau to focus his attention on what he identified in *d'Alembert* as the only other instruments capable of influencing a people's morals: 'the empire of opinion' and 'the appeal of pleasure' (264, 266/5:18–20). He rejected the Platonic-Stoic purging of passion, for 'the man without passions is a chimaera' and 'every well-regulated passion' is 'laudable in itself'. Rather than rejecting pleasure as such, he described and defended a form of pleasure that would be free of the 'poison' of both 'constraint and selfishness' (337, 343/5:107, 115). What Genevans needed, then, was a form of entertainment that would allow them to take pleasure in moderation (263/5:18).

Rousseau's approach to the theatre demonstrates his approach to useful political theory. Whereas the *Social Contract* demanded careful readers who would pay close attention to precise definitions and fine distinctions, *d'Alembert* was not a piece of 'speculative philosophy' addressed to an elite audience. Rather than attempting to 'make others think', he wanted to 'explain' a 'practical truth' that would be useful to his people as a whole. This popular intention informs his sceptical rejection of theoretical abstractions in the letter. In the first place, it was useless to consider whether the theatre, in general, was good or bad 'in itself'. Answering such a question required a standard of judgement. But because theatrical performances had to be agreeable, they were necessarily

---

[66] Citing Vernet (1756). Cf. Guyer (2014): 9–16, 295–301.

[67] Guyer (2014): 262–267.

[68] Jean le Rond d'Alembert, 'Geneva', in Rousseau, *LD*:254–255/*OC*5:4–7.

'made for the people'. As such, the only appropriate standard by which to judge the 'absolute qualities' of the theatre was its 'effects on the people'. In the second place, it was equally useless to think in terms of a generic people. Peoples are particular, exhibiting a 'prodigious diversity' of national character, moral temperament, and *moeurs* – the habitual practices characterising local ways of life. Finally, it was useless to think of human nature in the abstract. Laws, governments, religions, customs, even climates modify human nature to such an extent that the theorist must ask not 'what is good for man in general' but, rather, what is good for a particular people in 'this time or that country'. If 'man is one', politics is not. General qualities of the theatre could only be judged by or inferred from its effects in contexts that are both historically and geographically particular.

D'Alembert is one of the earliest published instances of Rousseau's use of the idea of a given people's 'general taste' to discuss the contextual embedding of judgement. I discuss the concept in more detail in the next chapter. Here, we should note that it helps to explain how a theatrical performance's ability to please depends on a given people's *moeurs*. The French concept of *moeurs* is notoriously difficult to translate; for our purposes, it helps to recall Rousseau's claim in *d'Alembert* that he would 'speak of *moeurs* or tastes indifferently'. They were not the same, exactly, but tastes and *moeurs* had a 'common origin' in judgement, and a change in one necessarily brought about a change in the other (264/5:18). This under-appreciated claim comes in the context of a discussion of modern French theatre. Molière and Corneille had been successful, he explained, because they had a unique ability to grasp the people's 'general taste'. In particular, they were attuned to the fact that the general taste had shifted from 'old' to 'new' modes of comic performance. But they fell out of favour when the general taste subsequently changed once again, making their previously popular comedies no longer agreeable to the people (277/5:34). This analysis is consistent with Rousseau's disagreement with Raynal's comment about the general taste, noted above: public writers should not forcefully clash with the general taste because they had to remain agreeable to be useful. It also explains that the theatre must respond to and promote a people's general taste; it can 'embellish' and 'follow' *moeurs* or sentiments, but it cannot alter or 'moderate' the people's taste, on which its ability to please depends (264/5:18). As such, diverse forms of theatre arise in accordance with necessarily diverse general tastes.

As the historical mutability of the general taste suggests, Rousseau approached the question of a theatre's suitability in Geneva in a way similar to the problem of modern liberty. In the ancient world, actors were like public priests and plays were like national history pageants that educated citizens

THE PROBLEM OF MODERN LIBERTY

121

to love their liberty. Crucially, they were public entertainment performed for public enjoyment. As institutions of public memory, moreover, these ancient theatrical performances constituted real objects of pleasure, inspiring the Greeks with 'ardent emulation' and 'sentiments of honour and glory' (308–309/5:71–73). In this way, ancient Greek theatre provided a supplement to virtue or a simulacrum of virtue such as Rousseau described in the first *Discourse*. In modern Europe, however, 'everything has changed' (317/5:82). He thus applied his sharp ancient/modern periodisation to the theatre in order to explain that specifically modern theatre had emerged from a process of historical change. And as with the problem of modern liberty, that process was comprised of both economic and aesthetic elements.

In aesthetic terms, the passage from ancient to modern forms of theatre was a passage from tragic and comic subjects to romantic ones. Ancient forms of theatre no longer please modern audiences. The heroes of ancient tragedy are unrealistic or 'chimerical' and the concerns of ancient politics are distant from those of modern states. As such, and in contrast to an important tradition in contemporary political theory, tragedy is no longer a useful guide for understanding modern politics.[69] Comedy, on the other hand, is more realistic. Aristotle famously noted that comic characters are 'lower' than tragic heroes and thus more like the ordinary members of the audience.[70] Rousseau agreed, adding a historical dimension to his treatment of comedy's realism. For precisely its grounding in popular taste meant that comic characters more closely resemble modern men, and its moral lessons have a 'more immediate' relationship to modern tastes.[71] Yet even the agreeableness of comedy has diminished among the moderns, who have become unable to 'maintain the strength of comic situations or characters'. As such, modern playwrights like Molière and Corneille succeed by reinforcing what Rousseau calls 'the love interest'. Appealing to the modern taste for 'Romances', they compete with each other to give more energy and colour to the 'dangerous passion' of love (285/5:43).

Precisely this need to reinforce the modern taste for romantic love stories means that the theatre no longer fulfils its ancient role of providing a supplement

---

[69] J. Peter Euben, *The Tragedy of Political Theory: The Road Not Taken* (Princeton, NJ: Princeton University Press, 1990). Bernard Williams, *Shame and Necessity* (Berkeley: University of California Press, 1993). Martha C. Nussbaum, *The Fragility of Goodness: Luck and Ethics in Greek Tragedy and Philosophy* (Cambridge: Cambridge University Press, 2001).

[70] Aristotle, *Poetics*, trans. Stephen Halliwell (Cambridge, MA: Harvard University Press, 1995): 35 (1448a17–18).

[71] Although Rousseau sees comedy's realism as cause for concern, we don't need to: the mix of fallible agents and fantastical solutions might make comedy a resource for political theorists interested in the transformative potential of a 'realistic' approach to political theory. I am grateful to Birte Löschenkohl for discussion of this point.

to virtue. The 'true beauties' have been 'eclipsed' in modernity. In their place, modern theatre substitutes 'little pleasurable accessories capable of impressing the multitude' (285/5:43). Their basis in love makes modern plays agreeable. But it also makes them a constant threat to dominate the audience. Love is dangerous because it overwhelms 'simple' or 'natural' sentiments, inflaming its audience members' hearts to feel 'continual emotion'. This experience is of course a pleasant one. But Rousseau argues that such pleasure is superficial and fleeting, one that 'enervates' and 'enfeebles'. For whereas ancient theatre constituted a real object of pleasure, modern theatre merely stimulates a desire that it cannot satisfy. It induces a demand for an object of pleasure it does not provide. Moreover, where ancient theatre performed a moral-pedagogical function, modern theatre does not even provide a criterion of judgement concerning the objects appropriate to the satisfaction of the desire it stimulates. In this way, the modern theatrical experience produces and reinforces the vulgar Epicurean view of pleasure that most of its audience members bring to it. That is, it undermines the basis of moderation or self-command, leaving its audience unable to resist their passions and constantly running after new sources of immediate gratification. While it may 'interest' the audience in virtue, this is only a 'sterile' interest that is able to 'satisfy *amour-propre*' without leading a viewer to practise virtue.[72] Indeed, far from motivating a taste for virtue, love stories lead modern agents to judge the satisfaction of those passions stimulated in the theatre to be 'preferable to virtue itself' (293, 290/5:52–53, 49).

In economic terms, whether the theatre is good or bad depends on the objects of pleasure available to agents in modern commercial societies. Part of Rousseau's rhetorical strategy is to present the theatre as a foreign invention. Playing on d'Alembert and Voltaire's support for it, he notes that the objects preferred in Paris are those of fashionable Epicureanism. There, imaginations are 'depraved by sloth, inactivity, the love of pleasure, and great needs'. But Parisians lack 'religion' or any other 'principle' that might guide their pursuit of pleasure. Instead, they pursue 'vanity, money, and sensuality' because they judge according to frivolous 'appearances'. The theatre is made for the French, for whom '*moeurs* and honour are nothing' and whose general taste is corrupt insofar as they derive pleasure only from their 'reputation' and are 'esteemed' only for their wealth (293–294/5:54). In other words, the theatre is for vulgar

---

[72] On vanity and pride as the two 'branches of amour-propre', see Rousseau, 'Plan for a Constitution of Corsica', *CW*11:153–154/*OC*3:935–938 (see also Afterword, n. 7). For discussion see Chapter 5 and Ryan Patrick Hanley, 'Enlightened Nation Building: The "Science of the Legislator" in Adam Smith and Rousseau', *American Journal of Political Science* 52:2 (2008): 219–234.

THE PROBLEM OF MODERN LIBERTY

123

Epicureans who fail to follow their master's teaching that happiness requires drawing pleasure from oneself. Like those cultural productions that Rousseau discussed in the first *Discourse*, the utility of modern theatre is deeply limited: for individuals whose judgements of pleasure are already corrupt, the theatre is useful to the extent that it distracts them from pursuing pleasures that are even more dangerous. In conditions of great luxury and inequality, modern theatre can at best prevent corrupt taste from further degenerating into outright criminality (298/5:59).

Rousseau is very clear in *d'Alembert* that Geneva is also modern in the sense of being commercial. The contrast with Paris demonstrates that the pleasures of the theatre are not truly agreeable – it reminds his compatriots to take pride in their homeland, offering an alternative source of pleasure. But Rousseau also contrasts Geneva with ancient Sparta. There, *moeurs* or tastes were united with laws in the hearts of the citizens, who not only observed but 'loved the laws'. While Genevans were not Parisians, they still lived in the 'lap of commerce' and their pursuit of pleasure was motivated by the 'love of gain' (300/5:61). Geneva was rich, with large-scale commerce and a developed division of labour. But inequality was limited, and the majority of the population enjoyed easy circumstances 'from hard work, economy, and moderation' (319/5:85). The political-economic dimension of Rousseau's critique of the theatre is not always appreciated. But it is precisely because he is attempting to be 'easy and intelligible' to a commercial people that he frequently confines himself to 'considerations of self-interest and money', for these are more 'palpable' and convincing to the majority of his 'vulgar' readers (298, 334/5:59, 103). His famous thought experiment about Neuchatel argues that the introduction of a theatre would be economically disastrous: starting from conditions of material equality, the introduction of a theatre leads to a slackening of work, an increase of expenses, a decrease in trade, the establishment of new taxes, and the introduction of luxury (295–298/5:55–59). He also devotes space to comparative demography, financial statistics, and daily population movement to show that Geneva could only support a theatre through taxation. Indeed, the theatre itself could be thought of as an especially bad tax, one that returned nothing to the people and that unequally burdened the poor while relieving the rich (322–323, 335/5:88–89, 103–104). By increasing inequality, then, the fashion for theatre leads to the faction that inevitably destroys republican government. Whether Rousseau's analysis is accurate or not, it is important to note that such economic considerations are entirely absent from Vernet's critique of the theatre and d'Alembert's defence of it.

Rousseau concludes *d'Alembert* with an idealised portrait of Geneva as a place where a refined Epicurean patriotism is still possible. The comparisons to

Paris and Sparta ground arguments aimed at persuading ordinary citizens that a theatre would be neither useful nor agreeable – it is not in their economic interest and it is not a source of real, lasting pleasure. But once again, Rousseau emphasises that the ordinary concern of modern citizens with private interest and personal pleasure is not evidence of moral failing. Rather, his analysis of the structural conditions of modern politics informs his goal to combine or balance the useful and the agreeable. We have already seen his account of how Julie brings about this combination in the household at Clarens. To conclude this chapter, then, I want to note some of Rousseau's examples of how it might be secured publicly.

Much of *d'Alembert* can helpfully be read as an attempt to persuade Genevans that they possess sources of real pleasure already within the city-state itself. The frivolous pleasures of the theatre are appropriate to Parisians whose taste is corrupt and whose liberty is eroded by monarchical government. It remained possible for Genevans to pursue 'natural' pleasures, however, because their sentiments retained their 'natural rectitude' owing to their relatively small population and rustic occupations (337/5:106). Men's clubs – or *circles* – allow each member to surrender 'without restraint to the amusements of his taste'; they cultivate bonds of 'friendship' by pursuing together no other object than 'pleasure and joy'. Group walks in the countryside, for instance, are not a frivolous pleasure because they serve a 'natural' purpose of exercise. And because these natural pleasures are 'simple' and 'innocent', they can be indulged in with moderation (324/5:90). Crucially, these agreeable pursuits are also politically useful. Although the *circles* are not without vices of intemperance like drunkenness and gambling, it is impossible for an entire city to be 'without failing and self-controlled in everything' (331–332/5:99). And in any case, the majority of members maintain strong family bonds. Indeed, the *circles* provide Geneva's male citizens with a setting for political discourse – they 'dare to speak of fatherland and virtue'. In this way, they instil 'good sense and judgment', combining 'pleasure and gaiety' with 'everything that can contribute to making friends, citizens, and soldiers out of the same men'. By harmonising tastes and the morals required for republican politics, then, the *circles* are traditional Genevan institutions that are 'most appropriate to a free people' (323, 329/5:90, 96).

Rousseau's famous account of republican festivals is his clearest example of how the useful can be combined with the agreeable in public settings. Here, we should recall his argument that modern theatre no longer provides a supplement to virtue because it no longer constitutes an object of pleasure capable of satisfying the desire it stimulates. The pleasures of modern theatre undermine political freedom because they are frivolous, 'exclusive', and private. Republics, whether ancient or modern, require a form of pleasure that is 'solid', inclusive, and public. Rousseau argues that public competitions, such as academic essay contests or sailing regatta, can function as modern analogues of the ancient Greek Olympic games. They are 'so useful and so agreeable' because, through them, participants 'become an amusement to themselves'. Constituting a satisfying object of pleasure, these public institutions prove that the combination of utility and agreeableness we saw in Julie's household is also a public possibility even under conditions of the modern division of labour. We have already seen that the economic limits on modern politics mean that Geneva cannot hope to recreate Sparta. But Rousseau goes on to argue that his compatriots *should* follow Sparta's example in the specific sense of the collective pursuit of civic pleasure. For in republican festivals, a 'secret patriotic charm' is achieved through 'simple' pleasures, without pomp, luxury, or display. Recalling his youth, he claims that these civic amusements taught him that 'solid happiness' is preferable to 'vain pleasures', instilling in him the taste for 'virtue, liberty, and peace' (344, 349–351/2:115, 122–25).

Rousseau's critique of the theatre thus culminates in examples of the modern recovery of the taste for virtue. The *circles* and republican festivals are the kind of public, collective pleasure that he takes to be a necessary condition of genuine moral and political freedom in modernity. By presenting them in *d'Alembert*, he attempts to persuade his compatriots that 'we' should draw both 'our pleasures and our duties from our state and ourselves' (343/2:115). But he recognises that problems remain. Most importantly, he admits that the republican festivals that moved him in his youth would not be so agreeable to many others. For, he notes, 'one must have eyes for seeing it and a heart made for feeling it' (351/2:125). In this sense, Rousseau suggests that he had a natural predisposition to good taste. To realise the potential for the refined Epicurean politics of taste he describes and advocates, though, this taste for virtue must be generalised. And if it can be generalised in Geneva, we must still ask whether and how it might also be possible in other contexts.

Conclusion

One answer that Rousseau gave to his problem of modern liberty was to invert the ancient priority of the public good. The idea that a citizen ought to 'will to sacrifice his interests to those of the public' has been familiar since Plato. But for Rousseau, it was grounded on a wholly unrealistic view of modern politics and moral psychology. 'No one wills the public good unless it agrees with his own', he wrote. The social division of labour had thrown modern citizens into relations of mutual dependence, interweaving the questions of individual and collective survival more tightly than ever before. In the modern condition, the private good had to be prior to the public good. His idea that a genuinely common interest could be generated from out of the clash of necessarily self-interested agents was, he admitted, a 'strange' one. This, in part, is because it inverts the ancient idea of an antecedently given public good. But it is also because a political theory grounded in a view of politics as irreducibly self-interested seemed to leave little room for morality and virtue, let alone the ancient ideal that politics might 'make people happy and good'.[73]

Rousseau's inversion of the ancient priority of the public good is consistent with his rejection of the rationalist account of moderation he encountered in Plato. The Platonic-Socratic view that most members of a given population are incapable of deferring gratification, even when it is in their best interest to do so, has historically been used to justify the division of society into distinct classes of rulers and ruled. In Freud's updated Platonism, for instance, because humans are not 'spontaneously fond of work' and 'arguments are of no avail against their passions', social order requires a non-producing class to control and restrain those producers who are incapable of self-control or *sophrosyne*.[74] Rousseau is widely celebrated for defending the interests of this dominated class. Kant famously credited Rousseau with teaching him to 'respect human nature' and with removing his 'blind prejudice' against 'the ordinary working man'.[75] For Nietzsche, Rousseau's popular sympathies were more political than ethical: against Voltaire's sycophantic defence of the aristocratic 'ruling classes and their values', Rousseau always remained a 'plebeian' who wrote to advance the material interests of the *canaille* – the rabble.[76]

This chapter has demonstrated the centrality of Rousseau's refined Epicurean model of moderation or temperance to his defence of the people. The needs of the body are the foundation of society, and the division of labour compels everyone to pursue their self-interest – the moderns are Epicureans. But the needs of the mind make society agreeable. And because all individuals are in principle capable of restraining their pursuit of pleasure, it is possible for everyone to learn that 'the only pure joy is public joy'. If 'the true

---

[73] Rousseau, 'Letter to Christophe de Beaumont', *CW*9:29/*OC*4:937.

[74] Sigmund Freud, *The Future of an Illusion*, ed. and trans. James Strachey (New York: Norton, 1961): 8. For discussion of this passage, and its contrast to Engels' account of class division, see G. A. Cohen, *Karl Marx's Theory of History: A Defence* (Princeton, NJ: Princeton University Press, 1978): 208–212.

[75] Immanuel Kant, *Sämmtliche Werke*, ed. G Hartenstein, Vol. VIII (Leipzig: L. Voss, 1868): 624. Cited in Ernst Cassirer, *Rousseau-Kant-Goethe*, trans. James Gutmann, Paul Oskar Kristeller, and John Herman Randall, Jr (Princeton, NJ: Princeton University Press, 2015): 2.

[76] Friedrich Nietzsche, *The Will to Power*, ed. and trans. Walter Kaufmann (New York: Vintage Books, 1967): 62–66, 75–76.

sentiments of nature reign only over the people' (*LD*:351/5:124), then it is possible to find political arrangements in which, as he famously put it, 'each, uniting with all, nevertheless obey only himself and remain as free as before' (*SC*:49–50/3:360). With taste as refined Epicureanism, that is, a modern politics of individual freedom could replace the ancient politics of class oppression. But what are the conditions of possibility that a given people, as a whole, might come to judge pleasure according to the criteria that Rousseau proposed to his compatriots? The next chapter answers these questions by recovering his neglected analogy between the general taste and general will.

5

The Foundations of Political Judgement: *Amour-propre*, General Taste, General Will

Introduction

This chapter argues that Rousseau's refined Epicurean account of taste plays a foundational role in the state theory of the *Social Contract*. One of the benefits of the conventionalist, Epicurean reading of the general will is that it emphasises the democratic leanings of Rousseau's thought. But while the general will is often seen as a model of popular political judgement, the brief encounter with the general taste in the previous chapter raised important questions regarding the people's capacity collectively to make sound aesthetic judgements. As we saw, refined Epicureanism is a materially grounded hedonism that roots moderation not in reason or faith but in voluptuousness, sensuality, and sentiment. It is therefore possible, in principle, for every individual to follow Julie's example and practise refined Epicureanism in their pursuit of pleasure. It was this position that Rousseau had in mind when he claimed that the people are uniquely able to follow the true sentiments of nature in their pursuit of pleasure. Yet he developed his position precisely because he believed that the division of labour in modern commercial society had distanced the vast majority of modern individuals from their natural sentiments. With utility and agreeableness separated as criteria of judgement, they instead mistakenly pursue the pleasures of fashion and vanity. In this context, rescuing the possibility of modern patriotism through a generalised refined Epicureanism was either a stubborn insistence or a significant theoretical achievement. Realising that possibility in practice, however, would require overcoming the errors of judgement that the culture of commercial society continually reinforced.

The idea of political judgement is central to the leading accounts of democracy in contemporary political theory. Deliberative democrats ground

THE FOUNDATIONS OF POLITICAL JUDGEMENT 129

the legitimacy of democratic decisions in the refined judgement of elite representatives or the collective judgement of the people.[1] For epistemic democrats, such deliberations are legitimate because these judgements are the instrumental means of arriving at an independent standard of correct decisions.[2] Criticisms of these approaches, in turn, often focus on the nature of political judgement itself. Melissa Schwartzberg's 'judgment democracy' adopts a 'deflationary' view of judgement, which rejects the idea of an independent standard as 'implausible and unachievable'.[3] Perhaps more radically, agonist critics highlight the conflictual nature of democratic deliberation and political realists emphasise that political judgements are historically and contextually conditioned.[4]

Proponents of these rival theories of democracy and judgement often enlist historical precedent for support. Agonists and realists turn to Arendt and Nietzsche, deliberative democrats to Mill, and, as Schwartzberg notes, 'the patron saint of epistemic democrats' is Rousseau.[5] This is somewhat surprising, for Rousseau's treatments of both democracy and judgement are widely understood to be ambiguous. He is not usually considered an ally of those interested in political judgement itself.[6] For some, he wants rather to *disarm* judgement: his concern with the rhetorical influence of demagogues leads him to ground popular sovereignty in a sentimental patriotism intended to eliminate the need for individual autonomous judgement.[7] Moreover, while the view of Rousseau as a 'totalitarian' thinker has largely disappeared from the literature, even sympathetic readers emphasise that his vigorous defence of democratic sovereignty is inseparable from his equally robust rejection of democracy as a

---

[1] John Rawls, *Political Liberalism* (New York: Columbia University Press, 1996), Jürgen Habermas, *Between Facts and Norms: Contributions to a Discourse Theory of Law and Democracy* (Cambridge, MA: The MIT Press, 1998).

[2] Joshua Cohen, 'An Epistemic Conception of Democracy', *Ethics* 97 (1986): 26–38; Hélène Landemore, *Democratic Reason: Politics, Collective Intelligence, and the Rule of the Many* (Princeton, NJ: Princeton University Press, 2012).

[3] Melissa Schwartzberg, 'Epistemic Democracy and its Challenges', *Annual Review of Political Science* 18 (2015): 187–203.

[4] Bonnie Honig, *Political Theory and the Displacement of Politics* (Ithaca, NY: Cornell University Press, 2016). Bernard Williams, *In the Beginning Was the Deed: Realism and Moralism in Political Argument* (Princeton, NJ: Princeton University Press, 2005).

[5] Schwartzberg (2015): 192.

[6] Leslie Paul Thiele, *The Heart of Judgment: Practical Wisdom, Neuroscience, and Narrative* (Cambridge: Cambridge University Press, 2006); Ronald Beiner, *Political Judgement* (London: Routledge, 2013).

[7] Bryan Garsten, *Saving Persuasion: A Defense of Rhetoric and Judgment* (Cambridge, MA: Harvard University Press, 2009).

form of government.[8] From this perspective, one way to preserve Rousseau's democratic credentials is to identify the general will as an embodiment of political judgement but, then, to separate it from the sentimental support that he considered a necessary condition of its emerging in a given state.[9]

This chapter rejects that argumentative strategy. Instead, I reconsider Rousseau's approach to political judgement without abandoning the role of sentiment in his state theory. I begin by outlining Rousseau's argument that judgement is an active rather than a passive faculty. Part of his attempt to delineate a non-deterministic materialism compatible with free will, he linked that argument explicitly to Epicureanism. This introduces my novel interpretation of the origins of *amour-propre* in aesthetic judgement. Together, these discussions prepare the ground for the chapter's central theoretical contribution: the recovery of an implicit analogy in Rousseau's work between the general will and the general taste. Few scholars discuss the general taste; those that do tend strategically to deploy pre-existing interpretations of the general will.[10] My approach is the inverse: I make the analogy explicit by, first, reconstructing Rousseau's idea of the general taste and, only then, reconsidering the general will in its light. This approach provides a valuable new perspective on the perennial debate over the nature of the general will. For if my reconstruction is correct, then it adds a significant argument by analogy: like the general taste, the general will is democratically determined by majority vote, not constrained by transcendent standards. That argument, in turn, provides a more fulsome account of Rousseau's place in the tradition of modern Epicurean political thought.

Before reconstructing the analogy in detail, we can note some of the basic features shared between the general will and general taste. We saw Rousseau use the idea of the general taste to discuss the contextual embeddedness of aesthetic judgement in *d'Alembert*. Almost all readers agree that the general will is the will of a particular community at a particular time: several

---

[8] Christopher Brooke, 'Isaiah Berlin and the Origins of the "Totalitarian" Rousseau', in *Isaiah Berlin and the Enlightenment*, ed. Laurence Brockliss and Ritchie Robertson (Oxford: Oxford University Press, 2016): 89–98. Tuck (2018).

[9] Benjamin Barber, *The Conquest of Politics: Liberal Philosophy in Democratic Times* (Princeton, NJ: Princeton University Press, 1989).

[10] Gabriela Domecq, 'L'ordre du goût chez Rousseau', *Astérion: philosophie, histoire des idées, pensée politique* 16 (2017): https://journals.openedition.org/asterion/2977?lang=en; Céline Spector, 'De Rousseau à Smith: Esthétique démocratique de la sensibilité et théorie économiste de l'esthétique', in *La valeur de l'art. Exposition, marché, critique et public au dix-huitième siècle*, ed. J. Rasmussen (Paris: Champion, 2009): 215–244; Blaise Bachofen, 'La Lettre á d'Alembert: principes du droit poétique?', in *Rousseau, politique et esthétique: Sur la Lettre á d'Alembert*, ed. Bachofen and B. Bernardi (Paris: ENS Editions, 2011): 71–92.

THE FOUNDATIONS OF POLITICAL JUDGEMENT 131

individuals share a single will directed to their common preservation, only if and for so long as they are 'united together and consider themselves a single body' (SC:121/3:347). Even those who argue that the general will transcends the decision of the community do not typically hold that it is universal or cosmopolitan.[11] As discussed, the general taste is similarly geographically restricted and peculiar for each nation or people with a distinct culture – the French have a taste for poetry and the fine arts while Genevans have a taste for liberty and virtue. The general taste also varies historically, both between ancient and modern theatre generally and between old and new comedy specifically. And because the foundation of the analogy is the common origin of both in individual judgement, taking it seriously also provides a more complete understanding of the democratic foundations of Rousseau's political theory.

This chapter also develops some of the implications of the analogy for contemporary theories of political judgement. Parsing the leading 'democratic' and 'transcendent' interpretations of the general will via the general taste clarifies the ambiguities in Rousseau's account of the former while revealing them to be mutually constitutive. Not only does his emphasis on sentiment and beauty push back against overly rationalist accounts of judgement typical of contemporary democratic theory; it also reveals him to have a stronger theory of political judgement than is usually understood, one that connects the individual and the community through a model of political judgement as inherently imbricated with aesthetic judgement. Some of his earliest critics recognised this connection. Insofar as contemporary political theorists attempt precisely to re-connect moral and aesthetic judgement to political judgement, the chapter further demonstrates the value of an historically informed political theory. Reconstructing the analogy also clarifies the importance of aesthetic judgements to Rousseau's state theory. His account of the censorship is usually considered an institution of elite judgement that stands in tension with the popular judgement of the general will. I argue that we should instead read the censorship as articulating the people's general taste. Rousseau's account of political judgement differs from contemporary versions of the analogy between political and aesthetic judgement because he provided a place for popular judgements of beauty *within* his state theory. For him, political and aesthetic judgement are not merely analogous in theory. Rather, good political judgement, in practice, depends on and reciprocally supports good aesthetic judgement.

---

[11] Sankar Muthu, 'On the General Will of Humanity: Global Connections in Rousseau's Political Thought', in *The General Will*, ed. James Farr and David Lay Williams (Cambridge: Cambridge University Press, 2016): 270–306.

Both the general will and general taste derive from individual acts of judgement. To make the analogy explicit, then, I begin by outlining Rousseau's account of judgement. A simple way of reconstructing the analogy is to see it as one between 'political' and 'aesthetic' judgement. I qualify this simple view below and complicate it more significantly in the conclusion. Initially, it provides a placeholder to prepare the ground for the discussion of the general taste that follows.

Judgement

We saw that Rousseau's concern with the political importance of judgement was evident as early as the first *Discourse*. He reduced the problem of luxury to one of mistaken criteria of judgement, and he blamed modern education in conditions of inequality for introducing a senseless preference for the merely agreeable over the useful. The analogy between the general taste and general will overcomes this opposition by securing a place in the state for judgements of both the agreeable and the useful. Here, we can simply note his general claim that the aim of education 'is less science than judgment'; the art of pedagogy consists in slowly revealing the 'relations' his pupil 'must know one day in order to judge well of the good and bad order of civil society' (*E*:338, 341/4:463, 466). Readers tend to emphasise the tensions between the view of domestic education in *Emile* and Rousseau's treatment of civic education elsewhere.[12] But in the *Political Economy*, the formation of citizens similarly requires cultivating judgements of utility and agreeableness, teaching them 'to love one object rather than another, and to love what is genuinely beautiful rather than what is malformed' (*PE*:155/3:259). Thus, both private and public education cultivate political judgement because it is 'the most necessary art' for both man and citizen (*E*:498/4:655).

Despite this evident concern, judgement is not a typical topic of discussion even among Rousseau scholars. There are several reasons for this neglect. Rousseau was initially sceptical about the nature of judgement and, especially, its relationship to free will. In the second *Discourse*, he introduced the faculty of 'perfectibility' precisely to defer judgement on the metaphysical foundation of the 'spiritual acts' deriving from 'the power of willing, or rather of choosing' (*DI*:141/3:142). We saw his earliest readers seize upon this passage as evidence of his accepting determinism and a materialist conception of judgement.

---

[12] Bjorn Gomes, 'Emile the Citizen? A Reassessment of the Relationship between Private Education and Citizenship in Rousseau's Political Thought', *European Journal of Political Theory* 17:2 (2018): 194–213.

THE FOUNDATIONS OF POLITICAL JUDGEMENT 133

Moreover, his most developed account of judgement appears in *Emile*'s 'Profession of Faith of the Savoyard Vicar', and the relationship between that text and Rousseau's own views is debated.[13] Indeed, it has been argued that there is no consistent account of judgement across all four books of *Emile*.[14] Finally, however one interprets Rousseau's account of judgement, the relationship of *Emile* more generally to his earlier work is controversial. Framing *Emile* and the *Social Contract* as the 'solution' to the 'problems' Rousseau identified in the *Discourses* has been a favoured approach since Kant.[15] But it raises the consistency dilemma regarding Rousseau's moral ideal of personal happiness and his political ideal of popular sovereignty. By demonstrating the importance of judgement and the general will – general taste analogy to Rousseau's state theory, this chapter offers new evidence for the coherence of his system.

The core of Rousseau's account is his argument that judgement is an 'active' rather than a 'passive' faculty. He was responding to the philosophical controversy surrounding the *Encyclopédie* article 'Evidence' (1756). There, François Quesnay asserted: 'to judge is nothing other than to perceive and to acknowledge the relations, quantities, and qualities or ways of being of objects'. On this principle, free will consisted entirely in the ability to suspend judgement in deliberation, to 'refuse or to surrender decisively' to a will determined by external sense objects.[16] The controversy was rekindled in 1758 by the publication of Helvétius' *De L'ésprit*.[17] Rousseau never rebuked Helvétius publicly but his marginal annotations demonstrate his intention to attack the text's foundational principle 'that human judgments are purely passive' and, instead, defend and 'establish the activity of our judgments'.[18] Helvétius' central thesis was that 'to judge is to sense'.[19] In *Emile*, the Savoyard Vicar responds by asserting: 'To perceive is to sense; to compare is to judge. Judging and

---

[13] Although my reading can afford to remain agnostic, I do think that the balance of the evidence suggests that we ought to accept Rousseau's affirming the Vicar's views as his own: *CW*9:139/*OC*3:694; *R*:21–23/*OC*1:1016–1018; 'Rousseau à Moultou, le 23 decembre 1761', *CC*9:341–343.

[14] Jean H. Bloch, 'Rousseau and Helvétius on Innate and Acquired Traits: The Final Stages of the Rousseau-Helvétius Controversy', *Journal of the History of Ideas* 40:1 (1979): 21–41.

[15] Immanuel Kant, 'Conjectural Beginning of Human History', in Immanuel Kant, *Anthropology, History, and Education*, ed. Günter Zöller and Robert Louden, trans. Allen W. Wood (Cambridge: Cambridge University Press, 2007). Ernst Cassirer, *The Question of Jean-Jacques Rousseau*, ed. and trans. Peter Gay (Bloomington: Indiana University Press, 1963).

[16] François Quesnay, 'Evidence', in Diderot and d'Alembert (1756): 6:146–57.

[17] Cp. Pierre-Maurice Masson, 'Rousseau Contre Helvétius', *Revue d'histoire Littéraire de La France* 18:1 (1911): 103–124.

[18] *CW*12:211/*OC*4:1129.

[19] Claude-Adrien Helvétius, *De l'esprit; or Essays on the Mind and Its Several Faculties* (London: M. Jones, 1809).

134   ROUSSEAU'S POLITICS OF TASTE

sensing are not the same thing.' Sensation merely presents objects to the mind. Judgement is the mind's active ability to compare, transport, or superimpose sense experiences in order to 'pronounce' on their differences, likeness, and their 'relations' in general. This ability, Rousseau insisted, is not external to the individual but internally produced (*E*:430–431/4:571–573).

Rousseau linked this defence of active judgement explicitly to the Epicurean account of sensation and error. In a passage preserved in one manuscript version of *Emile*, he did so to conclude that the source of our errors is in judgement.

> I say that it is impossible that our senses deceive us; for it is always true that we sense what we sense, and the Epicureans were right in that. Sensations only cause us to fall into error by the judgments it pleases us to join to them about the productive causes of these same sensations, or about the nature of the objects that they make us perceive (*apercevoir*), or about the relations that they have among them. But it is in this that the Epicureans deceived themselves (*se trompaient*), claiming that the judgment we made about our sensations were never false.[20]

This refinement of Epicurean epistemology was part of Rousseau's developing a non-deterministic materialism compatible with free will. His view in the second *Discourse* that one is 'free to acquiesce or to resist' natural sense impressions was compatible with the passive judgement thesis (*DI*:141/3:142). Castillon fastened on that account to accuse him of vulgar Epicureanism. Revisiting it in the light of Helvétius, Rousseau moved away from his radically sceptical position to argue that 'freedom is only a similar power or one derived from' the active power of judging and comparing (*E*:442/4:586). This was the foundation of his rejection of the 'modern' materialism of the *philosophes*.

Rousseau saw his account of active judgement as part of his refined Epicureanism. It was also the foundation of both freedom and virtue, for it secured the ability to regulate one's pursuit of pleasure. By undermining freedom, the passive judgement thesis was 'as fatal to good taste as to virtue'.[21] Rejecting it allowed him to confront a further challenge, for the criteria by

---

[20] Rousseau, *OC*4:1447, note 'a', 481. This passage is found in the manuscript of Emile preserved in Paris at the Palais Bourbon (ms 1428) but not in the manuscripts preserved in Geneva (mss fr. 205 and 224 and Rés. Cc 12). See also *E*:353–354, 430–432/*OC*4:481, 572–573. For discussion, see Terence Marshall, 'Epistemology and Political Perception in the Case of Rousseau', in *The Challenge of Rousseau*, ed. Eve Grace and Christopher Kelly (Cambridge: Cambridge University Press, 2012): 76–120.

[21] *CW*7:325/*OC*5:419.

THE FOUNDATIONS OF POLITICAL JUDGEMENT   135

which we judge pleasure change over time. Though partly dependent upon sensations, we have seen that he insisted that the variations in our values and desires also 'depend on us'. The central insight of his *Wise Man's Materialism* was that our active mental ability to interrupt the stream of sense impressions allowed us to bring the physical world into harmony with the moral world. We could actively compare sensations across time and space, form judgements about them, and derive principles and criteria from them (*C*:343/1:408–409). Rousseau never used the term aesthetics. But his reflections on judgement are further evidence of just how seriously he took the emerging idea of a 'science of what is sensed or imagined'.[22] And while his position on free will and materialism is sometimes hotly contested, what matters here is that he intended his account of active judgement to secure a foundation for taste, virtue, and freedom.[23]

Political judgement is notoriously difficult or even impossible to define. Some emphasise its uncertain epistemological status as a distinct faculty or concept.[24] Others argue that the conditions of ignorance and opacity that necessarily characterise all political actions render political judgement little more than a matter of chance.[25] These difficulties notwithstanding, the general will is often taken to 'model' political judgement. On one influential 'Kantian' or 'Hegelian' reading, the general will models the rational agency of individuals: the 'principles' guiding the general will reflect the 'content' or 'standpoint' of reason itself.[26] From another view, the general will is not a 'tool' for individual judgement but a 'model' of how a political community becomes aware of its shared interests: the general will emerges from conflicting private interests, which requires that citizens 'meet and act in common'.[27] From this perspective, Kantian readings effectively occlude what is specifically *political* about judgement in Rousseau.

The spectre of Kant also haunts the question of aesthetic judgement in Rousseau. Rousseau identified the essence of judgement as comparison; Kant's idea of subsuming particulars under universals is for him a kind of formal

---

[22] Alexander Gottlieb Baumgarten, *Aesthetica*, Vol. 2 (Frankfurt/Oder: Kleyb, 1750).

[23] See David Lay Williams, 'Rousseau on Inequality and Free Will', *Political Theory* 45:4 (2017): 552–565. Ryan Patrick Hanley, 'Rousseau's Virtue Epistemology', *Journal of the History of Philosophy* 50:2 (2012): 239–263.

[24] Peter J. Steinberger, *The Concept of Political Judgment* (Chicago, IL: University of Chicago Press, 1993).

[25] John Dunn, *The Cunning Of Unreason Making Sense Of Politics* (London: Basic Books, 2000).

[26] Neuhouser (2008): 191.

[27] Benjamin Barber, *The Conquest of Politics: Liberal Philosophy in Democratic Times* (Princeton, NJ: Princeton University Press, 1989): 204.

reasoning distinct from judgement.[28] Moreover, we must not attribute to Rousseau the view that aesthetic judgements are distinctly 'reflective' judgements; nothing in his work corresponds to Kant's distinction between these judgements made without reference to general rules and 'determinate' judgements made according to general rules.[29] As such, Arendt's famous extension to politics of Kantian aesthetic judgement cannot be applied analogously to Rousseau.[30] Nor, finally, does Rousseau take aesthetic judgements to be 'disinterested' – for him, judgements of beauty are inseparable from pleasure and politics. This is one reason why he is often placed in a 'Platonic' tradition of judging aesthetic objects according to moral and political criteria.

With these qualifications in mind, we can take Rousseau to distinguish between 'political' and 'aesthetic' judgements in two crucial ways. First, the general will and general taste emerge from distinct *modes* of judgement. Though the role of 'reason' in the general will is debated, Rousseau was sometimes willing to grant that 'the general will is in each individual a pure act of the understanding, which reasons in the silence of the passions' (*SC*:157/3:286).[31] We saw that he preferred to describe taste as providing 'spectacles to reason' or as the 'microscope of judgment'. These visual metaphors were designed to capture the unique combination of reason and sentiment in aesthetic judgements: sentiment 'brings small objects' within the reach of judgements according to rational concepts of beauty and goodness. Second, they operate according to the different criteria of judgement explored in Chapter 4. The political judgements that create the general will consider what is *useful*: the *Social Contract* is an account of how to combine 'what right permits with what interest prescribes, so that justice and utility not be disjoined', and the general will produces this 'admirable agreement between interest and justice' (41, 62/3:351, 374). The judgements that create the general taste consider what is *agreeable*: 'taste is exercised only in relation to things which are neutral or which are at most of interest as entertainment, and not in regard to those things connected with our needs'; the essay on 'true taste' in *Emile* concerns 'the choice of agreeable leisure', not what is 'useful' or harmful (*E*:512, 528/4:671, 690).

---

[28] Denise Schaeffer, *Rousseau on Education, Freedom, and Judgment* (University Park: Penn State University Press, 2014).

[29] Immanuel Kant, *Critique of the Power of Judgment* (Cambridge: Cambridge University Press, 2000).

[30] Hannah Arendt, *Lectures on Kant's Political Philosophy* (Chicago, IL: University of Chicago Press, 2014).

[31] See Arash Abizadeh, 'Banishing the Particular: Rousseau on Rhetoric, Patrie, and the Passions', *Political Theory* 29:4 (2001): 556–582.

THE FOUNDATIONS OF POLITICAL JUDGEMENT   137

Even while he distinguished political and aesthetic judgements analytically, however, Rousseau always emphasised their deep practical imbrication. This is perhaps clearest in his celebrated account of *amour-propre*. But as with the general will and Rousseau's state theory more generally, the aesthetic dimension of *amour-propre* is consistently neglected by his readers. This is surprising. For we saw that he identified *amour-propre*'s interaction with a mistaken vulgar Epicurean understanding of pleasure as central to the prevalence of domination and lack of freedom in modern commercial society. He also identified *amour-propre* as the 'genuine source of honour' and explained, in his discussion of the censorship, that the content of honour is itself derived from private judgement about what is beautiful. Before exploring the general taste and its analogy with the general will, then, I first explore how Rousseau's refined Epicurean account of taste elucidates the neglected aesthetic dimensions of *amour-propre*.

Amour-propre

The mutual imbrication of political and aesthetic judgement is especially apparent in Rousseau's account of the origin of *amour-propre* in the second *Discourse*. After isolated humans have settled into nations with shared ways of life, they begin to judge, or 'make comparisons'. These first judgements are made according to aesthetic 'ideas of merit and beauty which produce sentiments of preference'. In Rousseau's famous image, early humans judge song and dance competitions with a combination of reason and sentiment.

> Everyone began to look at everyone else, and to wish to be looked at himself, and public esteem acquired a price. The one who sang or danced the best; the handsomest, the strongest, the most skilful, or the most eloquent came to be the most highly regarded, and this was the first step at once toward inequality and vice: from these first preferences arose vanity and contempt on the one hand, shame and envy on the other.

The image introduces his argument that the ideas of 'consideration' or esteem at play in these incipient aesthetic judgements immediately generate political claims of 'right' and 'the first duties of civility'. The example grounds his general critique of status hierarchies in civil society, where one's 'advantage' comes to depend on one's ability to 'have or to affect' qualities that 'attract consideration' from others (*DI*:165–166, 170/3:169–170, 174–175). In other words, the image illustrates how it becomes useful to make oneself agreeable.

138   ROUSSEAU'S POLITICS OF TASTE

This analysis is repeated in *Emile*. There, in place of the Maypole Dance satire, he emphasised the relationship between inwardly directed self-love and outwardly directed erotic love, the moral side of the sexual passion. Without ideas of 'merit or beauty', humans would be unable to form erotic attachments. But with these ideas and sentiments, both sexes begin to develop preferences and a desire to be similarly preferred: 'to be loved, one has to make oneself loveable. To be preferred one has to make oneself more loveable than another, more loveable than every other, at least in the eyes of the beloved object.' Again, this desire to be granted preference stimulates our knowledge of our relations with others, our comparisons with and between them, and hence gives rise to 'emulation, rivalries, and jealousies'. And again, Rousseau used this account of moral-psychological development to illustrate 'where our *amour-propre* gets the form we believe natural to it, and how *amour de soi*, ceasing to be an absolute sentiment, becomes pride in great souls, vanity in small ones, and feeds itself constantly in all at the expense of their neighbours' (*E*:364–365/4:494).[32] In each case, then, *amour-propre* originates in our awareness of our relations to external objects, other humans, and ourselves; and in the comparisons we make between them. It becomes politically relevant, or dangerous, when we begin to make those comparisons according to ideas of merit or beauty. The development of *amour-propre* is coterminous with the origin of aesthetic judgement.

From this perspective, Rousseau's attempt in *d'Alembert* to persuade Genevans to reject the pleasures of vanity for those of pride was an attempt to redirect their *amour-propre*. In his advice to Corsica, Rousseau identified the two 'great motivations that make men act' as 'sensual pleasure' and 'vanity'. Satisfying one's vanity provided a type of pleasure distinct from sensual pleasure insofar as it was rooted in opinion. Those who performed their enjoyment of pleasure for others were not sensual but vain, vulgar Epicureans who are unable to taste any true pleasures beyond mere ostentation. But he immediately clarified that vanity was only one of the two 'branches of *amour-propre*'. The other was pride, which was also grounded in opinion. Crucially, his distinction between vanity and pride is also grounded in beauty: 'the opinion that puts a great value in frivolous objects produces vanity; the one that falls upon objects great and beautiful by themselves produces pride'. We saw that, when Rousseau rejected d'Alembert's proposed legal regulation of the theatre,

---

[32] On the development of Rousseau's account of the relationship between *amour-propre* and *amour de soi*, see Brooke (2012). For my purposes here, it matters only that Rousseau is consistent that *amour-propre* originates alongside aesthetic judgement. For *amour de soi* and its relationship to conscience, see Sonenscher (2020).

THE FOUNDATIONS OF POLITICAL JUDGEMENT 139

he instead focused on opinion and pleasure as the most effective means of influencing a people's morals. This accords with his advice to Corsicans that 'the arbiters of a people's opinions are the arbiters of its actions'. For their common source in *amour-propre* meant that a people would be either vain or prideful depending on whether their 'judgments' were directed towards either frivolous or beautiful objects.[33]

Amour-propre is one of the most frequently discussed topics in Rousseau. He distinguishes between two basic varieties of human self-love: *amour-propre* and *amour de soi*. On the traditional view, these are simply the 'good' and 'bad' form of self-love, with *amour-propre* a wholly negative sentiment that necessarily generates psychological distress and social conflict. The appeal of this view rests on the account of *amour-propre* in the second *Discourse*: *amour de soi* is a 'natural' form of self-love because it is 'unreflective', a concern for one's 'well-being' understood in 'physical' as opposed to mental or 'moral' terms; *amour-propre* is an 'artificial' form of self-love because it is 'reflective'. It is 'only a relative sentiment, factitious, and born in society'. Crucially, 'it inclines every individual to set greater store by himself than by anyone else, inspires men with all the evils they do one another, and is the genuine source of honour' (*SC*:218/3:219). Seeing *amour-propre* as a negative quest for superiority supports (quasi) 'totalitarian' readings of Rousseau's politics. In a political system in which citizens come to love themselves to the extent that they identify fully with the common self of the state, *amour-propre* is satisfied by giving citizens a sense of 'national superiority', preferring their people to all others.[34]

It is now common to distinguish between two different varieties of *amour-propre*. 'Simple' or 'basic' comparative self-love is a natural need for 'recognition' in which one desires simply to compare to all others as a moral equal. 'Corrupt' or 'inflamed' comparative self-love is a malignant desire for 'preference' or 'superiority' over all others. For 'revisionists', *amour-propre* remains a psychological and social problem but admits a variety of solutions. First, it can be satisfied or contented through 'general' or 'egalitarian esteem': the mutual recognition that comes from being recognised as an equal among equals. Equal esteem can be granted politically, as when one desires to be recognised as a co-citizen of a well-ordered republic. However, revisionists argue that political equality is grounded in and expresses a more fundamental moral equality. Second, *amour-propre* can be contented through 'special esteem'.

[33] Rousseau, 'Plan for a Constitution of Corsica', *CW*11:153–154/*OC*3:935–938. Cf. Ryan Patrick Hanley, 'Enlightened Nation Building: The "Science of the Legislator" in Adam Smith and Rousseau', *American Journal of Political Science* 52:2 (2008): 219–234.

[34] Shklar (1969). David Gauthier, *Rousseau: The Sentiment of Existence* (Cambridge: Cambridge University Press, 2006).

140 ROUSSEAU'S POLITICS OF TASTE

General esteem or 'respect' as a human being or citizen provides a background against which one is recognised for one's particular accomplishments, granting preference and superiority in ways that are compatible with psychological well-being and political stability. For Axel Honneth, *amour-propre* is contented through 'sources of social recognition that supplement the general will', such as marriage and the *Social Contract*'s civil religion. Here Rousseau emerges as a sort of proto-Rawlsian liberal, with different interpreters pursuing either 'Kantian' or 'Hegelian' readings of both Rousseau and Rawls.[35] For revisionists, then, while Rousseau's politics still prioritise cultural unity and conformity, they permit and provide sources of individual esteem or recognition in ways compatible with liberalism.

The most influential version of the revisionist reading centres on one passage in *Emile*.[36] After describing the generalisation of Emile's pity and before his essay on taste in Book IV, Rousseau describes the transformation of *amour-propre* into a virtue via its 'extension' to others:

> Let us extend *amour-propre* to other beings. We shall transform it into a virtue. The less the object of our care is immediately involved with us, the less the illusion of particular interest is to be feared. The more one generalizes this interest, the more it becomes equitable, and the love of mankind is nothing other than the love of justice ... It is of little importance to [Emile] who gets a greater share of happiness provided that it contributes to the greatest happiness of all. This is the wise man's first interest after his private interest, for each is part of his species and not of another individual. (*E*:409/4:547)

Traditionalist readers struggle to interpret this passage. If the 'only satisfying pleasure' of *amour-propre* is the 'oppression of others', then it is incompatible with virtue.[37] As such, traditionalists are left to suggest that, although Rousseau

---

[35] Axel Honneth, 'The Depths of Recognition: The Legacy of Jean-Jacques Rousseau', in Lifschitz ed. (2016): 200. Cf. Rafeeq Hasan, 'Rousseau on the Ground of Obligation: Reconsidering the Social Autonomy Interpretation', *European Journal of Political Theory* 17:2 (2018): 233–243; David James, *Rousseau and German Idealism: Freedom, Dependence and Necessity* (Cambridge: Cambridge University Press, 2013).

[36] Other scholars provide slightly different views, drawing on different texts: Timothy O'Hagan, *Rousseau* (London: Routledge, 2003): 163–180; Zev M. Trachtenberg, *Making Citizens: Rousseau's Political Theory of Culture* (London: Routledge, 1993): 132–143. For the wider historical background of the idea of transforming *amour-propre* into *amour de la patrie*: Nannerl Keohane, *Philosophy and the State in France: The Renaissance to the Enlightenment* (Princeton, NJ: Princeton University Press, 1980).

[37] Cassirer (1963): 75.

wrote *amour-propre* here, what he actually meant was *amour de soi*.[38] Revisionists relieve this interpretive embarrassment by arguing that to 'extend' *amour-propre* is 'to grant to others' that they are motivated by the same desire for 'equal moral dignity'.[39] Crucially, for this view, Emile's *amour-propre* is 'extended' to 'mankind' in general as distinct from any particular individual or set of individuals. This distinction grounds Frederick Neuhouser's interpretation that 'extending amour-propre to other beings' consists in according to them a kind of dignity that one's own *amour-propre* makes one seek for oneself, the dignity of a "human being" as expressed in the idea of moral equality'.[40]

Although the revisionist view has become the default position of Rousseau's readers, grounds for scepticism remain. The idea of extending *amour-propre* to others occurs throughout his texts. But this is the only place where he describes its extension to the idea of 'humanity in general' and he otherwise tends largely to resist a 'cosmopolitan' position.[41] As such, for some readers, this passage alone simply cannot bear the weight of the revisionist distinctions between 'neutral' and 'inflamed' *amour-propre* or 'egalitarian' and 'special' esteem.[42]

While neither school has reflected on Rousseau's evident concern with the aesthetics of *amour-propre*, taking it seriously reframes the contemporary debate. Befitting its development through aesthetic judgement, beauty serves as a means of transforming *amour-propre* into a virtue throughout *Julie*. In the short story appended to the novel's letters, the English gentleman Edward Bomstom establishes a pedagogical relationship with the beautiful prostitute Laura. The two eventually fall in love, and the climax of their drama comes with the girl breaking down in tears. Edward's response is instructive:

> Where is the man austere enough to flee the looks of a charming creature who demands of him no more than that he let himself be loved? Where is he whose honest heart does not swell a little at tears from two beautiful eyes? Where is the beneficent man whose useful *amour-propre* does not like to enjoy the fruit of its attentions? He had made Laura too estimable to have no more than esteem for her. (*J*:619/2:758)

---

[38] For this substitution, see Asher Horowitz, *Rousseau, Nature, and History* (Toronto: University of Toronto Press, 1992): 237; John Charvet, *The Social Problem in the Philosophy of Rousseau* (Cambridge: Cambridge University Press, 1974): 85. Cf. N. J. H. Dent, *Rousseau: Introduction to his Psychological, Social and Political Theory* (Oxford: Blackwell, 1988): 55.

[39] Dent (1988): 143–145.

[40] Neuhouser (2008): 224.

[41] Rousseau, 'Geneva Manuscript', *CW*4:81/*OC*3:288. Helena Rosenblatt, 'Rousseau, the Anticosmopolitan?', *Daedalus* 137:3 (2008): 59–67.

[42] Richard Tuck, 'A Spokesman for His Country', *TLS* (blog), accessed 9 July 2023. https://www.the-tls.co.uk/articles/a-spokesman-for-his-country/

The satisfaction of Edward's *amour-propre* is compatible with the virtues of austerity, honesty, and even beneficence. In this respect, it is similar to Emile's extension of *amour-propre*, which follows on and completes the prior generalisation of his pity, a process which makes him, like Edward, beneficent. But Edward is not motivated by considerations of general human dignity. He desires to be esteemed by one particular – and particularly beautiful – woman. His desire is compatible with virtue because the looks he receives from a woman he judges charming, the tears from eyes he judges beautiful, are physical signs of the moral sentiments they share. This is one of several examples throughout the novel in which what Rousseau calls 'exquisite *amour-propre*' is said to provide a pleasure that 'repays all austere virtues' (262/2:320). Thus, beauty makes *amour-propre* 'useful' by providing a reward for virtue.

This Epicurean view of virtue as the means to greater pleasure directly informs another of Rousseau's accounts of the 'extension' of *amour-propre*. The main characters of *Julie* are 'friends' who never attempt 'to shine in each other's eyes' because they 'know and love each other too much for *amour-propre*' to have much effect on them (11/2:16). However, Rousseau notes that every friendship, even between these 'simple but sensitive youths', is necessarily governed by 'a certain intensity of *amour-propre*' (225/2:275). In a helpful but neglected example, Julie's cousin Claire compares their relative standing in what she calls 'the empire of beauty'. She acknowledges that, with respect to their physical features, there is no doubt that Julie's beauty exceeds her own. Yet, despite this judgement, Claire claims to be 'more proud than jealous over it'. As she explains to Julie: 'the charms of your face . . . do not diminish those that I have, and I feel more beautiful with your beauty, more graceful with your graces, adorned with your talents. I deck myself in all your perfections, and it is in you that I make the best possible extension of my *amour-propre*.' Recognising Julie's superior beauty, she can 'yield' her relative position in the empire of beauty without being 'humble' (168/2:205–206).

These examples of the interaction of *amour-propre* and the pleasures of beauty problematise the revisionist interpretation of the extension of Emile's *amour-propre*. First, when Claire extends her *amour-propre*, she is not according to Julie the kind of dignity due to all humans as moral equals. This is not what she desires to be recognised in herself. Perhaps their friendship, a relationship grounded in love, allows Claire's *amour-propre* to be satisfied in a way that is compatible with virtuous pride rather than vain jealousy. Yet neither does Claire desire for her status as Julie's friend to be recognised. She desires to be recognised as beautiful, as more beautiful than others. Most remarkably, *Claire's amour-propre* is satisfied by recognition of *Julie's* superiority, over both herself and others. Crucially, this is not because Claire senses her own virtue,

THE FOUNDATIONS OF POLITICAL JUDGEMENT   143

or the propriety of her acknowledging Julie's natural superiority in beauty. Rather, Claire's *amour-propre* is contented because she has 'extended' it to the superior beauty of her more beautiful friend. This allows her to take pleasure precisely in Julie's unequal beauty, and the recognition – by both herself and others – of Julie's superiority. As the contemporary translation puts it, she has 'invested' her *amour-propre* in Julie's beauty and receives a dividend accordingly (148/2:206).

Second, we must note that the Tutor's stated aim in extending Emile's pupil's *amour-propre* is to put his newly acquired 'beneficence in action'. The point of his considering 'the species' is to make Emile's *amour-propre*, like Edward's, 'useful'. Edward's example reminds us that extending *amour-propre* 'activates' Emile's beneficence in the same way: being 'beneficent for the profit of others' gives Emile an 'inner enjoyment' (*E*:409/4:548). From this perspective, what Emile desires to be recognised in himself when he extends his *amour-propre* to the idea of mankind is not his fundamental moral equality but his superiority. The pleasure of feeling superior is the reward that motivates him to act beneficently.

These similarities with Rousseau's other accounts of its operation and extension to others suggests that it is a mistake to neglect the aesthetics of *amour-propre*. Neuhouser briefly notes that an appreciation of beauty plays 'some important role' in Rousseau's pedagogy. For him, Rousseau's civic education is an instance of general egalitarian esteem, where individual citizens receive honour by participating in the civic life of the particular people to which they belong rather than by performing feats of civic virtue. Citing Rousseau's statement that citizens are taught 'to love what is truly beautiful rather than what is malformed', Neuhouser's central interpretive suggestion is that Rousseau takes national identification to be a 'normative stance'. In his view, the love of the beautiful is not 'sentimental' but expresses a 'commitment' to 'normative ideals that distinguish the fine from the base'. This interpretation, he suggests, 'coheres nicely' with the fact that the last phase of *Emile*'s education is 'devoted to forming his aesthetic judgment'. Neuhouser does not specify precisely what the role of an appreciation for beauty might be for Rousseau's citizens. But he does claim that Rousseau advanced 'moral and aesthetic ideals' understood as 'abstract concepts' that ground 'principles' that, in turn, 'claim a more general validity than merely local practices and *mores*'.[43]

My reconsideration of the 'extension' passage may not refute the entirety of the revisionist position. But if it is at all correct, then it substantially shifts the burden of proof and demands further consideration of *amour-propre*'s

---

[43] Neuhouser (2008): 236–237.

relationship to beauty. The revisionist project generally tends to rationalise Rousseau in an explicit attempt to highlight his affinities with the German idealist tradition.[44] This may explain why Neuhouser supports his interpretation with what he calls Rousseau's 'definition' of beauty: both 'the morally good' and 'the beautiful', he claims, are defined not 'by what we love because it is useful to us nor [by] what we hate because it harms us'.[45] But in this passage, Rousseau is discussing taste rather than beauty, and we might hesitate to call it a 'definition' of either. Minimally, then, for these interpretations to support the 'coherence' suggested between Rousseau's accounts of private and public education requires a more detailed interpretation of his essay on taste.

The next section examines Rousseau essay on taste in detail. But I conclude this discussion of *amour-propre* by noting a final example of its aesthetic dimension, which highlights its place in Rousseau's politics of taste. In a thought experiment from *d'Alembert*, Rousseau describes a 'Winter Ball' at which young men and women meet and dance under the watchful eye of Genevan citizens. At the end of the evening, the city's elders crown one young woman Queen of the Ball. While they aim to reward the most 'virtuous' woman, it is always possible that they will select the most 'beautiful' woman.

> But even if modest beauty were sometimes favoured, what would be the great harm in that? Having more assaults to sustain, does it not need to be encouraged more? Is it not a gift of nature just as talents are? What harm is there if beauty obtains some honours which excite it to make itself worthy of them and can content amour-propre without offending virtue? (*LD*:347/5:119)

In this reformed version of the Maypole Dance, beauty allows *amour-propre* to be satisfied in a way that is compatible with virtue. Importantly, the thought experiment comes amid Rousseau's description of relative material equality and a moderate enjoyment of pleasure. It is this context that allows for the appreciation of beauty to be set with reference to virtues like modesty and, crucially, to be set publicly. In these conditions, artificial inequality is proportionate to natural inequality and the recognition of one's superior beauty is thus merited. As with the examples of the *circles* and republican festivals, here utility and agreeableness are appropriately balanced in the state. In short, the Queen of the Ball is a further image – or simulacrum – of how the taste for virtue might be cultivated in a society that is both commercial

---

[44] Cp. James (2013), Sonenscher (2020): 141–178.
[45] Neuhouser (2008): 244.

THE FOUNDATIONS OF POLITICAL JUDGEMENT

and yet still provides an economic and aesthetic context for the realisation of modern liberty.

The General Taste

Rousseau began his career as a composer and philosopher of music and the politics of taste were never far from his mind. As we have seen, he denied any contradiction between his critiquing the contemporary corruption of taste and cultivating those tastes whose progress he approved. His defence was grounded on an 'essential distinction' that, he insisted, his early critics had ignored – between good taste, which was useful for others, and bad taste, which was born of a prideful and false, purely selfish desire to be merely agreeable. Insofar as we neglect the centrality of judgements of taste to Rousseau's politics, we repeat the error of these critics. To guard against this mistake, we must foreground two of Rousseau's claims, both of which we have encountered before. First, his famous insistence in *Emile* that those 'who want to treat politics and morals separately will never understand' either (*E*:389/4:524). Second, he considered morals and tastes indistinguishable because, while they were not the same, their common origin in judgement meant that a change in one necessarily affected a change in the other (*LD*:264/5:18). Rousseau scholars have neglected this second claim for too long. For if understanding politics requires understanding morals, and morals and tastes are nearly indistinguishable, then understanding politics requires understanding tastes.

The democratic reading of the general taste developed in this section fits with Rousseau's celebration of popular judgement elsewhere. In the second *Discourse*, he celebrated the people's capacity as 'the genuine judge of morals . . . sometimes deceived, but never corrupted' (*DI*:222/3:223). In the *Social Contract*, this view of the people as moral arbiter lies behind his arguments in favour of aristocratic government.[46] Aristocracy is preferable to democracy because it requires 'fewer virtues' and permits moderate inequality. As such, it leaves the people 'content' while allowing those of individual 'merit' to govern beyond the narrow interests of their class or economic faction (*SC*:94/3:407–408). Crucially, this primary benefit of aristocracy requires the standard of individual merit to be popularly determined. The 'public voice' elevates only 'enlightened and capable men' to positions of power because, in contrast to monarchs, 'the people is much less often mistaken with this choice' (96/3:410). This idea that the people is a better judge of moral character than

---

[46] Cf. John P. McCormick, *Reading Machiavelli: Scandalous Books, Suspect Engagements, and the Virtue of Populist Politics* (Princeton, NJ: Princeton University Press, 2020): 109–143.

146 ROUSSEAU'S POLITICS OF TASTE

the prince is familiar in the republican tradition.[47] It suggests the following: if the people is the best judge of morals, and tastes and morals are indistinguishable, then the people must also be the best judge of tastes.

I have already remarked that Rousseau's account of the censorship provides a place for popular judgements of beauty and agreeableness in his state theory. In the second *Discourse*, he suggested that the ancient Roman censorship was an unrealistic model for the modern politics of self-interest. Now, 'the distinction between wicked and good men' had to be drawn by 'public esteem' (*DI*:222/3:222–223). The censorship discussion in the *Social Contract* develops this insight, insisting that it is 'useless' to distinguish between the people's moral values of honour and merit and the 'objects of its esteem' or 'choice of its pleasures'. In the key passage, Rousseau explains that 'one always loves what is beautiful or what one finds to be so, but it is in this judgment that one is mistaken; hence it is this judgment that has to be regulated'. Whatever the people esteems is determined by what each individual judges to be 'beautiful or fine'. But because these judgements are not given by 'nature' and are, rather, a matter of 'opinion', moral reform requires reforming the opinions that influence each individual's taste. Moral reform therefore requires regulating individual judgements of what is beautiful and, thereby, determining the choice of the people's pleasures (*SC*:141–142/3:418–419). In other words, the censorship's role is to express a standard of aesthetic judgement by which individuals can regulate their pursuit of pleasure.

The censorship is usually seen as an institution of elite judgement that undermines whatever democratic credentials Rousseau's theory of the general will might have earned him.[48] This view can be supported by his defence of connoisseurship elsewhere. Beyond his immediate contemporaries, he sometimes suggests that all peoples lack the capacity for aesthetic judgement. He once explained that 'to judge French Music well', one must consider it 'independent of what the populace of all stations thinks'. For the people necessarily lack 'reason and reflection' and, thus, judge artistic productions according to the 'false pleasures' they provide. Operating with a mistaken criterion, they always give 'badly understood approbation' to those musical performances of 'the worst taste'. Quoting Plato's *Laws* approvingly, Rousseau argues that 'the many' are correct that music must be judged by the criterion of pleasure; but the best music is that which 'pleases the best and best educated'.[49] From this

---

[47] Niccolo Machiavelli, *Discourses on Livy*, ed. Nathan Tarcov and Harvey Mansfield (Chicago, IL: University of Chicago Press, 1996): 157–158.

[48] Ethan Putterman, 'Rousseau on the People as Legislative Gatekeepers, Not Framers', *The American Political Science Review* 99:1 (2005): 145–151 (149).

[49] Rousseau, 'Letter on French Music', *CW*7:143/*OC*5:292.

THE FOUNDATIONS OF POLITICAL JUDGEMENT

perspective, the censorship would be one example of elite aesthetic judgement, the priority of which is a sort of trans-historical necessity.

I argue that we should instead read the censorship as articulating the general taste. The chapter begins with an allusion to the analogy reconstructed below. Rousseau emphasises that the censorship's declaration is itself derived from private judgements: just as the law declares the general will, so the censorship declares the general taste, here described as 'public opinion' or the 'public judgment' about what is beautiful and, therefore, both honourable and agreeable (SC:141/3:418). With no transcendent 'natural' standard of judgement, a central problem arises regarding the source of the criterion of 'the beautiful' that will regulate aesthetic judgement in the state. As we will see, my reconstruction of the general taste suggests that this criterion must be internally generated, not externally supplied. The analogy with the general will thus extends further: the censorship does not *impose* an aesthetic standard on the people; it is the institutional means through which the people *declares* its own standard. Indeed, the argument of this chapter suggests that Rousseau moved away from his early Platonic critique of the people's incapacity for musical judgement and that the view of popular taste informing the *Social Contract* was closer to his view in *d'Alembert* of the people's unique capacity to be ruled by natural sentiments.

To make the analogy explicit, we must turn to Rousseau's first detailed discussion of the general taste. This occurs in the comprehensive *Dictionary of Music* on which he worked for over twenty years. That Rousseau saw his refined Epicurean account of taste as important to that work is indicated by its epigraph, taken from Book V of *De rerum natura*: discussing the dangers of the pleasures of vanity, Lucretius described how in society our 'taste is changed from its ancient condition'.[50] In his entry on taste, Rousseau explains that each member of a culture has both a particular and a general taste. Each is a specific form of the human capacity of taste, according to which individuals judge objects to be 'beautiful and good'. Expressions of one's particular taste are judgements that refer these objects solely to one's subjective preferences of beauty. As such, there is a necessary 'diversity' of particular tastes – where some judge a simplistic melody beautiful, others prefer instead an overwhelming harmony. Repeating the cliché, Rousseau notes that there is 'no dispute to be made' about matters of particular taste.

In contrast to the diversity of particular tastes, the general taste is that on which all properly educated judges agree. When critics refer to 'good taste' in the judgement of aesthetic objects like music, they are referring to the

---

[50] Rousseau, *Dictionary of Music*, CW7:27/OC5:158.

148 ROUSSEAU'S POLITICS OF TASTE

general taste thus understood. The general taste *is* subject to dispute because it is not merely subjective but fundamentally comparative and intersubjective. Rousseau explains that 'good taste' is not immediately given by 'nature' but, rather, always mediated by 'opinion'. It is therefore crucial that, although the general taste expresses the 'agreement' of aesthetic judgements, 'unanimity' of opinion is practically impossible. Conflicting critical judgements about aesthetic objects – whether a musical composition or performance is good or bad – either implicitly or explicitly refer to the general taste of a given culture. To know which of these judgements is correct is to know whether the object in question does or does not conform to the general taste. The critic thus confronts a situation of conflicting aesthetic judgements analogous to the citizen's situation of conflicting political judgements. Here, Rousseau appeals to majority vote to end the conflict: regarding the general taste 'we may dispute upon it, because there is only one that can be true: but I see no other means of ending the dispute than that of counting the votes, when one no longer agrees on that of nature'.[51]

The *Dictionary* thus provides a discussion analogous to the famous account of outvoted minorities in the *Social Contract*, explored below. In a shared experience of an aesthetic object like a concert, some judge the performance good while others judge it bad. Each of these conflicting aesthetic judgements is a comparison of one's personal sentiment with what one judges the general taste to be. As with political judgements, there is no natural standard to which one can appeal to settle the dispute. Therefore, the only way to know which sentiment is correct is to adopt a procedure of majority vote. If the result of that vote is that the piece is bad, then this means simply that my sentiment that the piece was good was mistaken, and what I took to be the general taste was not so.

It is not immediately clear whether Rousseau thinks the general taste transcends this procedure or is determined by it. One reason for this ambiguity is that the *Dictionary* simply takes the general taste as a standard to which individual aesthetic judgements refer – it does not address the general taste's *formation*. For this, we must turn to the essay on taste in *Emile*. While Rousseau does not refer to *la goût générale* in the essay, he is explicitly concerned with the formation of a given culture's taste *in general*, and with the socio-political conditions required for that general taste to be 'good' in the sense of being 'well-expressed'. The audience of the *Dictionary* is the cultured observer or critic, whom Rousseau intends to educate in the narrow question of judging music as a specific form of art. His purpose in *Emile* is to outline his 'principles

---

[51] Rousseau (1779): 428–429/*OC5*:842–843.

THE FOUNDATIONS OF POLITICAL JUDGEMENT 149

of taste' just as the *Social Contract* outlines his principles of political right. Thus, he crucially extends the capacity for aesthetic judgement to the people as a whole. Perhaps this explains his earlier recourse to connoisseurship. It may also be why in *Dialogues* he highlighted the essay's importance as special evidence of the 'pure intention' and 'love of virtue' animating his 'system' (*D*:24/1:689).

Despite these different concerns, Rousseau's recourse to majoritarianism to settle conflicting aesthetic judgements is consistent. At the outset of the essay, he abandons the microscope metaphor in favour of a definition emphasising the social construction of taste: taste is simply 'the faculty of judging what pleases or displeases the greatest number'. In turn, he defines 'good taste' as 'the conjunction of the most general tastes'. He had previously noted that the 'simplest' tastes are 'the most natural' and 'more universal'. As such, the general taste will be 'good' when the 'greatest number' of individuals in a given society have tastes that are 'the most general' in the sense of being 'simple' (*E*:512, 294/4:671, 408).

The essay identifies three cultural conditions required for the formation of a good general taste. Because taste is a kind of judgement and to judge is to compare, cultivating taste requires opportunity for comparison. The first condition is thus a society that is large enough to facilitate comparison by presenting a diversity of both objects of judgement and of individual judgements. This allows for the diversity of particular tastes out of which arises the agreement characteristic of the general taste. The second condition is that a given culture values 'amusement and idleness' over 'business'. Because judgements of taste concern objects of 'amusement' that are 'not connected with our needs', individuals must be encouraged to regulate their actions according to 'pleasure' rather than 'self-interest'. In the terms of Rousseau's critique of 'senseless' education in the first *Discourse*, this condition preserves the agreeable alongside the useful as criteria of judgement. The third condition is most important: the formation of a good general taste requires a society in which inequality is kept within moderate bounds, the 'tyranny of opinion' limited, and what Rousseau calls 'voluptuousness' has more power over judgements than does 'vanity' (512–514/4:672–673). For a large society to promote or value pleasure over self-interest is necessary but insufficient because the people is incapable of judging musical performance if they hold a 'false' understanding of pleasure. The formation of a good general taste therefore requires, further, that the greatest number regulate their choice of leisure according to the appropriate understanding of pleasure – namely, as voluptuousness.

This discussion makes voluptuousness the real foundation of Rousseau's distinction between good and bad taste. First, he defined voluptuousness negatively by contrast to vanity. Voluptuaries understand that true pleasure is to be found in objects or forms of leisure that are agreeable independently of their being valued by others. Like Julie, they enjoy to enjoy, not to be approved. As he puts it, 'real voluptuousness' is a pleasure found in goods 'apart from prejudices and opinion'. Second, he identified the goods of real voluptuousness as those of 'sensuality' rather than 'moral goods' rooted in 'the good disposition of the soul'. This distinction is crucial. Because real voluptuousness is not that of the so-called 'higher' or 'intellectual' pleasures, it provides a criterion by which every individual can, in principle, regulate their aesthetic judgements. Emile's 'affections and tastes' are fixed on the 'beautiful of all sorts', which he comes to feel and to love. His 'natural appetites' are uncorrupted, and he seeks happiness in his 'pure and healthy heart' rather than through wealth; he has good taste effortlessly. His Tutor provides an example of a lesser ideal that is 'more evident and closer to the morals of the reader'. But both adopt the same 'constant practice': both are 'sensual and voluptuous rather than proud and vain'; they are 'temperate out of sensuality'. Both, in other words, are refined Epicureans. Together, they demonstrate that every individual, irrespective of social station, education, or natural virtue, can enjoy 'true taste' and natural amusements: 'The man who has taste and is truly voluptuous has nothing to do with riches. It suffices for him to be free and master of himself' (517–518/4:677–678). Because real voluptuousness is sensual – not moral – and grounded in individual sentiment – not an abstract idea – it is 'simple' and therefore general. It thus provides a genuinely democratic foundation for the formation of a good general taste.

Rousseau presents these conditions in order to explain how, in their absence, the majority vote will fail to express a good general taste. When the conditions are secured, the general taste will be good because the majority will judge according to the simple criterion of pleasure as voluptuousness. Rousseau suggests an analogy with the account of factions in the *Social Contract*, where the majority vote fails to express the general will when individuals make political judgements according to the views of factional interests. As he described it, faction effectively changes the *object* of political judgement: 'instead of saying with his vote, *it is advantageous to the State*, he says, *it is advantageous to this man or to this party that this or that opinion pass*' (*SC*:122/3:348). Analogously, the majority vote fails to express a good general taste when individual aesthetic judgements are determined by the pleasures of 'fashion'. When fashion predominates in a given society, individuals seek the pleasures of 'distinction' rather than of voluptuousness, regulating their choice of leisure according to a mistaken criterion of pleasure. If fashion does not corrupt individual aesthetic judgements, then 'good taste is that of the greatest number'. But fashion causes

THE FOUNDATIONS OF POLITICAL JUDGEMENT   151

the people to be mistaken in their judgements of agreeableness. As Rousseau puts it here, when fashion leads, 'the object of taste changes':

> Then the multitude no longer has judgment of its own. It now judges only according to the views of those whom it believes more enlightened than itself. It approves not what is good but what they have approved. In all times, see to it that each man has its own sentiments, and that which is most agreeable in itself will always have the plurality of votes. (*E*:513/4:672)

This passage is the very core of the analogy and demonstrates its explanatory value. As *faction* corrupts the general will, so *fashion* corrupts the general taste. In the cases of both political judgements of the general will and aesthetic judgements of the general taste, Rousseau's central concern is to guard against the corruption of individual judgement, grounding the general agreement of all on the judgement of each.

It might be thought that the analogy breaks down with the condition of a 'large' society, for Rousseau famously thought that for a society to be ruled by a general will it must 'be very small' (*SC*:116/3:431). But the analogy holds insofar as Rousseau clarifies that the cultivation of taste in large societies simultaneously threatens its corruption. What is called 'good taste' is cultivated in Paris. But the general taste in Paris is 'bad' because it has been corrupted by what Rousseau calls 'excessive delicacy' (*E*:514/4:674). In Paris, one encounters an array of aesthetic objects and engages in critical discussion. But this cultivation goes too far, for 'excessive delicacy' or 'refinement' means a radical particularisation of aesthetic judgements. Here, the metaphor of taste as microscope or spectacles is pejorative: Parisian men of letters are unable to see past their own noses. When aesthetic judgements are only myopic expressions of subjective preferences, then taste is 'less uniform' and it becomes impossible to determine 'what pleases the greatest number'. In other words, as Gabriella Domecq argues, 'the taste of the greatest number is nothing more than the sum of particular tastes without anything in common. There are as many tastes as individuals but no point of union.'[52] Although Rousseau never directly extends the analogy to the 'will of all', we might say that, at this extreme point of a complete lack of agreement, the general taste is so corrupted that it has dissolved into something like the 'taste of all'.

The analogy with the general will is further suggested by the third condition required for the formation of a good general taste – that of moderate inequality, limited 'tyranny of opinion', and voluptuousness over vanity.

---

[52] Domecq (2017).

152 ROUSSEAU'S POLITICS OF TASTE

By moderate inequality, Rousseau means that 'artificial' inequalities of wealth or power should be 'proportionate' to 'natural' inequalities of merit or virtue (*DI*:131/3:131–132).[53] He asserts that the 'true models of taste are in nature'. In a 'natural' condition, aesthetic judgements are made according to individual sentiments of pleasure: the 'objects we love' are those we find agreeable. A society characterised by only moderate inequality allows for the artificial approximation of such a natural criterion. But in societies characterised by great inequality, natural models become entirely inaccessible and no longer function as a criterion of judgement. Then, considerations of 'interest' or 'vanity' replace individual sentiments of pleasure: the 'objects we love' are those that we find useful or approved by others.

In the above passage about fashion, the majority determines its judgement according to the judgement of those 'it believes more enlightened than itself'. With great inequality, it is specifically 'the artists, the nobles, and the rich' to whom individuals refer in their aesthetic judgements, taking pleasure in the objects that please those who dominate them:

> The rich, in order to display their wealth, and the artists, in order to take advantage of that wealth, vie in the quest for new means of expense. This is the basis on which great luxury establishes its empire and leads people to love what is difficult and costly. Then what is claimed to be beautiful, far from imitating nature, is beautiful only by dint of thwarting it. This is how luxury and bad taste become inseparable. Wherever taste is expensive, it is false. (*E*:513/4:673)

Extreme particularisation of aesthetic judgements dissolves the general taste by eroding agreement – a political analogue might be rampant egoism destroying the general will by causing citizens to stop considering themselves as a single body. Inequality, oppressive opinion, and vanity do not so much erode agreement as render that agreement false – the political analogue is factional voting, for both stem from the corruption of individual judgement.

This discussion of the formation of a good general taste clarifies that the content of the general taste does not transcend but is determined by the majority vote. It might be argued that Rousseau's references here to 'the agreeable in itself', 'nature', and 'beauty' support a transcendent interpretation of the general taste. After all, if 'bad' taste is 'false' taste, then this might be because the general taste is something that exists with an independent content about

---

[53] Frederick Neuhouser, *Rousseau's Critique of Inequality: Reconstructing the Second Discourse* (Cambridge: Cambridge University Press, 2014): 16–26.

THE FOUNDATIONS OF POLITICAL JUDGEMENT 153

which individual judgements can be mistaken. As we will see, this is precisely the form of argument made in the transcendent interpretation of the general will. Does Rousseau's appeal to 'the agreeable in itself' suggest that the solution to the problem of corrupt aesthetic judgements is to conform one's aesthetic judgement to substantive values? If the general taste is constrained by a transcendent idea of beauty or nature, for instance, then perhaps, by analogy, the general will is constrained by a transcendent idea of justice.

It is crucial to recognise here that Rousseau explicitly rules out any appeal to substantive criteria as a solution to the problem of conflicting aesthetic judgements. The source of aesthetic pleasure is our sentiment of the relations of convenience between ourselves and an object. One way of explaining this sort of pleasant experience was to ground it in the 'perfection' of the object, such that one's experience of the object allows access to the kind of transcendent order that the French classical tradition called *La Belle Nature*.[54] But this is not Rousseau's view. First, his understanding of 'Nature' is opposed not to culture per se but to culture that is corrupt in the sense of being 'vain'. Nature is not as an objective reality or transcendent standard but an individual disposition to pursue pleasure (*E*:163/4:248). Second, Rousseau also defined 'Beauty' in subjective terms in his notes for *Emile*: 'abstract beauty is nothing at all, nothing is beautiful except through relations of convenience, and a man who has only himself as a measure of these relations, only judges of his affections'.[55] This passage does not appear in the final text. But it makes sense of his grounding taste in sensuality rather than rationality. It also clarifies his insistence that cultivating taste means learning 'to judge the beautiful by inspection' rather than examining 'principles and rules', so that one comes 'to feel and to see . . . the very good and the very beautiful' (*J*:47/2:59). That which is 'agreeable in itself', then, is not a substantive value: it is relative only to one's individual affections; it stands in contrast to the agreeable as dictated by fashion or vanity. It is characterised by the freedom of individual judgement, in contrast to judgements dictated by the artists, the great, and the rich who dominate unequal societies.

The General Will

The fundamental question of all Rousseau interpretation is 'what is the general will'? Readers typically answer that question in one of two ways. Citizens are

---

[54] Annie Becq, *Genèse de l'esthétique française moderne 1680–1814* (Paris: Albin Michel, 1994): 79–94.

[55] 'Fragments to *Émile*', *CW*11:17/*OC*5:482.

154   ROUSSEAU'S POLITICS OF TASTE

asked whether a particular proposal in the assembly conforms to the general will and vote accordingly. For some readers, the general will is something that transcends the political community. On this view, the result of the vote can be either right or wrong because there is an independent criterion that is antecedent to and can in principle be detached from the empirical procedure of the vote. The general will is thus 'discovered' by democratic politics. For others, the general will is simply a democratic decision that the people make together in the assembly: the votes are counted, and the successful proposition embodies the general will. The general will's content is not an antecedent matter of fact, it does not transcend, nor can it be detached from the empirical procedure of the vote – and so it does not provide a criterion against which the result of the vote can be judged right or wrong. The general will is thus 'created' by democratic politics.[56]

The above reconstruction of the general taste helps to clarify this debate. Interpreters of the general will neglect the analogy.[57] But as I have suggested, it extends to both Rousseau's account of outvoted minorities and his distinction between the general will and the will of all. The rival interpretations of the general will centre on precisely these issues. I have also noted that making the analogy explicit highlights the importantly diagnostic purpose of Rousseau's discussion – just as he described how *fashion* corrupts the general taste, so is his account of the will of all intended to explain how *faction* corrupts the general will. As such, I argue that reading the general will from the perspective of the general taste offers a significant argument by analogy for a democratic reading of the general will.

Describing the problem of outvoted minorities, Rousseau writes: 'the fact that I am in the minority proves neither more nor less than that I was mistaken, and that what I thought to be the general will was not' (*SC*:124/3:441). This is often taken as evidence for the transcendent reading. For many, it seems obvious that if I can be mistaken about the general will, that must be because 'it is an actually-existing something about the content of which I can err'.[58] This assumption is most familiar from those who read Rousseau as providing an epistemic justification of majority rule. The strongest version reads the general will as anticipating Condorcet's jury theorem: there is a substantive common good; citizens' judgements about its content are not always accurate; the vote

---

[56] Christopher Brooke, 'Aux limites de la volonté générale: silence, exil, ruse et désobéissance dans la pensée politique de Rousseau', *Les Études philosophiques* 83:4 (2007): 425–444. Christopher Bertram, 'Rousseau's Legacy in Two Conceptions of the General Will: Democratic and Transcendent', *The Review of Politics* 74:3 (2012): 403–419.

[57] Shklar (1969): 227, 185. Cf. Strauss (2014).

[58] Brooke (2007): 427.

THE FOUNDATIONS OF POLITICAL JUDGEMENT 155

in the assembly provides a reliable proxy for that content. Here, the process of voting is not 'a means of combining divergent interests' but, instead, 'a process that searches for "truth"' – the truth about the common good.[59] A more nuanced approach sees Rousseau's argument for majority rule as not 'truly epistemic' because, for him, 'the right answer in politics is always obvious' so long as citizens are unselfish and pure of heart. This places Rousseau some distance from Condorcet, but the general will nevertheless remains 'an independently given reality' or a 'procedure-independent standard of correctness of majority decisions'.[60]

Against the transcendent interpretation and the epistemic reading it often grounds, democratic readers emphasise the wider context of the chapter. Rousseau argues that it is 'a consequence of the contract itself' that 'the vote of the majority always obligates all the rest'. He first introduced this argument in Book I: the contract itself 'unites' a 'multitude' of 'scattered men' into a 'society' or 'people', an 'aggregation' into an 'association'. It does so by instituting majority rule: Rousseau insists that consent to the initial contract must be 'unanimous' because, if it were not, 'why would the minority be obliged to submit to the choice of the majority' – 'the law of majority rule is itself something established by convention and presupposes unanimity at least once' (49/3:359). The 'contract itself' is an agreement to be determined by majority rule.

Rousseau describes the 'essence of the social compact' in the next chapter: 'Each of us puts his person and his full power in common under the supreme direction of the general will; and in a body we receive each member as an indivisible part of the whole' (50/3:361). The 'contract itself' thus produces the general will, to which individuals alienate their natural freedom. Together, these passages clarify that to be 'under the supreme direction of the general will' is to be 'obliged to submit to the choice of the majority'. This is because, on the democratic reading, the general will is whatever the 'choice of the majority' will turn out to be in the future.

In the disputed passage from Book IV, Rousseau explains his reasoning further. The vote of the majority always obligates the minority because what each individual is voting on is 'not exactly whether they approve or reject' the proposed law but, rather, whether it 'is in conformity to the general will, which is theirs; everyone', he continues, 'states his opinion about this by casting his ballot, and the tally of the votes yields the declaration of the general

---

[59] Bernard N. Grofman and Scott L. Feld, 'Rousseau's General Will: A Condorcetian Perspective', *American Political Science Review* 82:2 (1988): 567–576 (596).
[60] Landemore (2012): 69–75.

will' (124/3:441). On a transcendent reading, this passage indicates that, in voting, each citizen is judging whether the proposed law is or is not 'in agreement with an independently given standard of political rightness, also called the common interest or the common good'. The result of the vote is taken to stand as the most reliable 'proxy' for the content of the general will.[61] On the democratic reading, the common good is simply whatever the public-spirited majority decides it is. The outvoted citizen is wrong, and the majority is right for no other reason than that it is the vote of the majority. Here, each citizen is exercising his judgement about whether the proposal is or is not in agreement with a standard that is itself created by the process of voting. As one of Rousseau's contemporary admirers put it, when I vote 'I can be wrong and consequently vote against my will, which is aimed at the maintenance and prosperity of the association. It is just the same, whatever the number of votes allied to mine, if the majority is not on my side. The will of the majority is therefore the expression of the general will.'[62] The tally of the votes merely alerts the outvoted citizen to the fact that the content of the general will was something other than what he thought it would be.

If my reconstruction of the general taste is correct, then it adds a significant argument by analogy to the democratic reading of this passage. Critical sentiments that a musical performance is good or bad are judgements about its conforming or not to what rival critics take to be the content of the general taste. Conflicting aesthetic judgements are resolved by majority vote, just as the outvoted citizen agrees to have their political judgement determined by majority vote. In each case, there is no antecedently given 'natural' standard to appeal to. Rather, the vote itself gives the general will and general taste content, telling citizens and critics whether they were correct in their judgement of what that content would turn out to be. That this analysis 'presupposes that the qualities of the general will are still in the majority' (124/3:441), moreover, is analogous to Rousseau's argument that the formation of a good general taste requires that the majority judge according to the appropriate understanding of pleasure as voluptuousness.

The second disputed passage is Rousseau's distinction between the general will and the will of all. Famously, Rousseau explains that the general will 'looks only to the common interest', whereas the will of all is 'nothing but a sum of particular wills'. He continues: 'if, from these same wills, one takes away the plusses and the minuses, which cancel each other out, what is left as the sum of

---

[61] Ibid.: 69.

[62] Jean-Baptiste Sallaville, *De l'organisation d'un État Monarchique, Ou Considérations Sur Les Vices de La Monarchie Françoise, et Sur La Nécessité de Lui Donner Un Constitution* (Paris: Desray, 1789).

THE FOUNDATIONS OF POLITICAL JUDGEMENT 157

the differences is the general will' (*SC*:60/3:371). Not all readers acknowledge that Rousseau used these expressions interchangeably. He did so on at least two occasions, both of which mirror the familiar claim about 'the law, which is nothing but the expression of the general will'.[63] In the *Political Economy*, he described the law as a 'salutary organ of the will of all' (*PE*:146/3:248). More strongly, he wrote: 'the will of all is therefore the order, the supreme rule, and this general and personified rule is that which I call sovereign'.[64] From this perspective, it is perhaps unsurprising that Rousseau does not describe a 'taste of all' that could be directly analogous to the will of all.

How should we understand this distinction if Rousseau was sometimes willing to collapse it? The distinction is part of Rousseau's argument that the general will does not 'err': 'the general will is always upright (*droit*) and always tends to the public utility'. Conversely, 'the people's deliberations' are not 'always upright (*droit*)' because, while the people can never be 'corrupted', it is 'often' possible to 'cause it to be mistaken' (*SC*:59/3:371). On the epistemic reading, that the general will is 'always upright' means, as we have seen, that the general will is always 'correct' about a fact. Other transcendent readers argue, instead, that the general will is not *epistemically right* but *morally upright*. The crucial feature here is that the source of the general will's rectitude is a transcendent moral standard. The general will 'must conform to an eternal idea of justice'; because the idea of justice is eternal, conformity to it gives the general will 'substantive' content. The moral uprightness of the general will is then 'a simple deduction drawn from definitions': the general will 'must be just, in order to be a general will'. This, in turn, explains why the people can be 'mistaken' in its deliberations: the people will articulate 'merely' the will of all if and when it 'deviates from the idea of justice'.[65]

Democratic readers have two related arguments in response to this ethical variety of the transcendent reading. First, there is the traditional argument that, when Rousseau refers to justice in the *Social Contract*, he does so 'in a purely formal sense pertaining to order and generality'.[66] Proponents of this view agree that Rousseau means here that the general will is 'upright' in a moral rather than epistemic sense. On their reading, however, the source of that rectitude is not eternal but historical and pre-eminently political. The 'common interest' to which the general will 'looks' is defined procedurally,

[63] Rousseau, 'Considerations on the Government of Poland', *CW*11:194/*OC*3:984.
[64] Rousseau, 'Letters Written from the Mountain', *CW*9:232/*OC*3:807.
[65] David Lay Williams, 'The Substantive Elements of Rousseau's General Will', in Farr and Williams eds (2016): 219–246 (234).
[66] John T. Scott, 'Politics as the Imitation of the Divine in Rousseau's "Social Contract"', *Polity* 26:3 (1994): 473–501 (490–491).

without reference to transcendent standards. The common interest is whatever the will of the majority decides it is, provided that the majority is sufficiently public-spirited; and to be sufficiently public-spirited is simply to be committed to following the will of the majority. Thus, Rousseau subordinates justice to law because the general will is a 'practical replacement' for justice.[67]

This Epicurean conventionalist account of justice and the general will grounds the democratic reading of the distinction with the will of all. The 'will of all' is simply the private wills of separate individuals considered as a multitude not as a people; the 'general will' is the will of the people created when they contract together. In any given community there are particular wills that necessarily diverge on any consideration of what is in the common interest. If asked, for instance, whether sumptuary laws conform to the general will, some individuals will 'yes', others 'no', and these 'pluses' and 'minuses' are the 'differences' that cancel one another. If there are sixty 'yeses' and forty 'noes', then the general will is declared by the sum of twenty 'yeses'.[68] On this view, the general will is always for the common interest. But to determine its content requires a procedure from which will emerge a 'sum of the differences'. As Rousseau explains in the next paragraphs, this procedure is the majority vote, which gives content to the common interest and, in this sense, creates the general will. Even where Rousseau appeals to the 'common interest which unites' the voters (62/3:374) he is evidently referring to the interest in self-preservation that provides the initial motivation for the contract itself – the citizens' common interest in submitting to majority rule as the means of being 'free, yet governed'.[69] This reading has the benefit of explaining those instances in which Rousseau collapses the distinction: the 'will of all' is the 'sovereign' and 'supreme rule' because the majority vote, by summing the differences, makes it 'general and personified' in law.

The core contrast between the transcendent and democratic accounts of the will of all concerns the rival interpretations of Rousseau's idea that one can 'often' cause the people to be 'mistaken'. For both, this mistake is an error in judgement. On the transcendent account, because the common interest has

---

[67] Arthur Melzer, *The Natural Goodness of Man: On the System of Rousseau's Thought* (Chicago, IL: University of Chicago Press, 1990).

[68] Adapting Tuck (2017): 52. Cp. Gabriella Radica, 'Le vocabulaire mathématique dans le Contrat social, II, 3', in *Rousseau et les sciences*, ed. B. Bensaude-Vincent and B. Bernardi (Paris: L'Harmattan, 2003): 257–275.

[69] Brooke (2007): 429. As Brooke points out (428), this common interest gives each citizen a general will that is 'constant, unalterable and pure' for as long as they remain citizens, under a contract the terms of which never change, which aims at pure, simple ends of 'peace, union, equality' (*SC*:121–122/3:437–438).

THE FOUNDATIONS OF POLITICAL JUDGEMENT   159

substantive content, this error consists in citizens' selfishly considering their personal interest at the expense of the common. The solution to this 'mistake', then, is to take the bearing of one's personal interest from the antecedently given common interest – to correct one's 'deviation' by 'conforming' to a substantive idea of justice. Democratic readers invert the problem and solution. As there is no natural, pre-political community united by a 'common interest', the politics of the general will is a politics of the collective determination of the common interest by majority vote. The crucial feature of this view is that, in order for the procedure actually to generate the common interest, each citizen is required to consider only his personal interest. This is the democratic reading's central contrast with the transcendent interpretation: the procedure will be 'good' if the citizens are committed to majority rule and, hence, cast their votes according to their own rather than factional interests.[70] As Rousseau writes, the politics of the general will presupposes that each citizen 'thinks of himself as he votes for all' (61/3:373). The solution to the 'mistake', then, is to ensure that each citizen exercise judgement for himself.

We have already seen that Rousseau was equally concerned with the people's mistaken aesthetic judgement. As with the general will, so the majority vote fails to express a good general taste if the people are judging according to a false criterion of pleasure, rooted in vanity or fashion. That his appeal to majority vote to determine the general taste in the *Dictionary* was addressed to 'well-educated' musical judges makes his extension of majoritarianism to the people as a whole more remarkable. In *Emile*, a good general taste requires that the greatest number make judgements of agreeableness according to the criterion of voluptuousness. When they are mistaken, it is not because they are selfishly pursuing their own sentiment but because they fail to feel what their own sentiment actually *is*. The solution to their mistake, similarly, is not to conform to an objective moral idea but, rather, to express their subjective sentiment of sensuality.

The analogy with the general taste also alerts us to the central problem that Rousseau identified in the formation of good popular judgement. For, as noted above, just as *fashion* causes the people to be mistaken in its aesthetic judgement, so *faction* corrupts the general will. Immediately following his introduction of the will of all, Rousseau writes:

When factions arise, small associations at the expense of the large association, the will of each one of these associations becomes general in relation

---

[70] Cp. Douglass (2015): 131–136 for a more substantive reading of what it means for a citizen to consult the common interest here.

160 ROUSSEAU'S POLITICS OF TASTE

to its members and particular in relation to the State; there can then no longer be said to be as many voters as there are men, but only as many as there are associations. The differences become less numerous and yield a less general result.

As in the previous example, citizens are asked whether sumptuary laws conform to the general will. But in this case, they allow their judgement to be determined by factional interests: those who vote 'yes' defer their judgement to religious ascetics; those who vote 'no' defer their judgement to luxury manufacturers; and the vote yields fewer 'differences' to be summed. Rousseau's solution to the problem of faction is not to appeal to a transcendent notion of justice or to a substantive common good. Rather, he argues that having the general will 'expressed well' requires that 'there be no partial society in the state, *and every citizen state only his own opinion*'. Just as a good general taste requires each individual to express his own sentiment, so the only means of ensuring that 'the general will is always enlightened, and that the people make no mistakes', is to preserve the individual judgement of each citizen (60/3:372).[71]

This democratic account is consistent with the treatment of faction across Rousseau's corpus. In the reflections on *Poland* (1772), for example, Rousseau writes: 'the law, which is but the expression of the general will, is indeed the resultant of all the particular interests combined and in balance by virtue of their large number'. The general will is created by voting procedure, which combines and balances the many individual, particular wills. But, as Rousseau immediately clarifies, the existence of factions will cause the procedure to fail to express the general will: 'corporate interests, because of their excessive weight, would upset the balance, and should not be included in it collectively. Each individual should have his vote, no [corporate] body whatsoever should have one.'[72] The analysis in the *Political Economy* is identical: when 'the people is seduced by private interests, which the credit or eloquence of some clever persons substitutes for those of the State: [then] the general will will be one thing, and the result of the public deliberation another' (*PE*:144/3:246). From this perspective, Rousseau's distinction between the will of all and the general will serves an above all *diagnostic* purpose. With it, that is, he explained how the people is caused to be mistaken: the majority vote will fail to express the general will if and when citizens fail to give their own opinion on the proposal

---

[71] Cf. Gopal Sreenivasan, 'What Is the General Will?', *The Philosophical Review* 109:4 (2000): 545–581.

[72] Rousseau, 'Considerations on the Government of Poland', *CW*11:194/*OC*3:984.

THE FOUNDATIONS OF POLITICAL JUDGEMENT 161

in question and, instead, allow their judgement to be determined by another individual or group of individuals – a faction.

The continued appeal of the transcendent interpretation stems from unease over this account. The democratic reading suggests that Rousseau was consciously rejecting the most readily available solution to the problem of faction. As we saw in the previous chapter, Rousseau inverted the ancient priority of the public good, grounding his political theory of the modern state in utility and self-interest. As I show below, reconstructing Rousseau's concept of the general taste and making explicit his implied analogy with the general will helps to make sense of the moral foundations of his state theory, in a way that retains his own sense of its strangeness.

Conclusion

Judith Shklar famously described the general will as Rousseau's 'most successful metaphor'.[73] By interpreting the metaphor in light of the analogy, this chapter has clarified some of the ambiguities arising from his recourse to figurative language. It also problematises epistemic democracy's strategic deployment of the transcendent interpretation of the general will. For while it may not be possible to settle the dispute definitively, my argument by analogy for the democratic reading shifts the burden of proof and prompts transcendent interpreters to account for the general taste. I have thus far been concerned to make explicit an analogy that Rousseau left implicit. By way of conclusion, I want furthermore to suggest that Rousseau's account of censorship was an attempt to think beyond the analogy, in a way that allows us to see it as his own.

One of the benefits of the Epicurean reading of Rousseau is that it opens up the range of ways in which he approached the problem of the moral foundations of politics. His political thought starts from the Epicurean premise that humans are not naturally sociable, that durable moral consensus is impossible without the coercive structure of the state. As such, while understanding politics required understanding morals, politics had both historical and normative priority. But if voting the general will constitutes the people's common interest and gives citizens reasons to see the laws which govern them as their own, they still require 'sentiments of sociability' to feel the real coincidence of their self-interest with the interest of the common self of the state. Understanding this gap between morals and politics required distinguishing very sharply between them analytically. The *Social Contract* addresses only the 'political

---

[73] Shklar (1969): 184.

laws' that 'constitute the form of government', saying little about the 'most important' laws 'of morals, customs, and above all of opinion' (*SC*:81/3:394). Similarly, the general will sets the parameters only of 'civil freedom'. While Rousseau adds 'moral freedom' to the 'credit of the civil state', he only hints at the full sense in which 'obedience to the law one has prescribed to oneself is freedom' (*SC*:54/3:365). His version of autonomy is thus more 'abrasively political' and less 'moral' in the sense of 'other-regarding' familiar from Kant.[74]

The competing interpretations of the general will diverge over precisely how moral Rousseau took his central political idea to be. For him, 'the transition from the state of nature to the civil state produces a most remarkable change' because it endows our 'actions with the morality they previously lacked' (53/3:364). On the democratic reading, the substance of this moral transformation lies in each individual's new-found willingness to abide by the outcome of majority votes. On some versions of the transcendent interpretation, it lies rather in each individual's new-found willingness to act in accordance with a set of rational moral principles. To commit to majoritarianism is less lofty, but it can appear remarkable starting from an Epicurean account of sociability.[75]

Reconstructing the general taste and making explicit the analogy with the general will suggests that Rousseau saw aesthetic judgement as a way of narrowing the gap in this framework. His so-called practical writings gesture in this direction: his claim about the interchangeability of taste and morals was part of his advice to Geneva, and his constitutional recommendations to Corsica and Poland include institutions designed to cultivate 'reflective detachment' from both political and aesthetic values.[76] As I have suggested, Rousseau's account of the censorship brings his concern with aesthetic judgement to the very heart of his state theory. In *Poland*, a biennial censorial committee draws up a roster of virtuous peasants to whom some government ministers occasionally assign privileges, and from which others select a 'number fixed by law to be enfranchised' as citizens. And while Rousseau laments that such a committee has 'never yet existed', he argues that its introduction would accomplish the

---

[74] Michael Sonenscher, 'Jean-Jacques Rousseau and the Foundations of Modern Political Thought', *Modern Intellectual History* 14:2 (2017): 311–337 (317). Cf. Richard Velkley, 'Transcending Nature, Unifying Reason', in *Kant on Moral Autonomy*, ed. Oliver Sensen (Cambridge: Cambridge University Press, 2012): 89–106.

[75] Melissa Schwartzberg, 'Voting the General Will: Rousseau on Decision Rules', *Political Theory* 36:3 (2008): 403–423.

[76] Schaeffer (2014): 179–190. Cf. Ryan Patrick Hanley, 'From Geneva to Glasgow: Rousseau and Adam Smith on the Theater and Commercial Society', *Studies in Eighteenth-Century Culture* 35:1 (2006): 177–202.

THE FOUNDATIONS OF POLITICAL JUDGEMENT 163

'goal of extirpating luxury' not by the necessarily ineffectual means of sumptuary laws but, rather, by impressing in the depths of citizens' hearts 'healthier and more noble tastes'.[77] Thereby, individuals of personal merit might come to fill legally defined ranks after having been judged according to the publicly articulated criterion of taste. From this perspective, political and aesthetic judgements in Rousseau are not merely analogous in *theory*. Rather, good political judgement in *practice* requires and reciprocally supports good aesthetic judgement.

The foregoing reconstruction demonstrates that Rousseau included a place for aesthetic judgements of beauty and agreeableness even in the most abstract version of his state theory. It also clarifies the foundations of political judgement in Rousseau, for the analogy with the general will allows us to see how the censorship solves the problem of popular aesthetic judgement without recourse to connoisseurship. The general taste allows the people to correct its false judgement of pleasure by generating the criterion of beauty according to which citizens moderate their pursuit of pleasure. This moderation prevents citizens' developing strong desires for wealth or luxury which, in turn, secures the material foundation of moderate equality that Rousseau called 'the basis of the entire social system' (*SC*:56, 78/3:392, 367). The core of the analogy is the claim that material equality is the condition of the possibility that judgements of utility, on the one hand, and agreeableness, on the other, might each be made in the appropriate way – namely, according to general standards created by the judgement of every particular individual. The general taste regulates the general will *not* by ensuring that citizens subordinate their personal interest to the common interest but, rather, by tempering the desires that generate factions. Recovering the analogy thus highlights both the source of moderation in Rousseau's state and its role in preventing the faction and fashion that always threaten to undermine it.

If this argument is at all persuasive, then it complicates what I called above the 'simple' distinction between 'political' and 'aesthetic' judgements. For if there is a place for both the general will and general taste in Rousseau's state, then 'political' judgements in Rousseau are always (already) 'aesthetic'. That is, political judgement always concerns both utility and agreeableness, interest and pleasure, justice and beauty. Note, too, that readers committed to the transcendent interpretation of the general will need not reject the general taste analogy. My account of the relationship between political and aesthetic judgement does not require that one accept the democratic reading of the

---

[77] Rousseau, 'Considerations on the Government of Poland', *CW*11: 227–229, 179/*OC*3: 1025–1028, 965).

164   ROUSSEAU'S POLITICS OF TASTE

general will. But on the interpretation offered here, because when the declaration of each is 'good', the general taste and general will are declared the same way – namely, democratically – we don't need to look beyond politics to any transcendent standard. All we need to do, as Rousseau says, is count the votes.

Many contemporary political theorists have expressed their dissatisfaction with the account of political judgement in theories of deliberative democracy. In its place, they strive to reconnect aesthetic, moral, and political judgement, often invoking historical precedent for support. As noted above, Hannah Arendt turned to Kant's *Critique of Judgment* to suggest her own analogy. For her, political judgement is like Kantian aesthetic judgement insofar as neither are 'rule governed' in the sense of applying universal standards of truth or reason. There is, she claimed, an irreducible element of 'freedom' from universal rules at the heart of political and aesthetic judgement alike.[78] More recently, Linda Zerilli has developed this insight 'to reclaim judgment as a practice of democratic citizenship'. She critiques deliberative democrats for erroneously denying the 'real relevance to political life' of shared aesthetic sensibility and sentiments, which she traces to these theorists' 'neo-Kantian' account of judgement. Against this view, Zerilli builds her defence of citizens' 'ordinary' ways of judging matters of 'common concern' on the foundation of Arendt's alternative 'Kantian' analogy between political and aesthetic judgement.[79]

Comparing Rousseau's and Arendt's respective analogies is instructive. His emphasis on sentiment, judgements of beauty and agreeableness, and their relationship to judgements of utility and interest, similarly cautions against the overly rationalist view of judgement familiar from deliberative and especially epistemic theories of democracy. But Rousseau's analogy is not at all concerned with subjective freedom from universal rules. As mentioned, nothing in Rousseau is analogous to Kant's distinction between 'determinate' and 'reflective' judgements. The point of his analogy is that general criteria of judgement can be created from individual judgements, provided that these latter are not determined by others. And as I have suggested, he seriously attempted to bridge the gap between theory and practice in a way that Kant and Arendt did not.

Following up these threads would require separate investigations. But I hope that this chapter will persuade – or convince – readers that Rousseau's idea of the general taste has been neglected for too long. Reconstructing it

---

[78] Arendt (2014).

[79] Linda M. G. Zerilli, *A Democratic Theory of Judgment* (Chicago, IL: University of Chicago Press: 2016): 146, 2.

THE FOUNDATIONS OF POLITICAL JUDGEMENT 165

accomplishes the difficult feat of providing a genuinely new perspective on the perennial debate on the nature of the general will. Making the analogy explicit highlights Rousseau's consistent appeal to majoritarian procedures to settle conflicts of judgement and, thereby, bolsters his credentials as a democratic thinker. It also allows us to reconsider his account of censorship in the *Social Contract*, excavating an account of the popular judgement of taste that supports his republican defence of the people as the best judge of morals. Together, these elements of my reconstruction of Rousseau might be further developed to yield an account of political judgement that is lacking in contemporary theory – namely, as mutually constitutive and imbricated with aesthetic judgement.

Though neglected today, this connection between politics and aesthetics was crucial to Rousseau's early readers. We saw that it was evidence for some of the peculiarly Epicurean dimensions of his thinking about moral and political virtue; for others, it revealed his insights into the imaginative requirements of civil society and federalism.[80] But interpretations of Rousseau in the history of political thought diverge along lines analogous to those in political theory. In histories of modern natural law, the path from Hobbes to German idealism runs through interpretations of the general will that, whether democratic or transcendent, consistently neglect aesthetics.[81] Conversely, readings of Rousseau as a forerunner of modern Romanticism tend to 'aestheticize' or 'moralize' politics in ways incompatible with a democratic reading.[82] Taking the analogy seriously shows that this divergence is a mistake. The historical question of *when* the separation between politics, morals, and aesthetics was established has significant implications for the political question of how they might be reconnected today. One general claim of this book is that political theorists can benefit from thinking about what historians of political thought have seen in Rousseau. This perspective allows us to reject the false choice between competing readings of Kant in political theory or between natural law and Romanticism in intellectual history, and to consider instead the more synthetic view of politics, aesthetics, and judgement in Rousseau.

---

[80] Sonenscher (2020).

[81] Tuck (2018); Frederick Neuhouser, 'Freedom, Dependence, and the General Will', *The Philosophical Review* 102:3 (1993): 363–395.

[82] Irving Babbitt, *Rousseau and Romanticism* (London: Houghton Mifflin, 1919).

6

The Memorial Practice of Happiness: Temperance, Sensuality, and Rousseau's System

Introduction

In this chapter, I use the understanding of Rousseau's politics of taste developed in the foregoing to reconsider the consistency dilemma in a new light. We have seen that Rousseau's account of taste runs across all his major works. His concern with restoring equilibrium between judgements of utility and agreeableness is evident in his treatment of Julie's household, the city-state of Geneva, and even the abstract state theory of the *Social Contract*. His intention to persuade his readers to avoid the pleasures of vanity and fashion and, instead, pursue those of sensuality and voluptuousness is manifest in his descriptions of the first humans in the second *Discourse*, Julie's art of enjoyment, and the good taste of both Emile and his Tutor. But the autobiographies pose by far the greatest challenge to my interpretation of Rousseau's work as consistent in this respect. Axel Honneth helpfully describes that challenge in Hellenistic terms. Although Emile is educated in the art of political judgement and not made to remain in solitude, his ultimate dependence on others is incompatible with the 'philosophical motif' orienting the autobiographies – namely, for Honneth, the 'Stoic idea' of achieving a moral posture in which 'the social recognition of one's own merits and capabilities has lost all existential significance'.[1] On this reading, even if Rousseau's account of political freedom under the general will is compatible with those of domestic flourishing and personal autonomy, his descriptions of solitary happiness in the autobiographies reveal the truth of the incompatibility thesis.

My aim in what follows is to demonstrate that Rousseau's autobiographies are consistent with his more straightforwardly political writings because

---

[1] Honneth (2016): 192, 205.

THE MEMORIAL PRACTICE OF HAPPINESS   167

they, too, instantiate his ideal of refined Epicureanism. The autobiographies pose two closely related difficulties for any interpreter of Rousseau's political thought. One concerns their position in his *oeuvre*: How do his descriptions of individual flourishing in the autobiographies relate to those of republican virtue in his more overtly political writings? The other concerns his account of flourishing itself: Does Rousseau present a consistent account of personal happiness and, if so, what are its defining features? Faced with these difficulties, a standard approach – especially in Anglophone political philosophy – is simply to ignore the autobiographies or to downplay their importance relative to his more straightforwardly normative work.[2] Instead, I explore the latter difficulty in a way that develops a new perspective from which to reconsider the former.

Those willing to wade into the autobiographies typically emerge with one of two competing interpretations. 'Romantic' readers emphasise the importance of *sentiment* to Rousseau's celebrations of solitude. On this view, his retreats to the countryside were a means to the end of the 'transparency' of unmediated experience, the fullness of 'being' in metaphysical 'wholeness', or 'communion' with self, others, or nature.[3] 'Rationalist' readers instead emphasise the prominence of *reason*. For them, Rousseau's solitary activities were designed to impart a 'rational order' to the soul, or to achieve a happiness or 'wisdom' that is 'philosophical' in the sense of being grounded in reason.[4] If these are somewhat stylised ideal types, it is nevertheless the case that even those readers who acknowledge the interplay of sentiment and reason tend to suggest that Rousseau ultimately gives priority to one over the other.

That Rousseau's overarching concern with pleasure and aesthetic judgement extends to his view of solitude is suggested in his description of happiness as resulting from the practice of 'reverie'. The term is rooted in the idea that 'to dream' is to engage in a uniquely 'abstract and profound' mode of thought with the non-utilitarian aim of 'occupying oneself agreeably'.[5] A reverie is,

---

[2] Cohen (2010), Neuhouser (2008), Dent (1988).

[3] Jean Starobinski, *Jean-Jacques Rousseau, Transparency and Obstruction*, trans. Arthur Goldhammer (Chicago, IL: Chicago University Press, 1988); Laurence D. Cooper, 'Nearer My True Self to Thee: Rousseau's New Spirituality – and Ours', *The Review of Politics* 74:3 (2012) 465–488; Marcel Raymond, *Jean-Jacques Rousseau: La quête de soi et la rêverie* (Paris: J. Corti, 1962); Jason Neidleman, 'Rousseau's Rediscovered Communion Des Coeurs: Cosmopolitanism in the Reveries of the Solitary Walker', *Political Studies* 60:1 (2012): 76–94.

[4] David Lay Williams, 'The Platonic Soul of the "Reveries": The Role of Solitude in Rousseau's Democratic Politics', *History of Political Thought* 33:1 (2012): 87–123; Heinrich Meier, *On the Happiness of the Philosophic Life: Reflections on Rousseau's Rêveries in Two Books* (Chicago, IL: Chicago University Press, 2016); Strauss (1947).

[5] Chevalier de Jaucourt, 'Penser, Songer, Rêver', in *Encyclopédie, ou dictionnaire raisonné des sciences, des arts et des métiers, etc.*, ed. Denis Diderot and Jean le Rond d'Alembert. University

consequently, 'agreeable' and 'sweet', with an inherent pleasure stemming from the 'letting go' of one's imagination.[6] For Condillac, for example, what pleases us in reverie is the lack of order in our ideas. That pleasure increases in an accordant physical environment – like the wild countryside – and decreases in a discordant one – like a highly cultivated garden. Similarly, we might read a work like Montaigne's *Essais* with pleasure in reverie but with frustration in another state of mind. Crucially, our experience of pleasure in reverie is not only mental but also physical or 'voluptuous'.[7] For Rousseau, too, reverie is a kind of useless pleasure, experienced in the mind first and the body second but stemming, ultimately, from the interaction between them characteristic of the imagination. Understood in this way, enjoying the pleasures of reverie is dangerous for individuals and communities alike. It threatens personal psychological distress, for letting go of the imagination could always devolve into 'extravagance' or even the 'delirium' of mental illness.[8] But even if one's pursuit of its pleasures was not carried to such extremes, reverie was a problem for sociability. Dreaming can of course be synonymous with distraction, and to engage in reverie would be at best 'impolite' in good company.[9] The most obvious way to avoid such breaches of propriety is therefore to engage in reverie alone. From this perspective, the pleasure of reverie is radically selfish, exclusive, and implies a rejection of cultural norms and political authority. Clearly, then, it poses an especially acute problem for Rousseau's aim of ensuring that what one judges pleasant and agreeable is also morally and politically useful.

This chapter argues that Rousseau's autobiographies outline an account of personal happiness as resulting from what I will call an Epicurean memorial practice. For Rousseau, happiness requires a certain attitude to pleasure that is cultivated by a series of practices utilising the mental faculties of memory and imagination. I argue that these are best understood as practices of *askesis* – a way of working on the self through 'inner exercises of thought and will' designed to bring about an ethical transformation.[10] In describing

---

of Chicago: ARTFL Encyclopédie Project (Autumn 2017 Edition), Robert Morrissey and Glenn Roe (eds), (12): 311. Cp. John Locke, *Essay Concerning Human Understanding*, ed. Roger Woolhouse (Oxford: Penguin, 1997): 214.

[6] 'Rêverie', *Le Dictionnaire de l'Académie française. Nouvelle Édition. T.2* (Nismes: Baume, 1786): 441.

[7] Etienne Bonnot de Condillac, *Essay on the Origin of Human Knowledge*, ed. and trans. Hans Aarsleff (Cambridge: Cambridge University Press, 2001 [1746]): 218.

[8] 'Rêverie', *Dictionnaire française*, 441.

[9] Denis Diderot (attributed), 'Rêver', in *Encyclopédie* (14): 228.

[10] Pierre Hadot, *Philosophy as a Way of Life: Spiritual Exercises from Socrates to Foucault*, ed. and trans. Michael Chase and Arnold Davidson (Oxford: Blackwell, 1995). Cf. Maria Antonaccio,

THE MEMORIAL PRACTICE OF HAPPINESS 169

these practices autobiographically, Rousseau hoped to teach his readers how to keep what is useful and good in the pleasures of reverie while avoiding what is harmful and bad.

I begin by reconstructing his defence of the coherence of his system in his final autobiography, *Rousseau, Judge of Jean-Jacques: Dialogues* (1776). At the heart of that defence is his now familiar account of good taste as a means of mitigating the potential for the pursuit of pleasure to devolve into vulgar hedonism, which he presents under the name 'temperate sensuality'. He also utilised the same ethos of critique he previously applied to Pope, combining a rational appreciation of argument with a sentimental appreciation of beauty and emphasising the need to contextualise parts within wholes. This critical ethos is important for understanding both his method of autobiographical writing and the pedagogical intentions of his descriptions of pleasure and happiness. I then show that the accounts of happiness across his autobiographies similarly aim to combat vulgar Epicureanism. He distinguished the *sensation* of pleasure from the *sentiment* of happiness and described how the latter required experiencing appropriate types of the former. He was particularly intrigued by our ability to use memories of past pleasures to temper our tendency to anticipate future pleasures through imagination. This approach to recollected pleasure, which has always been understood as distinctly Epicurean, is a core feature of Rousseau's refined Epicurean account of taste. As such, the orienting idea or philosophical motif of the autobiographies is not Stoic but distinctly Epicurean – namely, combatting through active memory the constant threat of vulgar hedonism to bring about a new relationship to self, others, and the natural world.

My account of the autobiographies is novel in two key respects. First, understanding happiness as emerging from a deliberate and intelligently adaptive form of mental activity with a rational structure pushes back against the romantic view of happiness as a kind of ecstatic experience resulting from the elimination of all boundaries between self and environment. Within my view, conscious mental exercises like recollection are not an obstacle to be eliminated but rather a necessary condition of the experience of happiness. Second, understanding the practices requisite to happiness as distinctively Epicurean pushes back against the rationalist view of happiness as grounded in an abstract or transcendent principle of reason. Within my view, Rousseau grounded temperance in sensuality precisely in order to avoid what he saw as the exaggerated faith in reason in the Platonic tradition.

'Contemporary Forms of Askesis and the Return of Spiritual Exercises', *The Annual of the Society of Christian Ethics* 18 (1998): 69–92.

170 ROUSSEAU'S POLITICS OF TASTE

Finally, I suggest that understanding happiness as a sentiment premised upon a refined Epicurean memorial practice demonstrates that Rousseau's view of solitude is compatible with his wider politics of taste. Like Epicurus before him, Rousseau suggests that the type of solitude advocated in and performed through his autobiographies might be compatible with shared sentiments in friendship and even wider social relations. This is a controversial interpretation, for the tension between solitude and sociability is a familiar theme in political thought.[11] Distancing oneself from public opinion, solitude facilitates critical reflection on and the potential change of one's values – of, for instance, pleasure and beauty. On one influential reading, because political authority rests on precisely these moral values, the solitary is not simply useless but pernicious, an example of apolitical quietism, cultural instability, or even revolution.[12] However, the previous chapters have demonstrated that orienting one's pursuit of pleasure by the appropriate criterion of temperate sensuality or refined Epicureanism is necessary to solve the problem of modern liberty. This perspective, I argue, allows us to see Rousseau's goal in the autobiographies as being precisely to reconcile the pleasures and happiness of solitude with sociability and, indeed, citizenship.

Temperate Sensuality and Rousseau's System

Rousseau's second major autobiography is widely neglected in the literature. But there are several reasons why *Dialogues* should be of interest to readers of Rousseau's political thought. Rousseau conceived of it as a justification of everything he wrote, and it contains one of his most forceful and revealing attempts to defend the coherence of his system. Late in the fictional dialogue between two characters about a third, the 'Frenchman' reports to 'Rousseau' on the results of his having read the works of 'Jean-Jacques'. Expecting a set of writings 'disconnected and full of contradictions', he instead found 'things that were profoundly thought out, forming a coherent system which might not be true but which offered nothing contradictory' (*D*:209/1:930).

Of particular interest here, the 'Frenchman' immediately explains that he reached this surprising conclusion by adopting the ethos of critique we saw Rousseau apply to Pope. First, he insists that the various parts of Rousseau's

---

[11] Horst Hutter, 'The Virtue of Solitude and the Vicissitudes of Friendship', *Critical Review of International Social and Political Philosophy* 2:4 (1999): 131–148; Guy Paltieli, 'Mill's Closet: J. S. Mill on Solitude and the Imperfect Democracy', *History of European Ideas* 45:1 (2018): 47–63.
[12] Most influentially, Strauss (1953): 292–293. For developments of Strauss' view, see Victor Gourevitch, 'A Provisional Reading of Rousseau's Reveries of the Solitary Walker', *The Review of Politics* 74:3 (2012): 489–518; Meier (2016).

THE MEMORIAL PRACTICE OF HAPPINESS 171

system must be contextualised within the larger whole: he understands that in order to 'make a sound judgment' about the system he must 'grasp the whole sufficiently' rather than 'picking apart a few scattered sentences here and there'. In this way, the 'Frenchman' protects himself from the charges of myopia that Rousseau famously levelled at French men of letters. Second, he appeals to an affective criterion of judgement. That is, he consults 'himself' and examines 'the dispositions of soul' produced in him by his readings of Rousseau's works.

Rousseau suggests that this hermeneutic approach allows the reader to access his intention in writing. The Frenchman is able to 'penetrate through' to the disposition of Rousseau's own soul during the time in which he wrote. This access to Rousseau's affective state, in turn, allows the Frenchman to ascertain 'the effect he proposed to produce' in his readers. In applying this 'poetic' mode of reading to the work of 'Jean-Jacques', the 'Frenchman' judges that Rousseau's works must be read in reverse. That is, he judges it necessary to grasp the correct order of the writings in order to follow 'the chain of their contents'. But because 'this order was the reverse of their order of publication', it was necessary to begin with his 'final writings' in order to begin with his first 'principles'. With this discussion, Rousseau not only insists that he has a system but, moreover, explains clearly how to read it and to judge its coherence (209–211/1:930–933).

In addition to the coherence of his system, Rousseau also specifies its content in *Dialogues*. He does so, first, by identifying the particular texts that constitute it. Sometimes, he narrows its scope, as when he identifies *Emile* as his most important and 'final' writing and explicitly excludes his subsequent public letters as mere 'personal' defences of his honour (211/1:933). But his general tendency is to broaden its scope. *Dialogues* opens with a discussion of his opera and musical theory, which are then related to the second *Discourse*, *Emile*, *Social Contract*, and, eventually, to 'the entire collection' of Rousseau's writings. From the perspective I have been developing, it is especially important that he singles out the essay on taste in Book IV of *Emile* for particular emphasis (25/1:689). In short, there is sufficient textual evidence to support a capacious understanding of the works constituting Rousseau's system. Indeed, he even repurposed the epigraph from Ovid that he had previously used for the first *Discourse*, providing intertextual evidence for including *Dialogues* itself in the system (1/1:657). And if that is the case, then any assessment of Rousseau's system really ought to begin precisely as I have done here – starting with *Dialogues*, and working one's way back.

Most significant for my arguments about the importance Rousseau placed on pleasure and happiness in his system, *Dialogues* clarifies the intention that unites it by specifying the content of the disposition he sought to produce in

172   ROUSSEAU'S POLITICS OF TASTE

his readers (213/1:934–935). The first indication of the disposition accessed by means of the poetic mode of criticism comes in Rousseau's presentation of his approach to writing. Because he is 'uniquely constituted', Rousseau insists, he must express himself in unique ways. As he explained, the originality of his writings resulted from his inhabiting 'an ideal world similar to ours, yet altogether different':

> Nature is the same there as on our earth, but its economy is more easily felt, its order more marked, its aspect more admirable. Forms are more elegant, colours more vivid, odours sweeter, all objects more interesting. All nature is so beautiful there that its contemplation, inflaming souls with love for such a touching tableau, inspires in them both the desire to contribute to this beautiful system and the fear of troubling its harmony; and from this comes an exquisite sensitivity which gives those endowed with it immediate enjoyment unknown to hearts that the same contemplations have not aroused.

Rousseau's familiarity with this ideal world was a 'characteristic sign' that marked all of his writings, which, in this sense, were simply attempts to reveal through the medium of prose something of his heightened sensitivity to beauty. Readers with a similar aesthetic disposition were among the 'initiates' who would immediately recognise his intentions (9–12/1:668–673).

The emphasis on sentiment and beauty in this account of the ideal world nicely captures the central idea behind refined Epicureanism, the taste for virtue, or what Rousseau called here temperate sensuality. Temperance or moderation is a sort of structural feature of this ideal world. As in the real world, inhabitants of the ideal world are motivated by their passions to pursue pleasure and happiness. But because their passions are 'simpler and purer' than are real ones, they need only to surrender to their natural inclinations for their actions to be 'good and right'. Their 'desire to contribute to this beautiful system' never devolves into excess, both because it is offset by their 'fear of troubling its harmony' and because their 'exquisite sensitivity' to beauty tempers their pursuit of pleasure by providing 'immediate enjoyment'. In other words, the inhabitants of the ideal world are refined Epicureans whose aesthetic disposition allows them to be 'sensuous and voluptuous' without indulging in 'opulence'. Temperate sensuality is thus an 'art of enjoyment', which consists in following 'nature and reason' rather than 'the estimation of men and the caprices of opinion' and, thereby, 'doing each day whatever seems good for themselves and beneficial for others' (9–12/1:1668–1673). As a standard of critical judgement, then, temperate sensuality is thus not simply an *affective* but,

THE MEMORIAL PRACTICE OF HAPPINESS   173

moreover, a fundamentally *aesthetic* criterion. It is an art of judgement that is just as much an art of reading and writing as it is an art of enjoyment.

Of course, the ideal world is not the real world. As Rousseau puts it, the inhabitant of the ideal world is a 'man of nature' who 'would be sought in vain amongst us' (214/1:936). Yet it is a crucial feature of temperate sensuality that it is a *realistic* ideal. In the first place, the inhabitants of the ideal world are not abstract intellects but passionate and embodied hedonists. Moreover, recall the dual nature of the character of 'Jean-Jacques'. His inhabiting the ideal world marks his originality as an 'author'. But he is also a 'man', and the central question of *Dialogues* is precisely the relationship between his identities of 'author' and 'man', respectively.[13] Even considered as a 'man', 'Jean-Jacques' practices a species of temperate sensuality that facilitates his aesthetic appreciation of natural beauty. In order truly to enjoy the sensual pleasure of natural beauty, as a 'man', crucially requires him to engage in a series of practices grounded in the senses. That is, his sensations are 'tempered' because they are 'mixed' – those that are 'purely material' have less appeal because they are combined with those that are 'intellectual' and all, together, 'act more moderately on him' (114/1:807). In this case, the realism of temperate sensuality consists in the way that it mediates between body and mind – we might therefore think of it as a practice of Rousseau's 'materialism of the sage'. Pleasure is appreciated appropriately here because, while it is a material sensation, it is also rooted in the mind's active mental ability to interrupt the stream of physical sense impressions. The ideal world is an image derived from comparing sensations across time and space, forming judgements about and principles from them, and according to which we can then regulate our pursuit of pleasure.

As Rousseau recognises, there is something paradoxical about effectively closing the gap between temperance and sensuality in this way. He knew well that precisely this approach had traditionally been derided as a sort of 'irrational' or 'unthinking' temperance practised by the vulgar lovers of gain. It was what he called in the first *Discourse* nothing but 'a refinement of intemperance' (*DSA*:8/3:9). But the account of temperance in *Dialogues* effectively reconfigures the Platonic spectrum discussed in Chapter 1. Rousseau claimed that the mixture of material and intellectual sensations allowed him to enjoy a sensuality that was 'lively' yet 'never impetuous'; as such, he was best described as 'temperate rather than sober'. For this account to hold, however, he insisted that 'this term sensuality must be confined to the meaning I am giving it'. That is, his sensuality is temperate because it could 'not be extended to those

---

[13] Cf. Antoine Lilti, 'The Writing of Paranoia: Jean-Jacques Rousseau and the Paradoxes of Celebrity', *Representations* 103:1 (2008): 53–83.

174 ROUSSEAU'S POLITICS OF TASTE

showy voluptuaries who make a vanity of being so, or who in their wish to exceed the limits of pleasure fall into depravity' (*D*:114/1:808). The 'wisdom' of this approach was noted by his contemporaries: Jaucourt even cited it in the *Encyclopédie* entry on temperance.[14] It also permits Rousseau to describe the practice of temperate sensuality by characters of varying degrees of 'ideal' abstraction from the 'real' world: 'Jean-Jacques' practices temperate sensuality as both an 'author' who inhabits an ideal world and a real 'man'. The main characters in Rousseau's great pedagogical treatise are characterised in a similar way: Emile's passions are as 'natural' and 'pure' as an inhabitant of the ideal world, whereas those of his Tutor are 'more evident and closer' to those of 'Jean-Jacques' the man, and the characters of 'Rousseau' and the 'Frenchman' in *Dialogues*. As with refined Epicureanism, the ideal of temperate sensuality is *realistic* because it can, in principle, be adopted by any reader of Rousseau's system (*E*:517/4:677).

Autobiographical Happiness

One way that Rousseau attempted to realise the popular potential of temperate sensuality was by guiding readers of his autobiographies to adopt it as a standard for ethical judgement and practice. As exercises of self-justification, not straightforward recordings of events, the autobiographies guide his readers in their evaluation of his personal moral character (*LM*:574/1:1133). They are also rhetorical performances of Rousseau's own moral self-criticism and, as such, should be considered pedagogical texts. As he described his aim in *Confessions*, self-knowledge required comparison and a new 'rule' of judgement: 'in order for one to learn to evaluate oneself, I want to provide at least one item for comparison, so that each can know himself and one other, and this other will be myself' (*C*:585/1:1149). I want to suggest that he wrote all of his autobiographies in a similar spirit: by guiding his readers' judgement about his own motivation, he sought to educate them in the practice of self-criticism on the path to ethical self-understanding.

The autobiographies accomplish their pedagogical purpose by developing the relationship between temperate sensuality and happiness suggested in *Dialogues*. As he explained in *Emile*, every intentional human action is directed towards pleasure and happiness. If we were able to live only according to our natural inclinations, then our happiness would consist simply in the use of free will. But achieving happiness is not so 'simple' as this, for we develop our opinions about its content by interacting with others in and through

[14] Jaucourt (1765): 59.

THE MEMORIAL PRACTICE OF HAPPINESS 175

social institutions. Infected by the 'poison of opinion', we mistakenly come to believe that happiness is constituted by goods rooted in vanity rather than by natural goods of 'health, freedom, and the necessities of life'. The actions we take to achieve happiness – that is, all of our actions – will be free only when we have reformed our opinion about its content (*E*:216, 324/4:310, 444). The autobiographies describe this process of moral reform in detail, teaching readers to adopt temperate sensuality as a standard of judgement.

Rousseau offered his clearest account of happiness later in *Emile*. The 'road of true happiness', he wrote,

> is not precisely in diminishing our desires, for if they were beneath our power, a part of our faculties would remain idle, and we would not enjoy our whole being. Neither is it in extending our faculties, for if, proportionate to them, our desires were more extended, we would as a result only become unhappier. But it is in diminishing the excess of our desires over the faculties and putting power and will in perfect equality.

This equilibrium of desires and faculties is natural, insofar as it characterises the moral psychology of infants. But sexually mature humans are torn between happiness and unhappiness because the 'superfluous' faculty of imagination 'outstrips' all the other faculties, extends our view of realistic possibilities and, thereby, 'nourishes the desires by the hope of satisfying them'. As Rousseau puts it, 'the real world has its limits; the imaginary world is unlimited. Unable to enlarge the one, let us restrict the other, for it is from the difference between the two alone that are born all the pains which make us truly unhappy' (*E*:211–212/4:304–305). As we have seen, *Dialogues*' 'ideal world' is a world of the imagination restricted in just this way: it is grounded in the reality of passionate, embodied hedonists, but it suggests the ideal possibility of finding an equilibrium between the desire for pleasure and the ability to secure it. With the imagination in play, this natural equilibrium cannot be recovered, any more than the ideal world can be made real. But if our pursuit of pleasure in the real world is regulated by an image of happiness such as in the ideal world, then that equilibrium can be approximated.

Rousseau's general principle that happiness is achieved by restricting the imagination has been made to fit a variety of interpretations. On one reading, it provides the moral-psychological foundation for Rousseau's rejection of modern luxury and insistence on a reversion to a radically austere political economy and culture; on another, the imagination must enjoy an array of unnecessary pleasures so wide that it threatens to devolve into a radical individualism incompatible with social and political life as such. If the former reading concedes rather

176   ROUSSEAU'S POLITICS OF TASTE

too much to 'diminishing our desires' and the latter to 'extending our faculties', this is because neither adequately attends to Rousseau's understanding of 'equilibrium'. As Stephen Salkever rightly notes, Rousseau never identified a 'single principle or way of life' as 'the sole or best path to happiness'. Instead, he offers 'a series of images or pictures of different ways of life, all of which are claimed to be productive of the kind of balance that characterizes human happiness' and each of which 'may be appropriate for particular kinds of individuals at particular times'.[15] This equilibrium can only be approximated because its precise content cannot be antecedently specified in theory – it must be determined by practical judgement in diverse contexts. The autobiographical accounts of happiness educate Rousseau's readers to make these judgements.

Rousseau's defence against misinterpretation by vulgar or unsympathetic readers is consistent across his autobiographies. He describes an account of happiness that refines the potential abuse of the pursuit of pleasure in much the same way as in the ideal world thought experiment. But his accounts of happiness in the autobiographies are unique in their emphasis on the passage of *time*, especially as it concerns the relationship of memory and anticipation to pleasure and happiness. His critical ethos is also present across the autobiographies, both in his preoccupation with how he had previously been and might subsequently be read, and through its relation to an ethic of composition. For as we will see, Rousseau conceived of autobiographical writing as a practice of *askesis*, or self-formation, through which the ability to deploy pleasant memories in the present is cultivated over time to bring about an ethical transformation.[16]

In these ways, Rousseau's autobiographies constitute what I call an Epicurean memorial practice of happiness. While other scholars have identified Epicurean elements in the autobiographies, they have mostly neglected the role of time and memory in this connection.[17] It is often noted that Rousseau agreed with Locke when he argued, in *Emile*, that 'the identity of the "I" is prolonged only by memory, and in order to be actually the same, I must remember having been' (*E*:445/4:590). But it is also well known that Locke's

[15] Stephen G. Salkever, 'Rousseau & the Concept of Happiness', *Polity* 11:1 (1978): 27–45 (41–42). On judgement and happiness see Schaeffer (2014): 40–43, 100–106. My account of Rousseau's pedagogical aim to cultivate his reader's judgement by means of autobiographical narrative could be seen as analogous to Schaefer's account of his aim for the narrative of Emile's cultivation of judgement.

[16] On *askesis* see Michel Foucault, *The Hermeneutics of the Subject: Lectures at the Collège de France 1981–1982*, ed. Frédéric Gros, trans. Graham Burchell (New York: Picador, 2005).

[17] See Victor Gourevitch, 'Rousseau on Providence', *The Review of Metaphysics* 53:3 (2000): 565–611 (603–604); Sonenscher (2008): 151; Vivasvan Soni, *Mourning Happiness: Narrative and the Politics of Modernity* (Ithaca, NY: Cornell University Press, 2010): 240–251. Hadot (1995): 259, 225, 209; 222–224.

THE MEMORIAL PRACTICE OF HAPPINESS 177

view follows the Epicurean position that our knowledge of our existence as an integrated self is provided, in Lucretius' words, by the 'memory that connects us with our former selves'.[18] Rousseau may have been thinking of Locke rather than Lucretius here. Nevertheless, it is useful for us to read his view of personal identity as part of his general Epicurean approach to happiness. For we will see that Rousseau, unlike Locke but like Epicurus, held that it is indeed possible to achieve a steady state of happiness.[19]

In Epicurean ethics, our orientation to both past and future figures prominently in the attainment of happiness, or *ataraxia*. Epicurean *ataraxia* is a steady state characterised by the absence of pain, which itself is the highest pleasure. The most pernicious pain is the mental disturbance of anxiety about the future, in the form of both unrestrained desire for pleasure and fear of death and the gods. Epicurean philosophy therapeutically corrects one's opinions about the true nature of pleasure, death, and the gods, thereby removing pain and preparing for *ataraxia*.[20] It is somewhat less often noted that the Epicureans relied on memory to overcome the anxieties of anticipation.[21] First, Epicurus instructed his followers to memorise his fundamental teachings, writing that happiness consists in a release from anxiety and 'a continual remembrance of the highest and most important truths'.[22] Second, he advocated the active recollection of

---

[18] Cf. Lucretius, *DRN*:3.847–851. Locke's famous account of personhood has been seen as a modern version of this Epicurean idea: see Locke (1997): 392 and James Warren, 'Lucretian *pangenesis* Recycled', *Classical Quarterly* 51 (2001): 499–508. Rousseau read Locke's *Essay* in Pierre Coste's 1729 French translation. See Catherine Glyn Davies, *Conscience and Consciousness: Self-awareness in French Philosophical Writing from Descartes to Diderot* (Liverpool: Liverpool University Press, 1990): 27–38.

[19] For Rousseau's disagreement, see John T. Scott, 'Rousseau's Unease with Locke's Uneasiness', in Grace and Kelly ed. (2012): 295–311. On this disagreement as a reversion to the classical Epicurean position, see Holley (2017): 638, 640.

[20] Epicurus, 'Letter to Menoeceus': 649–59 (§122–135) and 'Sovereign Maxims': 665 (§139–141). That Rousseau's descriptions of his happiest memories are framed or interrupted by painful emotions attests to his view of happiness as premised on the elimination of pain, which is both very difficult to achieve and only temporary. On these painful emotions, see Starobinski (1988): 342–346, 362ff., for Rousseau's attempt 'to change pain into pleasure' through autobiography as a means of 'clarifying transmutation' (362). For an insightful analysis of the positive moral and political effects of painful memories and sentiments like remorse and regret in *Émile*, see Martin McCallum, 'Nostalgic Enlightenment: Rousseau on Memory and Moral Freedom in *Émile* and "Lettres morales"', *The Journal of Politics* 81:4 (2019): 1254–1265.

[21] For a helpful way in to the importance and distinctive role of memory in Epicurean ethics see James Warren, *The Pleasures of Reason in Plato, Aristotle, and the Hellenistic Hedonists* (Cambridge: Cambridge University Press, 2014): 196–201.

[22] Epicurus, 'Herodotus': 611 (§80–82). Cf. Epicurus, 'Vatican Sayings', 17, 19 in *Hellenistic Philosophy: Introductory Readings*, trans. and ed. Brad Inwood and L. P. Gerson (Indianapolis, IN: Hackett, 1988): 29–30.

178   ROUSSEAU'S POLITICS OF TASTE

pleasant experiences in the past as a means of securing pleasure in the present. As Plutarch described in his critical account, the Epicurean sage practised 'vividly remembering and keeping in himself the sights, feelings, and movements associated with pleasure'.[23] Rousseau captured the idea clearly when he wrote in *Confessions*: 'my memory, which retraces only pleasant objects, is the happy counterweight to my frightened imagination, which makes me foresee only cruel futures' (*C*:233/1:278).

Rousseau's adoption of these Epicurean positions informs his understanding of autobiographical writing as a memorial practice of happiness. One obvious implication of the Epicurean account of memory is that our status as moral agents, both in our own and in others' eyes, comes critically to depend on the way in which our actions are related across time in narrative. Indeed, this is why Rousseau remarks that an account of one's actions and moral character is necessarily 'a sort of historical account' (*LM*:574/1:1134). The accounts of happiness in his autobiographies apply Rousseau's general principle that 'the true road of happiness' lies in establishing equilibrium between desires and faculties, which crucially involves 'restricting' the world of the imagination within appropriate limits.

The following sections argue that Rousseau's autobiographical accounts of happiness share a common narrative structure.[24] As we will see, they begin with a description of mental anxiety before a retreat into solitude secures self-sufficiency, understood as equilibrium of both physical and psychological needs and faculties. With this equilibrium secured, Rousseau actively recalls past pleasures. Enjoying re-presented pleasure facilitates reflexive control of the imagination, and enjoying the pleasures of an active imagination facilitates happiness. Appreciating this common structure, in turn, allows us to see apparent contradictions in the accounts as in fact further instances of Rousseau's memorial practice. It also, moreover, clarifies Rousseau's view of the political implications of the pursuit of personal happiness in solitude.

---

[23] Plutarch, *Moralia*, Vol. XIV, trans. Benedict Einarson and Phillip H. De Lacy (London: Harvard University Press, 1967): 33. Cf. Cicero, *Tusculan Disputations*, trans. J. E. King (London: Harvard University Press, 1971): 523, 576, and *De finibus bonorum et malorum*, trans. H. Rackham (London: William Heinemann, 1940): 45, 61.

[24] I refer throughout to: (a) his letters to Malesherbes, written over January–February 1762; two descriptions of happiness in *Confessions* – (b) one from Book VI, written sometime between 1765 and 1767, and (c) one from Book XII, written sometime over 1769 to 1770; and (d) the account of happiness in the 'Fifth Walk' of the Reveries written in 1778. Rather than a close reading of each, I present a synthetic reconstruction of all to achieve greater analytical clarity. My claim that they share a common narrative structure does not deny that specific differences of detail may differentiate them.

THE MEMORIAL PRACTICE OF HAPPINESS   179

It is important to be clear at the outset that Rousseau's abiding intention to write 'useful' work extends to his autobiographies. As we will see, he
thought they would be useful for both individuals and political communities.
The earliest of the texts I consider in this section is a series of four letters written in response to Malesherbes' judgement that Rousseau was 'the unhappiest
of men'.[25] But while Rousseau was touched by his friend's consideration, he
was distressed at the thought that 'the public will judge the same'. Giving
an account of himself by 'exposing the true motivations' for his behaviour
was meant not only to demonstrate that he had achieved happiness but also,
and moreover, to motivate others to follow his example. If only the fate he
had enjoyed were known more widely, he wrote, 'everyone would want to
make a similar one for himself' (*LM*:577/1:1138). Rousseau appears earnestly
to have held that evaluating his standing as a moral agent would educate his
readers to personal happiness and, thereby, engender social and political peace.

Rousseau believed that instructing others in the art of happiness would
be politically useful in this way because he took happiness and freedom to be
theoretically consistent and practically compatible. I noted above that, while
he famously never defined moral freedom in the *Social Contract*, his version
of autonomy is more self-centred and political than is Kant's. He gave more
content to his idea when he wrote in the *Letters from the Mountain* that 'freedom
consists less in being able to do what you will than in not being subject to the
will of others' (*CW*9:260–261/3:841). In another of the letters to Malesherbes,
he presents an argument for the relationship between freedom and happiness
in the same terms. Having explained that his taste for solitude was motivated
by his 'indomitable spirit of freedom', he clarified that by 'solitude' he did
not mean radical isolation. Indeed, he immediately identified 'intimate friendship' as a good of solitude compatible with freedom, for unlike the obliga-
tions incurred by the exchange of 'benefits' in society, in friendship one is
free because 'one follows one's heart and everything is done'. And Rousseau
agreed with Epicurus that the sociability of friendship is not only compatible
with freedom but supportive of happiness as well. Crucially, he concluded the

---

[25] The second of these letters has become the most famous of Rousseau's correspondence, con-
taining his description of the 'illumination' on the road to Vincennes that led to his conclusion
that 'man is naturally good and that it is from [social] institutions alone that men become
wicked'. *LM:*575/*OC*1:1135–1136. On Malesherbes, see Raymond Birn, 'Malesherbes and
the Call for a Free Press', in *Revolutionizing Print: The Press in France 1775–1800*, ed. Robert
Darnton and Daniel Roche (Berkeley: University of California Press, 1989): 50–66, and
E. P. Shaw, *Problems and Policies of Malesherbes as Directeur de la Librairie in France, 1750–1763*
(Albany: State University of New York Press, 1966). For Rousseau and Malesherbes, see Leo
Damrosch, *Jean-Jacques Rousseau: Restless Genius* (New York: Mariner Books, 2005): 250–251,
324–335, 353–358.

180   ROUSSEAU'S POLITICS OF TASTE

argument by defining happiness in nearly identical terms to freedom: the kind of happiness he wanted to enjoy was, like freedom, correctly understood not as the ability 'to do what I want' but, rather, as the ability 'not to do what I do not want' (*LM*:573/1:1132).

The Pleasure of Painlessness

Happiness for Rousseau, as for Epicurus, is predicated on the elimination of pain. Whatever else might be said about the veracity of his self-presentations, there is little doubt that Rousseau endured frequent bouts of physical pain. He suffered from a congenital malformation of the bladder, the persistence of which led to his intense dislike of physicians. He often complained that fever, indigestion, and the general 'breakdown' of his body made it painful to write for long periods. In the autobiographies, he links his physical infirmity with the difficulty of his birth, which had caused the death of his mother (*LM*:577, 572/1:1137, 1130).[26] Just as for Epicurus wisdom and happiness is found in 'the pleasures of the stomach', so for Rousseau the experience of, philosophical reflection on, and rhetorical communication of happiness is impossible without first eliminating physical need and pain. As he remarked to Malesherbes, one 'talks poorly about happiness when one is suffering' (577/1:1138).

Rousseau also agreed with Epicurus that psychological pain was an even greater barrier to happiness than was physical discomfort. He used the term *inquiétude* to describe the general phenomenon of anxiety; it is important to be clear about what he meant by it. In one view, *inquiétude* is an ineliminable feature of human nature itself. The French term was used to translate 'uneasiness', the psychological pain that Locke argued all human action was intended to remove.[27] But Locke's account of agency was famously tragic, for

---

[26] See William Noyes, 'The Insanity of Jean Jacques Rousseau', *The American Journal of Psychology* 3.3 (1890): 406–429.

[27] Coste used *inquiétude* to translate Locke's uneasiness, that 'lack of ease and tranquillity in the soul' that must be overcome in order for happiness to become a possibility: John Locke, *Essai philosophiques concernant l'entendement humain*, trans. Pierre Coste (Amsterdam, 1729): 176, n. 1. Cf. Robert Mauzi, *La philosophie de l'inquiètude dans la literature et philosophie francaise au XVIIIe siècle* (Paris: A. Colin, 1960) and Claire Fauvergue-Simon, *La philosophie de l 'inquiétude de Leibniz à Diderot* (DEA: Université de Toulouse-le-Mirail, 1998). Coste explained his choice by referring his French audience to a passage from the *Apology for Raymond Sebond* in which Montaigne criticised Epicureanism – 'that sect of philosophy which has most cried up pleasure' – for presenting happiness as 'a state so stupid as to be without sensation': Locke (1729): 193. The passages from Montaigne on the role of pleasure and pain in happiness to which Coste referred his readers of Locke are immediately followed by a discussion of Epicurus' memorial practice. See below, n. 33.

THE MEMORIAL PRACTICE OF HAPPINESS 181

he also argued that *inquiétude* was perpetual: because we are bound to consider ourselves in a future state, we are bound either to desire to continue our present enjoyment or to fear losing it, and to act accordingly. Thus, a steady state of happiness such as Epicurean *ataraxia* is fundamentally impossible.[28] In a different view, *inquiétude* has rather less to do with ontological striving than with social discomfort. The *Encyclopédie* defined it as an 'agitation of the soul' felt most frequently by one whose 'duties, situation, or fortune are contrary to their instinct, tastes, or talents'. One experiences *inquiétude* as a feeling of needing to act differently from the ways in which one is forced by the habits of sociability. It is almost always the effect of discontent with oneself, self-doubt, and placing too great a value on one's property and relationships. In this view, *inquiétude* is a sort of debilitating psychological dependence that could in principle be overcome through a combination of individual and social reform.[29]

Rousseau's autobiographical presentations of *inquiétude* consistently link social turmoil to psychological pain in this way. He rejected the view associated with Locke and his followers, reverting instead to the classical Epicurean position that it was indeed possible to secure pleasure and happiness by removing physical pain and *inquiétude*. His treatment of *inquiétude* follows from two conclusions he drew from what he presents as his experience of it. First, he claimed to have discovered the source of human vice and suffering in 'the false opinions of men'; these false opinions made him unhappy, and his psychological pain came more from his situation than from himself (576/1:1136). Second, he simultaneously concluded that his 'extreme agitation' was not rooted in his 'present situation' but, rather, in 'a disordered imagination, ready to take fright over everything and to carry everything to the extreme'. The two claims functioned together: the 'importunities' of the times exacerbate his own; societal 'upheaval' coincides with the onset of his 'illnesses', 'madness', and 'delirium'; suffering or witnessing 'injustice' generates both 'disdain' for his contemporaries and 'discontent' with himself alike (572–573/1:1130–1132). Happiness,

---

[28] Locke (1997): 235–241. On Locke's debt to Epicureanism and Lucretius compare Lisa T. Sarasohn, 'The Ethical and Political Philosophy of Pierre Gassendi', *Journal of the History of Philosophy* 20.3 (1982): 239–260 and James Tully, *An Approach to Political Philosophy: Locke in Contexts* (Cambridge: Cambridge University Press, 1993). Locke's account of happiness continues to be read as a sort of Epicureanism, updated on the premises of modern natural science, and politicised via Hobbes' account of agency as rooted in the perpetual striving of 'power after power'. Such a reading grounds Leo Strauss' notion of 'political hedonism', which is in many ways central to his influential histories of modern political thought: see my 'Theory, Practice, and Modernity'. For Locke's debt to Stoic ideas of appropriation, see Duncan Kelly, *Propriety of Liberty: Persons, Passions and Judgement in Modern Political Thought* (Oxford: Princeton University Press, 2011): 46–48.

[29] Denis Diderot (attributed), 'Inquiétude', in *Encyclopédie* (8): 773.

182   ROUSSEAU'S POLITICS OF TASTE

then, is a hard-won achievement premised on overcoming *inquiétude* by reciprocally reforming one's opinions and tempering one's imagination in a process
of moral transformation.

Rousseau's account of his retreat from Paris on 9 April 1756 is especially
revealing in this respect. While he engaged in protracted debate with his many
critics after the first *Discourse* rocketed him to literary celebrity in 1751, he quickly
grew weary of his role as public intellectual of the Parisian Enlightenment. The
accusations aroused by the publication of the second *Discourse* – of materialism,
atheism, and vulgar Epicureanism – were rather more serious. Combined with
the personal pain of his break with Diderot, this motivated Rousseau to embark
on what he later described as a 'general review of my opinions':

> I was living among modern philosophers who hardly resembled the ancient
> ones. Instead of removing my doubts and curing my uncertainties, they had
> shaken all my most assured beliefs concerning the questions which were
> most important to me, for these ardent missionaries of atheism, these over-
> bearing dogmatists, could not patiently endure that anyone should think
> differently from them on any subject whatsoever. (R:21/1:1015–1016)

He issued this critique of the Parisian *philosophes* after the period he would
come to describe as his 'six years at Montmorency'. His time outside of Paris
from 1756–1762 marks the interval between the publication of the second
Discourse and the *Social Contract* and *Emile* and includes the drafting of *Julie*. It
was unquestionably the most intellectually productive period of his career. If
his autobiographies are to be believed, it was also during this time of solitude
when he learned the art of happiness.

Each of Rousseau's accounts of happiness presents solitude as a means of
re-establishing equilibrium of needs and faculties. Securing physical needs provides a material foundation on which to overcome psychological pain: 'reas-
sured on the question' of how he would 'subsist', he was without *inquiétude*
'on any other' (C:535/1:639). Solitude eliminates *inquiétude* in two ways.
First, it allows one to avoid the competitive clash of interests in society; by
removing the 'necessity' of ever 'harming someone else for one's own advantage', it ensures that one may remain 'in no way wicked for others' (LM:576,
580/1:1137/1142). Second, it enables one to reflect on the nature of pleasure
and the source of one's desires. The retreat into solitude is a movement in
both physical and affective or cultural space: the sort of freedom one enjoys
in solitude is a reflective critical distance from public opinion. In solitude,
Rousseau learns that what he once thought were goods of nature were merely
goods of opinion: he learns that 'fortune', 'fame', 'reputation', or 'honour'

THE MEMORIAL PRACTICE OF HAPPINESS 183

are unnecessary pleasures rooted in vanity (572–573/1:1134–1137). He discovers instead his taste for the natural pleasures of rest, a meal, botany, walking, or music (578–579/1:1139–1142). In other words, he becomes a refined Epicurean. Indeed, solitude itself becomes a source of pleasure (R:41/1:1040). And while he identified his reputation as a leading figure of the Parisian *salons* as a cause of *inquiétude*, he nevertheless recognised that it had allowed him to earn a living as a musical copyist and thus supported him on his solitary retreats from the capital. Whereas in Paris his so-called friends sought to make him happy according to their false opinions of pleasure and happiness, in solitude Rousseau pursues and achieves happiness according to his natural tastes and temperament. Solitude allowed Rousseau to be 'free', as well as 'good and happy', because it allowed him to return to the internal goods already within his grasp; after the examples of Epicurus and Pope, Julie and Emile, Rousseau wrote 'I have not looked for my felicity far away, I have looked for it near me and I have found it there' (*LM*:576–577/1:1137–1138).

Memory and Imagination

Rousseau describes the harmony of physical and moral needs and faculties as the foundation on which actively to deploy the faculty of memory to secure further sources of mental pleasure. We have seen that he argued against the *philosophes'* reductive materialism that judgement was an active rather than a passive faculty. He did something similar with memory. Helvétius had asserted that, like judgement, 'to remember' is 'only to sense'. Rousseau responded that 'to sense an object that is present and to sense an object that is absent are two different operations'. Memory was the ability intentionally to recall an absent sensory object. Like judgement, it was an active faculty.[30] Each of his accounts of happiness is prefaced by a description of a specific memory of pleasant sensations. The pleasures he 'recalls most often and most willingly' are those of his retirement: a walk or a sunrise, his dog and cat, a friend or lover. In some cases, recalling his past experiences of pleasure simply allows Rousseau to forget his present suffering, as when his 'sweet remembrances' distract him from the sudden onset of physical pain. But beyond mere distraction, Rousseau was most interested in the way that past experiences could become new sources of pleasure precisely by being recollected in the present, generating 'charm' or 'exquisite sentiments' (578–579/1:1139–1142).

This particular approach to memorial pleasure has always been recognised as distinctively Epicurean. Epicurus notoriously claimed that he was happy

[30] *CW*12:204/*OC*4:1121.

184 ROUSSEAU'S POLITICS OF TASTE

despite enduring rather intense physical pain on his deathbed because his recollection of past philosophical conversations with friends had removed all mental pain.[31] Perhaps unsurprisingly, that claim has never been considered very plausible.[32] In the *Apology for Raymond Sebond*, for instance, Montaigne drew on the critical tradition to argue that memory was far too unreliable and ambivalent a faculty to secure present pleasure, for it 'sets before us, not what we choose, but what it pleases. Indeed, there is nothing that imprints a thing so vividly in our memory as the desire to forget it.'[33] In his essay 'On Solitude', Montaigne instead celebrated the ability of the imagination to provide new sources of pleasure.[34] But it is important not to suggest a stark opposition here. For Rousseau, it is never a question of *either* memory *or* imagination. Rather, the two faculties work together to provide mental access to non-present sensory experience in reverie (579/1:1141). Memory draws on past experiences of pleasure while imagination looks to the future in anticipation and, together, they secure mental pleasure in the present. Once more, then, Rousseau can be seen to follow an idea unique to Epicureanism – namely, that 'the expectation of pleasures hoped for is combined with the recollection of pleasures already realized' to provide an 'unbroken tissue of pleasures' in the present.[35]

The imagination can become an active source of new pleasures only with physical needs satisfied and mental pleasure secured through memory. The imagination is no less ambivalent a faculty than memory: *reverie* threatens sociability because it threatens to devolve into imaginative extravagance; imagining ourselves in a future state grounds Locke's idea of perpetual uneasiness; and Rousseau's general principle of happiness requires restricting the imagination. But while the imagination is a superfluous faculty, it cannot be eliminated. Instead, it must be tempered by memorial practice. By securing a source of pleasure in the present, memorial practice ensures that the search for imagined pleasure will not relapse into 'disordered' *inquiétude* and unhappiness. The traditional view that 'the imagination can only make us unhappy' overstates Rousseau's position; rather, he seeks not to 'shackle' but to 'redirect' the

---

[31] Epicurus, 'Letter to Idomeneus': 549 (§22). Cf. Cicero, *De finibus bonorum et malorum*, trans. H. Rackham (London: William Heinemann, 1940): 189.

[32] Warren (2014): 196–201.

[33] Michel de Montaigne, *The Complete Essays of Montaigne*, trans. Donald M Frame (Stanford, CA: Stanford University Press, 1966): 365; citing Cicero, *De finibus* II.c.3. This is the passage, noted above, to which Coste had referred readers of his translation of Locke's *Essay* to indicate to them what Locke had intended by 'uneasiness'. See above, n. 27.

[34] Montaigne (1966), 179–183.

[35] Cicero (1971): 523; (1940): 61.

THE MEMORIAL PRACTICE OF HAPPINESS 185

imagination 'in ways that does not threaten human happiness'.[36] Recollected pleasure thus overcomes the typical problems associated with the imagination and its pleasures in reverie. The source of temperance is pleasure itself.

Rousseau describes three central ways in which the imagination might actively be deployed to provide new sources of mental pleasure. The uniqueness of imagination resides in its relating physical inputs from particular sensations to general ideas, and turning general ideas into particular sensations with emotional content (*E*:490–491/4:645–647; *DI*:148/3:149–150). Rousseau's celebration of 'nature' in the autobiographies is perhaps the most famous example of his use of this capacity. With his imagination, Rousseau moves 'from the earth' to 'all the beings of nature' and, thus, enjoys 'everything that is beautiful in the perceptible world, and that is imaginable in the intellectual world'. The imagination mediates between intellectual and physical experience: the general idea of nature produces a concrete sensory experience, 'a sort of sensual pleasure' or 'delights' the likes of which even 'the most voluptuous people have never known'. Rousseau is celebrated and derided in almost equal measure for his unrestrained accounts of the emotional response generated by this agreeable experience. 'I loved to lose myself in imagination', he wrote; the 'ecstasy' and 'raptures' made him weep and 'cry out, "Oh great being! Oh great being"' (*LM*:579/1:1141). Crucially, Rousseau describes these pleasures as embodied, sensual, or voluptuous, and distinguishes them from the pleasures of philosophy. The *askesis* he practices in solitude is not philosophy; it is the synthesis of reason and sentiment characteristic of good taste as refined Epicureanism. Finally, this imaginative process has a transformative moral effect. Solitude frees Rousseau from false opinions about pleasure to experience the true pleasures of nature, which alone are able to satisfy one's desires. This refined embodied understanding of pleasure facilitates a new appreciation of true luxury: just as Julie speaks the language of signs to replace the 'luxury of vanity' with the 'luxury of pleasure and sensuality', so in Rousseau's imagined integration with nature the 'gold of the broom and the purple of the heather struck my eyes with a luxury that touched my heart' (578/1:1140).[37]

A second main purpose to which Rousseau puts the imagination in his autobiographies is overcoming fear, understood as painful thoughts about the future. In the aforementioned appeal to imagination in 'On Solitude',

---

[36] Robert Derathé, 'La Dialectique Du Bonheur Chez Jean-Jacques Rousseau', *Revue de Théologie et de Philosophie* 2 (1952): 81–96 (93). Martina Reuter, 'Jean-Jacques Rousseau and Mary Wollstonecraft on the Imagination', *British Journal for the History of Philosophy* 25:6 (2017): 1138–1160 (1142).

[37] Etienne Gilson, 'La méthode de M. Wolmar', in *Les idées et les lettres*, ed. Etienne Gilson (Paris: Vrin, 1932): 275–298.

186 ROUSSEAU'S POLITICS OF TASTE

Montaigne suggested that it was necessary 'to picture the evil that is to come, as far as my imagination can reach', in order to eliminate the fear of 'death, poverty, contempt, and disease'.[38] Rousseau adopted a similar approach: he imagined himself to be near death and resolved to confine himself to solitude until the end, and imagining that he might be so confined forever made him 'content' to live his entire life in solitude. For him, imagining death was a means of restricting his desires by focusing on the pleasures of the moment. Thus, his allusions to his death leave him 'without a moment's desire for any other state' or free to enjoy his time 'without plan or purpose', following 'the caprice of the moment' (R:42/1:1041; C:189, 535–579/1:226, 639–641). As this suggests, Rousseau's emphasis on following his whims or caprices in the pursuit of happiness is grounded in his memorial practice: partly because it helps to ensure that these whims are meaningfully one's own, memorial practice helps to ensure that following them does not devolve into vulgar Epicureanism or depraved voluptuousness. This approach informs his use of metaphors of imprisonment to describe the heights of his happiness (LM:573/1:1 132; R:41, 47/1:1040; 1048). It has always been recognised as a distinctly Stoic therapy. Epicurus preferred for his atomic theory to fill this role, reasoning that the anticipation of future pain would simply make that pain present. He did, however, suggest that recalling painful experiences from our past could provide us with pleasure in the present. Rousseau followed him in this, actively recalling 'regrets' and the 'things I repent' to experience 'the true pleasures of humanity' in the present (578/1:1139–1140). In this way, Rousseau's paradoxical conclusion that 'every consistent Epicurean is necessarily a Stoic' also applies to his choice of therapeutic practices in his autobiographical accounts of happiness.

Rousseau's eclectic approach is also evident in the third imaginative practice central to his accounts of happiness – his creation of imaginary societies. Montaigne's Stoic-inspired practices included the imagination of moral exemplars: present continually to your imagination, he wrote, those men 'in whose presence fools themselves would hide their faults; make them controllers of all your intentions; if these intentions get off the track, your reverence for those men will set them right again. They will keep you in a fair way to be content with yourself.'[39] Rousseau followed this approach: he retreated to solitude from the 'society of men' and imagined 'refuges of nature' from which he drove away 'opinion, prejudices', or 'factitious passions'; and he populated these imaginary spaces with 'chimerical beings . . . worthy of inhabiting them'. His imagined 'social circle' was thus a 'golden age' that served as a

[38] Montaigne (1966): 179.
[39] Ibid.: 183.

THE MEMORIAL PRACTICE OF HAPPINESS   187

principle of moral judgement. Positively, it tempered his imagination by providing him with a source of pleasure that was 'reliable' and 'charming' because he could 'cultivate it without effort, without risk'. Negatively, precisely its ease, agreeableness, and its accordance with his heart reinforced his 'disgust' with Paris and the other societies he had left behind (572; 578/1:1130–1131; 1140). Alongside imagining nature and death, then, Rousseau suggests imagining societies of moral exemplars as a way of tempering the disorders of an imagination that otherwise 'always ran on ahead' in order to achieve a 'cheerful imagination' (C:189–190/1:226; R:47/1:1047).

As mentioned above, it is imperative not to think of imagination and memory as radically distinct faculties. Rousseau typically presents them in opposing pairs with distinct temporal orientations: memory-past, imagination-future. But he also suggests that the imagination's tendency to 'run on ahead' can be tempered by intentionally deploying it to look 'back'. That is, the imagination also takes past memories as its object, creatively refining them to provide greater pleasure. But we should not see this pejoratively as little more than 'self-serving misremembrance'.[40] For as we will see, the interplay between memory and imagination through autobiographical writing is an importantly deliberate part of Rousseau's ethical practice of *askesis*. This practical perspective helpfully shifts our focus from epistemological questions of the (in)accuracy of a written representation of a memory of a past event to ethical questions of intentions and consequences, and of the extent to which the authorial refinement of a given memory is conducive to present happiness.[41]

---

[40] John M. Warner, *Rousseau and the Problem of Human Relations* (University Park: Penn State University Press, 2016): 149–151. Warner discusses an example from *Julie*: St. Preux writes to his friend Edward Bomston, reliving an important past experience of their friendship; but whereas St. Preux presently remembers with pleasure their having shared a strong connection, readers remember his earlier confession to Claire that he had initially been troubled by his distrust of Bomston. For Warner, this is a distinction between an event and its subsequent misrepresentation by false memory ('what actually happened there' and 'simply inaccurate accounts of the events being remembered'). Considering memory as a practice of *askesis*, in which autobiographical writing can play a crucial role, allows us to read this example differently: it is a more complex distinction between two written recollections of an event, written from two different 'futures' after the event, for two different readers, by a fictional character in a novel written by Rousseau, which itself begins with his disavowing his authorship.

[41] My account of Rousseau's memorial practice harmonises with Jason Neidelman's arguments that Rousseau approaches 'truth' not from an 'epistemological' but an 'ethical' perspective, in which philosophical speculation and literary activity 'must be made to serve the ethical imperative of human happiness'. Jason Neidelman, 'The Sublime Science of Simple Souls: Rousseau's Philosophy of Truth', *History of European Ideas* 39:6 (2013): 815–834 (817). Cf. Starobinski (1988): 197–198.

Writing Happiness

Rousseau's account of imaginary pleasures is indicative of his approach to writing as itself a source of pleasure. Authorial pleasure consists in the first place of agreeable sensations. The imaginary beings whose company he enjoyed were of course the characters Rousseau created for the novels he composed in solitude. Writing letters to his real friend Malesherbes is a source of pleasure because, Rousseau admitted, he enjoyed talking about himself – although, not with just anyone; which is why he often 'abused' his pursuit of the pleasures of autobiographical disclosure to Malesherbes (*LM*:577, 580/1:1138, 1142). He was most interested, however, in the ability of autobiographical writing to access not sensations but sentiments. According to Rousseau, the vulgar materialism of Helvétius and the *philosophes* was unable to grasp the unique activity of sentiments, both psychologically and politically, because it reduced sentiment to sensation. This was a mistake, for while sensations affected a particular sense organ, sentiments were felt throughout the entire sensory apparatus. As such, the pleasures and pains of sentiment outweighed the pleasures and pains of mere sensation.[42] Unlike sensations, moreover, sentiments could not be clearly identified with any material objects. As an author, one could describe and express past actions or speech, but it was a genuine challenge to express what was 'only tasted, only felt without my being able to point to any other object of my happiness but this sentiment itself'. For happiness 'did not lie in any assignable object'; it was wholly internal and 'did not leave me for a moment'. His descriptions of the sentiment of happiness are often introduced by a sort of incantation: 'retrace once more for me your charming course; move more slowly in my memory, if this is possible, than ever you did in your first rapid flight' (*C*:189–190/1:226). A sentiment that was only briefly experienced can be accessed and prolonged by being actively represented in memory, and autobiographical writing is the means of securing that sentiment in the present.

The practice of autobiographical writing cultivates Rousseau's ability to remember pleasant sensations and agreeable sentiments over time. One of the most famous passages in the autobiographies is his recollection of his experience of the sentiment of happiness on the Île de Saint-Pierre in 1765:

> But if there is a state where the soul can find a resting-place secure enough to establish itself and concentrate its entire being there, with no need to

---

[42] Rousseau, 'Notes on Helvétius', *CW*12:204/*OC*4:1121. Cf. Marshall (2012), Salkever (1978): 39–40, 44–45.

THE MEMORIAL PRACTICE OF HAPPINESS 189

remember the past or reach into the future, where time is nothing to it, where the present runs on indefinitely but this duration goes unnoticed, with no sign of the passing of time, and no other feeling of deprivation or enjoyment, pleasure or pain, desire or fear than the simple sentiment of existence, a feeling that fills our soul entirely, as long as this state lasts, we can call ourselves happy, not with a poor, incomplete and relative happiness such as we find in the pleasures of life, but with a sufficient, complete and perfect happiness which leaves no emptiness to be filled in the soul. (*R*:46/1:1046)

This description from the 'Fifth Walk' in the *Reveries* is the second recorded memory of that experience. The first comes in Book XII of *Confessions* and was written sometime between 1769 and 1770. The descriptions share the narrative structure reconstructed above, and their comparison allows us to see Rousseau engaged in the practice of gradually refining his memories of past pleasures to secure his present happiness. This evidence of utilising memory through autobiographical writing as a memorial practice, in turn, clarifies the discrepancies between the two accounts.

In Book XII, what Rousseau described as a 'sweet reverie' that has inspired 'the most intense delight' is once again made possible by his being 'isolated from other men . . . shielded from their insults . . . forgotten . . . abandoned, in a word, to the joys of idleness and the contemplative life'. Once more, self-sufficiency in necessities tempers the agitation of imagined *inquiétude*. Indeed, in this state of self-sufficient tranquillity, Rousseau's botanical studies occupied him in the present and prevented the 'fevered workings of the imagination or the boredom of total inactivity' from wresting him from his enjoyment of the present moment. With physical self-sufficiency once again procuring mental tranquillity by tempering his imagination, Rousseau began to imagine death in the absence of fear. And this preparation for death entailed and supported his enjoyment of the present moment. Just as he had claimed in the letter to Malesherbes to have taken pleasure in his tasks only when he felt able to put them off indefinitely, here in Book XII Rousseau remembers himself having been free 'to begin a hundred times and to finish none . . . to while away the whole day without plan or purpose and to follow in everything the caprice of the moment' (*C*:534–537/1:637–641).

This familiar narrative structure recurs in the 'Fifth Walk'. Rousseau's happiness is founded upon material self-sufficiency, for life on Saint-Pierre is said to be the ideal situation 'for the happiness of those who like to live within narrow bounds'. Yet again, the requisite harmony between desires and faculties is achieved only through social retreat: with few residents and even fewer

190 ROUSSEAU'S POLITICS OF TASTE

roads to bring travellers, Rousseau's retreat is 'fascinating' for 'solitary dream-
ers' like himself. Characteristically, the reader is presented with Rousseau's
anxious imagination prior to his arrival in this secluded idyll, for we are told
that he was 'troubled by forebodings'. Again characteristically, however, his
self-sufficient solitude tempers his imaginative projections and allows him to
contemplate death in the absence of fear, for he then imagines with pleasure
the possibility that he might 'be shut up here for the rest of my days'. Solitude
facilitates Rousseau's limitation of his desires, a state of moderation necessary
for happiness. Thus, whilst he spent only two months there, Rousseau says that
he could have spent 'all eternity there without a moment's boredom', for those
two months were 'the happiest of my life, so happy that I would have been
content to live all my life in this way, without a moment's desire for any other
state' (*R*:41–42/1:1040–1042).

Despite these evident similarities, there is a difference between Rousseau's
two accounts of happiness on Saint-Pierre that, although seemingly minor, is
of crucial importance. As we have seen, the final account in the 'Fifth Walk'
closely follows the first. Rousseau remembers his having resolved to 'end my
days there', just as he remembers 'thinking that I would have all the time in the
world to settle in, I began by making no attempt at all to install myself'. Recalling
his being without his inkstand and having 'no communication or correspondence with the outside world', he even goes so far as to remember having left
all of his scattered belongings and his books packed in the boxes in which they
had arrived: 'living in the house where I intended to end my days, as if it had
been an inn which I was to leave the following day' (82–83/1:1041–1042).
Through the metaphor of the inn, then, Rousseau's final depiction of happiness
is founded on his consideration of each day as his last.

In the earlier account in *Confessions* XII, however, Rousseau remembers
that he specifically requested that his 'books and belongings' be delivered to
him. Importantly, this memory is itself the foundation for the recollection of a
particularly unpleasant memory:

> After breakfast I would write, hurriedly and grudgingly, a few wretched
> letters, thinking longingly all the while of the happy moment when I
> would never have to write another. I would busy myself with my books
> and papers for a few minutes, unpacking and arranging rather than reading
> them; and this rearranging . . . was a way of whiling away pleasantly a few
> hours, after which I would become bored and abandon it.

Here Rousseau remembers his experience of pleasure being interrupted by the
onset of the psychological pain of boredom; he remembers that his inability

THE MEMORIAL PRACTICE OF HAPPINESS   191

to abandon his concern with others in society and for projects in the future –
represented by his books and letters – rendered impossible the happiness for
which he longed. Indeed, this earlier account from Book XII is peppered with
terms of mental pain absent from the final account in the *Reveries*. Thus, he
remembers that 'every day spent away from the island seemed to me a day
subtracted from my happiness' because 'past experience had made me fearful'.
The 'ardent desire to finish my days on the island' that recurs in the 'Fifth
Walk', was in his first memory 'inseparable from the fear of being forced to
leave', and the calm aroused by the sight and sound of crashing waves was
'troubled by the anxiety that I might lose it'. Indeed, he remembers in Book
XII, 'this *inquiétude* soon reached the point where it spoiled all sweetness'
(*C*:538–541/1:643–646).

The chronological comparison of Rousseau's two descriptions of the same
event in his life helps to clarify some persistent interpretive issues surrounding his
autobiographical accounts of happiness. Some commentators have cited the discrepancies between these accounts as evidence for Rousseau's inconsistency or
even duplicity.[43] Our comparative perspective, however, allows us to see them
as instances of Rousseau's memorial practice. By contrasting his two depictions
of his time spent floating aimlessly on the lake at Saint-Pierre, moreover, we can
even suggest that Rousseau had become more adept at that practice. In Book
XII, Rousseau claims not to be able to 'tell or even to comprehend' the cause of
his experience of 'a joy so intense as to leave me trembling' (539/1:643). In the
famous passage from the 'Fifth Walk', Rousseau indeed told how he compre-
hended the cause of that intense joy – namely, as the experience of the sentiment
of existence. Indeed, we might say that all of the anxiety, trouble, foreboding,
and fear – the *inquiétude* that persists throughout the memory in Book XII, does
so because Rousseau had not then been able, as he remembered having been in
the *Reveries*, to deploy memory in an artful enough manner so as to enjoy the
sentiment of existence in an uninterrupted present moment.[44]

Other commentators have argued that the most distinguishing characteristic
of Rousseau's account of happiness is its fundamental passivity. Jean Starobinski

---

[43] See Jean Starobinski and Annette Tomarken, 'Rousseau's Happy Days', *New Literary History*
11:1 (1979): 147–166.

[44] This reading harmonises with that of Christopher Kelly, who similarly both emphasises the
interplay of memory and imagination in each account and suggests that the interaction between
them shows that Rousseau's 'imaginative recollection' in the *Reveries* 'involves embellishment':
Rousseau's Exemplary Life: The Confessions as Political Philosophy (Ithaca, NY: Cornell University
Press, 1987): 234–235. Cf. Victor Gourevitch, 'A Provisional Reading of Rousseau's Reveries
of the Solitary Walker', *The Review of Politics* 74:3 (2012): 489–518, who cites both Lucretius
on Epicurean *ataraxia* and the account in *Confessions* in his reading of the 'Fifth Walk' (500–
501, n. 10–11).

suggests that Rousseau advocates a passive 'abandonment to memory'.[45] Pierre Hadot puts it in Hellenistic terms: happiness for Rousseau is a 'passive, almost mystical state', which differentiates it from that of the ancient Epicureans for whom 'the transformation of one's view of the world was intimately linked to exercises which involved concentrating one's mind on the present instant'.[46] But comparing the accounts of happiness on Saint Pierre shows that Rousseau's memorial practice of happiness is inseparable from the very activity of writing itself.[47] As we have seen, writing allows Rousseau to relive his past experiences of happiness through memory. 'In wanting to recall so many sweet reveries', he wrote, 'I relived them instead of describing them. This is a state which is brought back by being remembered and of which we would soon cease to be aware if we completely ceased feeling it' (R:9–10/1:1003). Moreover, each description itself prolongs this remembered pleasure in the present in which Rousseau is writing it. As mentioned, his account of Les Charmettes in *Confessions* begins with an incantation:

> Precious and regretted moments, ah! Retrace once more for me your charming course; flow more slowly in my remembrance . . . What can I do to prolong this simple and touching narrative at my pleasure, to retell the same thing over and over and not bore my readers by their repetition, any more than I bore myself by endlessly repeating them. (189/1:225)

In addition to prolonging what were in the past only fleeting pleasures, writing also allows Rousseau to adorn them with genuinely new 'charming images'. His authorial activity allows him to both taste the 'same pleasures' and derive 'even greater pleasure' from them (R:48/1:1049). Finally, this memorial practice of writing secures transmission of re-presented and augmented pleasure into a future in which it can be repeatedly recalled and enjoyed in reading. Of the *Reveries* as a whole, Rousseau wrote, 'as the moment of my departure approaches, I will recall in reading them the pleasure I have in writing

---

[45] Starobinski (1988): 194. Cf. P. Hoffman, 'La mémoire et les valeurs das les Six Premiers Livres des *Confessions*', *Annales J.-J. Rousseau* 39 (1972–77): 79–93.

[46] Hadot (1995): 259.

[47] My reading shares certain affinities with those emphasising a kind of dialectical relationship or play between activity and passivity: Pierre Burgelin, 'Introduction and Notes' to *Émile, ou de l'éducation*, by Jean-Jacques Rousseau (Paris: Pléiade, 1969) and J.-F. Perrin, *Le chant de l'origine: la mémoire et le temps dans les Confessions de Jean-Jacques Rousseau*, Studies on Voltaire and the Eighteenth Century, Vol. 339 (Oxford: Oxford University Press, 1996): 56–65. For a helpful updating of this active/passive debate, which my account supports, see Martin McCallum, 'Eyes Turning Towards the Light: Nostalgic Memory and Nascent Community in Rousseau's Emile', *History of Political Thought* 38:4 (2017): 681–711.

THE MEMORIAL PRACTICE OF HAPPINESS   193

them and thus by reviving times past I shall as it were double the space of my existence' (8/1:1001). An unpublished fragment puts the point succinctly: 'in saying to myself, I have enjoyed, I enjoy again'.[48] In sum, Rousseau exercises reflective control over his past pleasure through representing the sentiment of happiness in memory, writing, and, finally, reading. Rather than seeing inconsistency and passivity, then, we ought rather to read the two accounts of Saint-Pierre as two instances of an Epicurean memorial practice designed to provide what Cicero called an 'unbroken tissue of pleasures'.[49]

Conclusion: Solitude and Sociability

When these charges of inconsistency and passivity are combined, they underpin the widespread understanding that Rousseau's vision of solitary happiness is radically incompatible with any form of sociable relations with others. Leo Strauss argued that whereas the ancient pursuit of happiness was grounded in a standard of truth that is objective and thus 'radically non-private', Rousseau's standard of the sentiment of existence is subjective and thus 'emphatically private'. As such, for Strauss, Rousseau ultimately privileges the avant-garde life of the artist over the political life of the citizen.[50]

At first glance, this charge may seem more difficult to answer on the basis of the foregoing analysis. We have seen that happiness requires solitude understood as a retreat from those false opinions that undergird corrupt modes of modern commercial sociability and produce *inquiétude*. As Rousseau noted in a different context, happiness is subjective and private to the extent that a sentiment can be evaluated only by the one who experienced it; external signs of happiness can never be certain.[51] But we have also seen that Rousseau's autobiographies are motivated by his concern to communicate the sentiment of happiness to others. What, then, if we approach the consistency dilemma from this perspective on the communicability of sentiments?

Most concretely, Rousseau's autobiographical accounts of happiness present a vision of solitude compatible with shared sentiments in friendship. Epicurus famously argued that friendship and self-sufficiency are compatible, rebuking the Stoics for suggesting that the wise man had no need of friends.[52] In a similar fashion, Rousseau's descriptions of happiness are embedded within descriptions of his enjoyment of sociability. We should not overlook his

[48] Rousseau, 'On the Art of Enjoying', *CW*12:58/*OC*1:1174.
[49] Cicero (1971): 523.
[50] Strauss (2014): 423.
[51] Rousseau, *CW*4:40/*OC*3:507.
[52] Epicurus, 'Vatican Sayings', 34 and 39 in Inwood and Gerson eds (1988): 30–31.

194 ROUSSEAU'S POLITICS OF TASTE

repeatedly effacing the presence of his domestic partner Thérèse Levasseur and her mother. From the present perspective, however, it is important that he never fails to note that his solitude was shared with the other members of his 'little household'. Indeed, he counts the fact that amongst them 'no image of servitude and dependence disturbed the benevolence that united us all' as a contributing factor in his 'true happiness' (*LM*:579/1:1142). Even the 'Fifth Walk' is immediately preceded by a description of sociable sentiments: talking, laughing, and singing together provided more enjoyment than 'modern rigamarole', allowing them to rest 'content with our day' and wishing for no other pleasure than that of repeating the same activities tomorrow (*R*:45/1:1045).

Similar sentiments are even shared with others beyond the household. Rousseau notes that having their most basic needs amply provided for allowed the locals nearby Saint-Pierre to enjoy a calm and peaceful sociability, describing how all 'the people who live round the lake meet and dance on Sundays during the wine harvest' (42/1041).[53] For Rousseau, solitude is properly understood as involving *both* being 'cut off from the rest of the world' *and* enjoying 'the company of a few people'. While this combination may seem superficially contradictory, it is only so amongst the 'men of the world'; the contradiction is resolved amongst friends living according to natural pleasures and sentiments. Company with others can then become 'attractive and pleasing' because it is compatible with the freedom to enjoy oneself – it need not 'absorb all my attention' (47/1:1048). In these conditions, it facilitates self-approval as a source of pleasure (*LM*:580/1:1142). Freeing us from false opinions about pleasure and happiness, solitude eliminates the discontent with one's self and disdain for others characteristic of *inquiétude* and, thereby, allows both the self and others to become genuine sources of pleasure.

Autobiographical writing also allows for this reconfigured relationship of self and others to be further extended to imagined communities of readers. We saw that Rousseau drew pleasure both from his relationship to the imaginary friends he created as characters for his novels and from describing his happiness in the letters he wrote to his real friends. The frenzied response to *Julie* is well known, and the letters he received from his female readers in particular indicate something of the wider circle of mutual sentiment it helped to create.[54] We should also note that some of his most effusive accounts of sentiment are

[53] Cf. Rousseau's famous account of the grape harvest in *J*:493–495/*OC2*:602–605, where country labour is described as combining 'public and private utility'.
[54] See, classically, Robert Darnton, 'Readers Respond to Rousseau: The Fabrication of Romantic Sensitivity', in *The Great Cat Massacre and Other Episodes in French Cultural History* (London: Allen Lane, 1984): 215–256.

THE MEMORIAL PRACTICE OF HAPPINESS 195

those that he recalls having shared with friends and lovers in the past.[55] And just as he took pleasure in rereading his works in private, so did he debut his autobiographies with public readings that allowed him to perform for an audience his written recollections and imaginations of sentiments both shared and private.[56]

This concern with the communicability of sentiment is central to Rousseau's understanding of the pedagogical purpose of the autobiographies. Just as he interpreted Pope as attempting to do years before, so did he try to use his own experience to show that 'the source of true happiness is within us and that it is not in the power of men to make anyone truly miserable who can will to be happy' (R:9/1:1003). We have already noted his claim that judgements of the coherence of his works must be based on the internal sentiment they express, for only this clarifies the intention or goal that unites them. In a similar spirit, he told Malesherbes that the writings he published in Paris were tinged with unhappy sentiments, a 'black bile' that gnawed at his heart and that 'made itself felt too much'; those he completed in solitude, however, revealed the 'serenity of soul' on which his readers could base a 'sure judgment' about his 'internal state'. Precisely this combination of unhappy and happy sentiments, he continued, was evidence that his 'three principal writings' – the first and second *Discourse* and *Emile* – 'are inseparable and form the same whole' (LM:572, 575/1:1131, 1136). This claim has often been cited to argue for the logical coherence of Rousseau's work by dividing it into an early 'critical' phase and a later 'constructive' phase.[57] But as we see here, Rousseau emphasised that the unity of his project has as much if not more to do with the taste and sentiment of the poet than with the reason and logic of the philosopher. Whether with friends and neighbours in solitude, with concrete or imagined others in writing, or with public audiences, then, Rousseau's concern with the communication of sentiments illustrates that, while the experience of happiness is

---

[55] For example, and to cite only *Confessions*: his friendship with his cousin Bernard (C:12–22/OC1:13–25); with Diderot (C:291–293/OC1:34–3-48); with Sophie d'Houdetot (C:370–381/OC1:440–454); his return to Mme de Warens' home (C:86–92/OC1:102–110); and his encounter with Zulietta, discussed above.

[56] On shared sentiments in reading, see J:16–17/OC2:22–23. *Confessions* was published posthumously but Rousseau performed public readings of excerpts from the manuscript on several occasions. See Lilti (2008), Christie V. McDonald, 'The Model of Reading in Rousseau's Dialogues', *MLN* 93:4, French Issue: Autobiography and the Problem of the Subject (1978): 723–732. On public readings in the *salons* and French Academy, see Jean-François de La Harpe, *Philosophie du dix-huitième siècle: Vol. 1/2* (1818): 100ff.

[57] Especially following Kant (2007): 160–175 (169–170), Cassirer (1963), and John Rawls, *Lectures on the History of Political Philosophy*, ed. Samuel Freeman (London: Harvard University Press, 2007): 191–249 (206ff.).

internal and private, it remains possible for it to be less emphatically so than Strauss suggests.

Of course, this does not adequately address the full implications of the incompatibility thesis advanced by Strauss and others. For even if Rousseau's account of solitude is compatible with friendship and the rustic sociability of village life, this says nothing of the psychological dispositions of citizenship and the sociability of modern commercial society. Indeed, especially for readers of Strauss, Rousseau's central concern with the legitimacy of state power distinguishes him as a 'modern' thinker who largely abandoned the 'ancient' concern with happiness.[58] Conversely, it has recently been argued that Rousseau understood the rational legitimacy of state power to require its compatibility with personal happiness.[59] However, both of these approaches neglect Rousseau's view of happiness as predicated on the enjoyment of the particular pleasures of temperate sensuality.

The plausibility of my claim that Rousseau's solitary pursuit of *ataraxia* through Epicurean memorial *askesis* forms a coherent part of his wider system, in a sense, rests on the analysis of the preceding chapters. The most abstract version of Rousseau's state theory is grounded in temperance and requires an institutional expression of the general taste. Precisely how temperate sensuality might be cultivated will necessarily vary across particular contexts: his description of 'public joy' in *d'Alembert* was an attempt to educate his compatriots' judgement, and the collective pleasures of Geneva's men's clubs and republican festivals would seem to be compatible with those explored in his autobiographies. To draw this chapter to a conclusion, I want to note that, although Rousseau understood solitude to be compatible with some measure of sociable relations with others, he was nevertheless aware of the remaining tension with the political commitments of popular sovereignty. He adopted two main strategies to address that tension. The first was a theoretical interrogation of the possible analogy between individual happiness and the happiness of a people or nation. But he rejected the idea of 'public happiness' as 'in itself a chimera', dependent upon the happiness of each member of a given state; the best one could say was that a people's happiness was found in independence.[60] The second was a more practical consideration of the relationship between the individual solitaire and the political community. This latter approach is perhaps obvious for anyone who describes happiness as a kind of refined Epicureanism,

---

[58] Soni (2010): 431–444 provides an account of happiness in the *Social Contract* that adopts Strauss' historical narrative.

[59] Hasan (2018): 233–243.

[60] *CW*4:40–44/*OC*3:507–511.

THE MEMORIAL PRACTICE OF HAPPINESS 197

for it has long been wondered just how wide an Epicurean community of friends might extend.[61] Epicurus famously argued that politics was a prison from which we must escape. But while he certainly considered friendship as an alternative principle to justice, he also seems to have thought that it could, in principle, be extended to any number of individuals who adopt the same way of life.[62]

Rousseau's celebration of solitary happiness is tempered by his insistence on the necessity of active social engagement. As we have just seen, one way that he described happiness was as the experience of the sentiment of existence, that 'precious sentiment of peace and contentment which alone would suffice to make this existence dear and sweet to anyone able to spurn all the sensual and earthly impressions that constantly distract us from it and trouble the joy it could give us in this life'. This image of the happy man is contrasted with that of the vulgar Epicurean who is 'agitated by continual passions' and, with 'only an obscure and confused idea of it', is 'unable to feel its true charm' (R:46/1:1047). In a letter to Malesherbes, he claimed that he enjoyed this sentiment when 'the active life has nothing that tempts me' (LM:573/1:1132). If my reading of his autobiographical accounts of happiness as evidence of his engagement in something like a refined Epicurean memorial practice is persuasive, then we can conclude that he improved at that practice over time. It is particularly intriguing, then, that he cautioned readers of the 'Fifth Walk' that it would not be 'desirable in our present state of affairs that the avid desire for these sweet ecstasies should give people a distaste for the active life which their constantly recurring needs impose upon them' (R:46/1:1047). With this reference to the modern division of labour, Rousseau's accounts of solitary happiness over sixteen years culminate in a gesture towards the practical necessity of the active life with others.

While politics is unavoidable, solitude properly understood can nevertheless be politically benign. Only God is capable of 'absolute happiness'; individuals' basic physicality left them to experience 'human felicity' (E:210/4:303). In the modern division of labour, this meant that they were locked into a system of interdependence in securing their material needs. More than that, social habit rendered imaginary luxury goods genuine needs for modern agents. Seen in this light, the pursuit of happiness in solitude is but a 'compensation' for those

---

[61] See Benjamin Farrington, 'Friendship versus Justice', in *The Faith of Epicurus* (London: Weidenfeld and Nicolson, 1967): 20–32. Cf. Fonna Forman-Barzilai, *Adam Smith and the Circles of Sympathy: Cosmopolitanism and Moral Theory* (Cambridge: Cambridge University Press, 2010).

[62] Epicurus, 'Vatican Sayings', 58 in Inwood and Gerson eds (1988): 31. Cf. John M. Rist, 'Epicurus on Friendship', *Classical Philology* 75:2 (1980): 121–129.

'unfortunate' individuals who have been 'excluded from human society'. This comparison with the necessity of social interdependence presents solitude as a decidedly second-best way of life, available to those who 'can no longer do anything in this world useful or good for others or for himself'. In the modern world, then, the lifestyle previously described in laudatory terms as the necessary condition for happiness is, ultimately, of less worth than politics. But while idle isolation turns to enforced exclusion, it does not threaten shared values or political authority.

Indeed, Rousseau went beyond making solitude safe for politics by describing a form of solitude that was morally and politically useful. In the *Reveries*, he suggests that happiness could be approached without a physical movement away from society: with 'the assistance of a cheerful imagination', practised individuals could recognise and seize rare opportunities to draw pleasure from internal sources in the present moment regardless of their physical proximity to others (*R*:47/1:1047). His clearest example of this process of solitude within society comes not in the *Reveries* but in the last of his *Moral Letters* (1757–1758) to Sophie d'Houdetot. His description there of consulting one's conscience shares the narrative structure of his autobiographical discussions of happiness: Sophie is instructed to turn away from the ceaseless distractions of public opinion, and to imagine nature to temper *inquiétude*. She is instructed to 'seek out solitude'. Once more, this solitude prepares for engagement in memorial practice: just as the refined Epicurean enjoys internal goods, so is Sophie instructed, 'please yourself in retreat by preparing pleasant memories, by obtaining your own friendship for yourself there and making yourself into good enough company for yourself that you can do without any other'.[63]

Rousseau's instructions to Sophie contain his clearest account of the moral and political utility of solitude properly understood. In the first place, the conscience itself is only activated through social interaction: 'it is from the moral system formed by the double relation to oneself and to one's fellows that is born the natural impulse of the conscience'.[64] Moreover, solitude is properly understood as a movement not in physical but primarily moral space. Sophie learns to isolate her 'soul', to circumscribe her affective responses within their natural limits, and to maintain a state of 'languor and calm'. She does so by taking 'short retreats' without ever leaving society – she learns the art of being 'alone in the middle of the social world'. An appropriate understanding of solitude thus mitigates the threat of misanthropy, ensuring that the solitaire does not become 'taciturn and unsociable'. On the contrary,

---

[63] Rouseau, *CW*12:201/*OC*4:1116.
[64] *CW*12:196/*OC*4:1109. On the 'double relation', see Sonenscher (2020): 121–132.

THE MEMORIAL PRACTICE OF HAPPINESS   199

solitude properly understood transforms the habits of sociability from a source of *inquiétude* into a source of 'greater sweetness'. The memories recalled in consulting the conscience are memories of the pleasure felt upon acting virtuously with and towards others. Through virtuous practices of beneficence, for example, *amour-propre* is provided with a natural gratification, and the desire for superiority is channelled to socially beneficial ends. Finally, the particular pleasure one draws from a contented conscience is the 'natural pleasure of doing good'. And because this pleasure is the 'first foothold for all the other virtues', consulting a contented conscience ensures that 'solitude turns to the profit of humanity'.[65]

---

[65] *CW*12:199/*OC*4:1113–1114. Cf. *E*:453/*OC*4:600 for conscience as the basis of the Vicar's claim that 'man is by his nature sociable, or at least made to become so'. For comment, see Laurence D. Cooper, *Rousseau, Nature, and the Problem of the Good Life* (University Park: Penn State University Press, 1999): 84–85.

Afterword: Revisiting Rousseau's Paradoxes

Shortly after the publication of the *Letter to d'Alembert*, Rousseau was criticised for failing to recognise that the division of labour rendered public education impossible in modern republics. His response from late November 1758 recalls the discussion of taste with which this book began:

> There is a great difference between craftsmen of other countries and ours: a Genevan watchmaker is a man to be introduced to everything; a Parisian watchmaker is only good at talking about watches. A worker's education tends to train his fingers, nothing more. However, the citizen remains; right or wrong, the head and heart are formed; there is always time for this, and this is what the institution must provide for. Here, Sir, I have the same advantage over you in particulars as you have over me in general observations. This state of the artisans is mine, the one in which I was born, in which I should have lived, and which I left only for my misfortune. I received this public education, not through a formal institution, but through traditions and maxims which, transmitted from age to age, give youth the enlightenment it needs and the sentiments it should have.

Over the course of six chapters, we have become familiar with the intellectual framework Rousseau deploys here. Parisian craftsmen were like modern men of letters: subjects of corrupt monarchies, dissecting flies, with a myopic focus on their watches. Genevan watchmakers had able fingers but saw beyond their workbenches: they could be introduced to everything because, as republican citizens, they were adept with both microscopes and telescopes. The choice 'between the public education of the Greek republics and the domestic education of monarchies' was therefore not a binary one, either/or. The goal had to

AFTERWORD   201

be to find a balance – or 'precisely the middle ground' – between ancient *and* modern, head *and* heart, reason *and* sentiment.[1]

Rousseau was replying to a compatriot who framed the problem of modern pedagogy as an echo of what I have called Rousseau's problem of modern liberty. 'What suited the Greek republics no longer suits ours', wrote the physician Théodore Tronchin. In the ancient world, 'the arts and crafts were unworthy of the citizen, and the artisan could not be a citizen'. But in the modern world, 'the arts give each citizen an object that is personal to him, an object that occupies him entirely, and which, by the nature of things, becomes his principal object'. There could 'be no public education' in Geneva, for Tronchin, because 'it would be incompatible with the arts and crafts, and without the arts and crafts, Geneva would starve'.[2] As readers following my discussion to this point will anticipate, Rousseau accepted the premise: Tronchin had drawn 'a very judicious distinction', for the modern need of a developed division of labour meant that ancient priorities had to be inverted. But it should now be equally obvious that Rousseau would reject Tronchin's conclusion: just as the public good could still, however strangely, be generated from the private good, so would some form of public education continue in modern Geneva.

The dynamic at the heart of this epistolary exchange can readily be expressed in the terms of my reconstruction of Rousseau's politics of taste as a kind of modern Epicureanism. Tronchin agreed with Jacob Vernet's view, discussed in Chapter 3, that Geneva was filled with vulgar Epicureans. Fathers who 'play, drink, and smoke' raised children who pursue their 'budding passions' without 'restraint', and mothers had 'their amusements and their *circles* too'. As I have emphasised, Rousseau accepted that the division of labour compelled individuals to pursue their self-interest and, thus, the moderns were Epicureans. Bombarded by a commercial culture that separated utility and agreeableness as criteria of judgement, they were also, increasingly, vulgar ones. But where the former condition was an unavoidable structural feature of modern politics, the latter could be combated. Rousseau rejected Vernet's recourse to political theology, insisting instead that the *circles* could be reformed and public amusements developed to allow citizens to enjoy the true pleasures of nature, both privately and collectively. He rejected Tronchin's abandoning public for domestic education for the same reason. As we saw in Chapter 5, public education taught citizens to appreciate beauty, correcting their political and aesthetic judgement, preventing their taste for fashion, and cultivating their taste

---

[1] 'Rousseau à Tronchin, le 26 novembre 1758', *CC*5:241–243.
[2] 'Tronchin à Rousseau, le 13 novembre 1758', *CC*5:219–221.

for natural pleasures. It was still possible, in other words, for the moderns to become refined Epicureans.

I have argued here that the coherence of Rousseau's system can be clarified once we appreciate precisely this interest in how modern agents might become refined Epicureans. This argument is disputed in the literature, with many new interpretations of Rousseau emerging that challenge all or part of it. Some readers may be disappointed by a lack of direct confrontation with these books. But if my engagement has been somewhat oblique, that is because I have found it more useful to attempt to provide an intellectual context for the debates occurring in them. That is, approaching Rousseau from the historical perspective developed here allows us to see why the contemporary debate takes the form it does. Much of that debate centres on the positive dimensions of *amour-propre* – whether in the more neo-Kantian terms of moral and political virtue under a *Rechtsstaat* – or the more Hegelian terms of recognition theory.[3] While I have discussed these readings, I have been primarily concerned to describe the genesis of the intellectual framework that Rousseau brought to his theorisation of *amour-propre*. In Part I, I reconstructed a neglected aspect of Rousseau's argumentative context, presenting the history of modern Epicureanism as undergoing a shift from atheism to aesthetics. This allowed me, in Part II, to reconstruct Rousseau's system in a way that foregrounds some of its neglected aspects, like judgement, pleasure, the imagination, and happiness. I hope thereby to have provided a new perspective from which to view his system, one that will allow other readers to integrate elements of it that might otherwise seem incongruous – and that I may not have discussed. This ability to help us see something old in a new way, it seems to me, is one reason that the history of political thought is so useful for political theorists.

I also hope that this book will allow political theorists to appreciate that much of what seems new about modern politics is in fact rather old. Rousseau's theory of the modern state speaks directly to our era of so-called 'populism', in which both public discourse and academic analysis often plays out as a rehearsal of repetitive controversies over the respectively 'economic' or 'cultural' determinants of political behaviour. As Istvan Hont so forcefully demonstrated, the 'commercial future' that Rousseau and his contemporaries 'imagined as plausible' has 'become our historical present'.[4] Economic inequality, international competition, and political centralisation – war, trade, and debt – are the problems around which contemporary politics revolves and the core concerns

---

[3] Along with the works discussed in Chapter 5, see Avi Lifschitz, 'Adrastus versus Diogenes: Frederick the Great and Jean-Jacques Rousseau on self-love', in Lifschitz ed. (2016): 17–32.

[4] Hont (2005): 156.

AFTERWORD   203

of contemporary political theory. Seeing Rousseau as an Epicurean, internal critic of commercial society allows us to appreciate just how astute his analysis of these problems was. But as I have argued throughout this book, we need to see Rousseau as a refined Epicurean, specifically, fully to appreciate the centrality of aesthetics to his efforts at developing 'useful' responses to them. For Hont, thinking about the politics of modern states meant thinking about both the political limits to economic innovation and the economic limits to political transformation. For Rousseau, on the reading presented here, thinking about the politics of modern states also means appreciating the extent to which addressing the problems of economic justice requires serious consideration of the possibilities of aesthetic judgement. That Rousseau's problems remain our problems is a genuine and important insight. But what follows from it is not altogether straightforward. This book will be useful if it can show political theorists that framing contemporary politics as a binary choice between culture or economics is, to a large extent, useless – and push us to consider instead their necessary, and deeply complicated, interaction.

My own blend of theoretical precision, historical imagination, and realistic political knowledge is somewhat different than that in Rousseau's approach to useful political theory. But I also hope that this book will help to demonstrate that his attempt to be useful was somewhat more successful than is typically thought. For Tronchin, the idea of refined Epicureans in Geneva was fanciful proof that Rousseau was unaware of just how vulgar they had become. But Rousseau was clear – his 'advantage in particulars' was empirical knowledge derived from his class background. Asserting its relevance was part of his more general defence of the moral capacities of ordinary people that, we have seen, he consistently grounded in his refined Epicurean model of temperate sensuality. More recent critics argue that Rousseau's political theory is useless in contexts other than eighteenth-century Geneva. He was adamant that his proposals were 'intended only for small republics' not 'large nations' (D:213/1:935). He also suggested that the only modern country capable of receiving good laws was Corsica, seemingly because he thought it could be agriculturally self-sufficient (SC:78/3:391).[5] The choice Corsicans faced was genuinely a binary one: while agriculture and commerce occurred in every country, they could not 'flourish' 'simultaneously' because a new government had to support either one or the other. In conditions closer to the Neuchatel thought experiment than Geneva, developing commerce would be so 'destructive of agriculture' that they were 'incompatible'. This advice is usually taken as proof that Rousseau could not

---

[5] Cp. Mark J. Hill, 'Enlightened "Savages": Rousseau's Social Contract and the "Brave People" of Corsica', *History of Political Thought* 38:3 (2017): 462–493.

have been a theorist of politics in commercial societies and that his could not have been a theory of the modern state.[6] Yet he also advised the Corsicans to manage the money supply through a kind of central bank.[7] Indeed, the best recent scholarship emphasises his account of how money and exchange could be used to mitigate the inequalities that would arise through the division of labour even in Corsica.[8] While more work would need to be done in this connection, my analysis of Rousseau's politics of taste could be expanded to support this more nuanced revisionist interpretation.

Of course, I also hope that my discussion has been agreeable. It is a daunting task to hold a reader's attention for the length of even a relatively short book, especially one about as gifted a writer as Rousseau so evidently was. As Tronchin noted, even when one agrees with Rousseau, it is probably impossible to express oneself as well as he did. Rousseau concurred, noting that even those who find it 'easy to counterfeit his turns of phrases' would not be able to 'express his feelings' (D:212/1:934). He was probably right that being useful requires the ability to please. It seems fitting, then, to draw to a close by returning to some aspects of Rousseau's writing that I find particularly enjoyable.

There is a sense in which I have been attempting to grasp the ideas behind some of Rousseau's paradoxes. Temperate sensuality, the Epicureanism of reason, and the taste for virtue are paradoxical expressions in the literal sense of going against (*para*) received opinion (*doxa*): that sensual pleasure is necessarily intemperate; that Epicureanism is a philosophy of the body; or that taste and virtue are always in conflict. I have argued that the hedonist view of self-command behind these expressions is consistent with some important analytical claims that Rousseau explored paradoxical structures to advance. For him, asking 'which came first' – society or language, agriculture or industry, chickens or eggs – was a way to emphasise their mutual interdependence. Moreover, Rousseau's texts themselves have long been seen as embodying paradoxes. His distinction between good and bad taste resolved the apparent paradox of critiquing the corruption of contemporary taste while writing operas and novels. While this particular paradox first arose in the wake of the

---

[6] Douglass (2018): 507–508; Sagar (2020): 163.

[7] Rousseau, 'Plan for a Constitution of Corsica', *CW*11:127, 139, 152/3:905–906, 920, 935.

[8] Pierre Crétois, 'Rousseau ou l'anti-mercantiliste', James Swenson and Christophe Litwin, 'Les finances publiques comme clef du gouvernment', and Christophe Litwin, 'L'économie de la puissance civile', in Jean-Jacques Rousseau, *Affaires de Corse*, ed. James Litwin and Christophe Swenson (Paris: Vrin, 2018): 317–377. Cf. Sonenscher (2020): 77–87; Hansong Li, 'Timing the Laws: Rousseau's Theory of Development in Corsica', *The European Journal of the History of Economic Thought* 29:4 (2020): 648–679.

AFTERWORD 205

first *Discourse*, we can also see the second *Discourse* as being structured by some paradoxical aims. His critical aim is well known. By juxtaposing a conjectural natural state of human beings against an artificial state in which 'a handful of people abounds in superfluities while the starving multitude lacks in necessities' (*DI*:188/3:194) we come to see our societies as being deeply illegitimate. Rousseau insisted that critique did not need to be constructive to be useful. But I have also discussed his more directly normative aim of providing a new criterion by which to judge modern societies – the equilibrium between physical and moral inequality, wealth and virtue. Rousseau's view was that such a balance could be at least approximated. If his normative position has been overshadowed by his critique, that is perhaps less a paradox than a fault of his readers, or further evidence of his rhetorical prowess.

One way to appreciate the deep paradox of the second *Discourse* is to consider what we can call Rousseau's sentimental or indeed aesthetic aim. After reading his conjectural account of 'our history', he wrote, we may be so 'discontented with our present state' that we 'want to be able to go backward'. This 'desire' or 'sentiment' is 'the praise of our earliest forebears, the criticism of our contemporaries, and the dread of those who will have the misfortune to live after us' (133/3:133). Rousseau's stated aim is to induce in his readers the feeling that we must return to our original condition because this feeling is itself the greatest critique of our present age. But he then, famously, proceeds to explain precisely why it is impossible to go back: we cannot 'return to live like bears in the forest' because 'our passions have forever destroyed our original simplicity' (203/3:207). From this perspective, Rousseau wants us to feel how deeply paradoxical a situation we've managed to get ourselves into. He tells us that we cannot go back. And yet he writes an entire book designed to make us feel that we must go back. How are we to make sense of a book written to make us want the very thing that it also teaches us is impossible?

The arguments of this book can help us to see why Rousseau might have thought it would be useful for us to recognise our paradoxical situation of wanting what we cannot have. A core component of his critique of commerce is precisely that it constantly stimulates desires it is unable truly to satisfy. Attending the theatre in this context can be dangerous because, when the performance ends, we seek out immediate gratification. But reading a conjectural history that both makes us want what we cannot have and, crucially, explains why we cannot have it, may bring us to discover the illusory nature of the pleasures we typically pursue – and are encouraged to pursue. We might see this as a kind of 'Socratic sentimentalism', in which the discovery that we cannot have what we want brings us to question whether we do, in fact, want what we think we do.[9] By analogy with Socrates' pursuit of wisdom, Rousseau's aim is not only to get us to question our apparent desires but to question ourselves and the values that guide our lives – to examine and become aware of ourselves as sentimental, pleasure-seeking creatures.

Seen in this way, Rousseau's aesthetic aims in the second *Discourse* are also part of his refined Epicurean politics of taste. Bringing us to question ourselves and our desires does not stop us from desiring – the Stoic extirpation of passion is, after all, a chimera. Rather, feeling our way through the paradox forces us to ask ourselves: what *can* we have, what *do* we want, what *should* we do? Rousseau's readers are often frustrated by what they take to be insufficiently comprehensive answers to such questions. But we have seen that, like Epicurus before him, Rousseau moved beyond this sort of 'aporetic' questioning.[10] His denial of particular providence is one reason why the second *Discourse* was initially received as an Epicurean text. Along with rejecting original sin, this rescued human agency and responsibility: all the misery and inequality we confront today is the unfortunate result of our own actions through history. If that means that it is up to us to change it, then, as has long been recognised, Rousseau's real answer is that politics is all there is, and we would do well to get on with it. I have argued that another crucial part of that answer has been largely under-appreciated – that ordinary agents *can* have pleasure because everyone can, in principle, practise refined Epicureanism. The politics of modern commercial societies is necessarily a politics of taste. As we get on with it, then, we should start by considering – individually and collectively – what it might mean to turn away from false pleasures of fashion and vanity, and instead pursue real pleasures rooted in nature.

It is fitting to end this book by having come to see Rousseau's second *Discourse* as an aesthetic attempt to turn his readers from vulgar to refined Epicureanism. We have arrived at this view by exploring my central themes of pleasure and judgement; and it encapsulates my central argument – that reading Rousseau's political thought in the context of modern Epicureanism allows us better to appreciate the aesthetic dimensions of his internal critique of commercial society and, thereby, his theory of the modern state. Moreover, this view further demonstrates Rousseau's consistency, for it also coheres

---

[9] See, despite some difference in interpretation, Eve Grace, 'Rousseau's Socratic "sentimentalism"', in *The Rousseauian Mind*, ed. Eve Grace and Christopher Kelly (London: Taylor and Francis, 2019): 13–22. Cf. Miriam Leonard, 'Rousseau's Socrates between Cato and Christ', *History of Political Thought* 37 (2016): 32–45.

[10] Cp. F. Javier Campos-Daroca, 'Epicurus and the Epicureans on Socrates and the Socratics', in *Brill's Companion to the Reception of Socrates*, ed. Christopher Moore (Leiden: Brill, 2019): 237–265.

nicely with one of his final descriptions of his philosophical system. As he wrote in *Dialogues*, his 'system may be false' but the 'intention' behind it is clear: he sought 'to rectify the error of our judgments to delay the progress of our vices'. The *Discourses* were designed to 'destroy that magical illusion' that makes us vulgar Epicureans, stupidly admiring false pleasures and scorning natural ones. He reiterated that the human race was 'happier in its original constitution' and insisted, once again, that 'human nature does not go backward'. These were the 'principles' on which his system was based. And if such a 'doctrine' was 'to be of some utility to others', he concluded, it was in helping them to become refined Epicureans – that is, 'in changing the objects of their esteem and perhaps thus slowing down their decadence' (D:213/1:934–935). In a similar spirit, this book will be useful if it can help others to see Rousseau slightly differently. My reconstruction of his system will likely be unable to change some readers' estimation of it. But I hope that it will allow others better to appreciate Rousseau's politics of taste as a kind of modern Epicureanism.

Selected Bibliography

Primary Sources

(i) Rousseau

Jean-Jacques Rousseau, *Correspondence Complète de Jean-Jacques Rousseau*, 52 vols, ed. Ralph Alexander Leigh (Geneva: Institut de Musée Voltaire, 1965–1971; Oxford: Voltaire Foundation, 1972–1977).

Jean-Jacques Rousseau, 'Letter to François Joseph de Conzié', in *Rousseau: Lettres philosophiques*, ed. Jean-Francois Perrin (Paris: Librarie Générale Français, 2003 [1743]): 45–58 (45).

Jean-Jacques Rousseau, *Oeuvres complètes de Jean-Jacques Rousseau*, 5 vols, ed. Bernard Gagnebin and Marcel Raymond (Paris: Gallimard, 1959–1995).

Jean-Jacques Rousseau, *The Collected Writings of Rousseau*, 13 vols, ed. Christopher Kelly and Roger D. Masters (Hanover, NH: University Press of New England, 1990–2010).

Jean-Jacques Rousseau, *The Complete Dictionary of Music*, trans. W. Waring (London: J. French, 1779).

(ii) Other

Alexander Gottlieb Baumgarten, *Aesthetica*, Vol. 2 (Frankfurt/Oder: Kleyb, 1758).

Pierre Bayle, 'Epicurus', in *The Dictionary Historical and Critical of Mr Bayle*, trans. P. Desmaizeaux (London: Knapton et al., 1734).

Abbé Du Bos, *Critical Reflections on Poetry, Painting and Music*, trans. Thomas Nugent (London: J. Nourse, 1748).

Antoine-Gaspard Boucher d'Argis, 'Droit de la Nature, ou Droit naturel', in *Encyclopédie* (1755), 5: 131–134.

SELECTED BIBLIOGRAPHY

John Brown, *Essays on the Characteristics of the Earl of Shaftesbury* (London: C. Davis, 1750).

John Brown, *Thoughts on Civil Liberty, on Licentiousness, and Faction* (Dublin: White and Saint, 1765).

Johann Jakob Brucker, *The History of Philosophy, from the Earliest Times to the Beginning of the Present Century; Drawn up from Brucker's Historia Critica Philosophiae*, trans. and ed. William Enfield (London: J. Johnson, 1791).

Louis-Bertrand Castel, *Amusements du cœur et de l'esprit, Géométrie naturelle en dialogues, Dissertation philosophique et littéraire* (Paris, 1738).

Louis-Bertrand Castel, 'Lettre sur la politique dans ses rapports avec la physique', *Journal de Trévoux* (1725): xxi, 698–729.

Louis-Bertrand Castel, 'Lettres a M. l'abbé de Saint-Pierre sur la véritable cause primitive et insensible de la pesanteur en général et de la chute des corps en particulier', *Journal de Trévoux* (1731): xxii, 2084–2095; 1732.i, 57–59; 1732.ii, 221–240.

Louis-Bertrand Castel, *Lettres d'un académicien de Bordeaux sur le fonds de la musique: a l'occasion de la lettre de M. R*** contre la musique françoise*, 2 vols (Bibliothèque de l'Arsenal, Paris; Bibliothèque Royale de Belgique, Brussels).

Louis-Bertrand Castel, *L'homme moral opposé a l'homme physique de Monsieur R***: Où l'on réfute le Déisme du jour* (Toulouse, 1756).

Louis-Bertrand Castel, *Seconde lettre philosophique pour rassurer l'univers contre les critiques de la première. En réponse à MM. Les auteurs des Réflexions sur les ouvrages de littérature* (Paris: Prault père, 1737).

Jean de Castillon, *Discours sur l'origine de l'inegalite parmi les hommes. Pour servir de reponse au discours que M. Rousseau a publie sur le meme sujet* (Amsterdam, 1756).

Abraham-Joseph Chaumeix, *Préjugés légitimes contre l'encyclopédie; et Essai de Refutation de ce Dictionnaire*, Vol. 1 (Brussels: Hérissant, 1758).

Cicero, *De finibus bonorum et malorum*, trans. H. Rackham (London: William Heinemann, 1940).

Cicero, *On the Nature of the Gods*, trans. H. Rackham (Cambridge, MA: Harvard University Press, 1933).

Cicero, *Tusculan Disputations*, trans. J. E. King (London: Harvard University Press, 1971).

Etienne Bonnot de Condillac, *Essay on the Origin of Human Knowledge*, ed. and trans. Hans Aarsleff (Cambridge: Cambridge University Press, 2001 [1746]).

Jean-Pierre de Crousaz, *A commentary on Mr Pope's principles of morality, or Essay on man*, trans. anonymous (London, 1742).

210 SELECTED BIBLIOGRAPHY

Denis Diderot, *Diderot's Early Philosophical Writings*, trans. Margaret Jourdain (London: Open Court, 1916): 33.

Denis Diderot, 'Droit Naturel', *Encyclopédie* (1755b), 5: 115–116.

Denis Diderot, 'Epicuréisme ou Epicurisme', in *Encyclopédie, ou dictionnaire raisonné des sciences, des arts et des métiers*, ed. Denis Diderot and Jean le Rond d'Alembert, 17 vols (Paris, 1751–1772 (1755a)): 5: 779–785.

Denis Diderot (attributed), 'Inquiétude', in *Encyclopédie* (8): 773.

Denis Diderot (attributed), 'Rêver', in *Encyclopédie* (14): 228.

Epicurus, 'Letter to Herodotus', 'Letter to Menoeceus', 'Sovereign Maxims', in Diogenes Laertius, *Lives of Eminent Philosophers*, Vol. II, trans. R. D. Hicks (Cambridge, MA: Harvard University Press, 2000).

Epicurus, 'Vatican Sayings', in *Hellenistic Philosophy: Introductory Readings*, trans. and ed. Brad Inwood and L. P. Gerson (Indianapolis, IN: Hackett, 1988).

Francois de Fénelon, *Telemachus, Son of Ulysses*, ed. Patrick Riley (Cambridge: Cambridge University Press, 1994).

Stéphanie Félicité de Genlis, *Alphonsine, ou la tendresse maternelle*, Vol. 1/4 (Paris: H. Nicolle, 1806).

Claude-Adrien Helvétius, *De l'esprit; or Essays on the Mind and Its Several Faculties* (London: M. Jones, 1809).

Chevalier Louis de Jaucourt, 'Penser, Songer, Rêver', in *Encyclopédie, ou dictionnaire raisonné des sciences, des arts et des métiers, etc.*, ed. Denis Diderot and Jean le Rond d'Alembert. University of Chicago: ARTFL Encyclopédie Project (Autumn 2017 Edition), Robert Morrissey and Glenn Roe (eds), (12): 311.

Chevalier Louis de Jaucourt, 'Tempérance', in *Encyclopédie, ou dictionnaire raisonné des sciences, des arts et des métiers*, ed. Denis Diderot and Jean le Rond d'Alembert (Paris: Briasson, 1751–1772): 16:59.

Immanuel Kant, 'Conjectural Beginning of Human History', in Immanuel Kant, *Anthropology, History, and Education*, ed. Günter Zöller and Robert Louden, trans. Allen W. Wood (Cambridge: Cambridge University Press, 2007).

Immanuel Kant, *Critique of the Power of Judgment* (Cambridge: Cambridge University Press, 2000).

Immanuel Kant, *Lectures on Ethics*, ed. P. Heath and J. B. Schneewind, trans. P. Heath (Cambridge: Cambridge University Press, 1997).

Immanuel Kant, *Notes and Fragments*, ed. Paul Guyer, trans. Guyer et al. (Cambridge: Cambridge University Press, 2005).

Immanuel Kant, *Sämmtliche Werke*, ed. G Hartenstein, Vol. VIII (Leipzig: L. Voss, 1868).

John Locke, *Essay Concerning Human Understanding*, ed. Roger Woolhouse (Oxford: Penguin, 1997).

SELECTED BIBLIOGRAPHY 211

Lucretius, *On the Nature of Things*, trans. W. H. D. Rouse, revised by Martin Ferguson Smith (Cambridge, MA: Harvard University Press, 1992).

Bernard Mandeville, *The Fable of the Bees: Or, Private Vices, Publick Benefits*, ed. F. B. Kaye, 2 vols (London: Oxford University Press, 1924).

Michel de Montaigne, *The Complete Essays of Montaigne*, trans. Donald M Frame (Stanford, CA: Stanford University Press, 1966).

Charles de Secondat, baron de Montesquieu, *Considerations sur les causes de la grandeur des Romains, et leur décadence* (Paris: Didot, 1802).

Laurence Nihell, *Rational Self-Love; or, a Philosophical and Moral Essay on the Natural Principles of Happiness and Virtue. With Reflections on the Various Systems of Philosophers* (London: W. Griffin, 1770).

Plutarch, *Moralia*, Vol. XIV, trans. Benedict Einarson and Phillip H. De Lacy (London: Harvard University Press, 1967).

Polybius, *The Complete Histories of Polybius*, trans. W. R. Paton (London: Loeb, 1922).

Alexander Pope, *Essai sur l'homme*, prose trans. Silhouette (Paris, 1736).

Samuel Pufendorf, *Le droit de la nature et des gens*, trans. Jean Barbeyrac (Amsterdam: Kuyper, 1706).

Samuel Pufendorf, *Of the Law of Nature and Nations*, trans. Mr. Carew (London: Knapton, 1729).

François Quesnay, 'Evidence', in Diderot and Jean le Rond d'Alembert (1756), 6: 146–157.

Hermann Samuel Reimarus, *The Principal Truths of Natural Religion, Defended and Illustrated, in Nine Dissertations: Wherein the Objections of Lucretius, Buffon, Maupertuis, Rousseau, La Mettrie, and Other Antient and Modern Followers of Epicurus Are Considered, and Their Doctrines Refuted*, trans. R. Wynne (London: B. Law, 1766).

Adam Smith, *An Inquiry into the Nature and Causes of the Wealth of Nations* (Indianapolis, IN: Liberty Fund, 1982).

Adam Smith, *Essays on Philosophical Subjects*, ed. W. P. D. Wightman (Oxford: Oxford University Press, 1980).

Adam Smith, *Lectures on Rhetoric and Belles Lettres*, ed. J. C. Bryce (Oxford: Oxford University Press, 2014).

Adam Smith, *The Theory of Moral Sentiments*, ed. D. D. Raphael and A. L. Macfie (Oxford: Oxford University Press, 2014).

Jacob Vernet, *Instruction chrétienne*, Vol. 1/5 (Geneva: Gosse, 1752).

Jacob Vernet, *Lettres critiques d'un votageur anglois sur l'article Geneve du Dictionnaire encyclopédique, et sur la Lettre de M. d'Alembert à Rousseau touchant les spectacles* (Copenhagen: Claude Philibert, 1766).

212 SELECTED BIBLIOGRAPHY

Jacob Vernet, *Réflexions sur les moeurs, sur la religion, et sur le culte* (Paris: Claude Philibert, 1769).

William Warburton, *A Critical and Philosophical Enquiry Into the Causes of Prodigies and Miracles, as Related by Historians: With an Essay Towards Restoring a Method and Purity in History*, 2 vols (London: Thomas Corbett, 1727).

William Warburton, *A Vindication of Mr. Pope's Essay on Man, from the Misrepresentations of M. de Crousaz. By the Author of The Divine Legation of Moses Demonstrated. In Six Letters* (London: J. Robinson, 1740).

Secondary Sources

Arash Abizadeh, 'Banishing the Particular: Rousseau on Rhetoric, Patrie, and the Passions', *Political Theory* 29:4 (2001): 556–582.

Hannah Arendt, *Lectures on Kant's Political Philosophy* (Chicago, IL: University of Chicago Press, 2014).

Blaise Bachofen, 'La Lettre á d'Alembert: principes du droit poétique?', in *Rousseau, politique et esthétique: Sur la Lettre á d'Alembert*, ed. B. Bachofen and B. Bernardi (Paris: ENS Editions, 2011): 71–92.

Annie Becq, *Genèse de l'esthétique française moderne 1680–1814* (Paris: Albin Michel, 1994).

Moishe Black, 'Lucretius tells Diderot: Here's the Plan', *Diderot Studies* 28 (2000): 39–58.

Moishe Black, 'Lucretius's Venus Meets Diderot', *Diderot Studies* XXVII (1997): 29–40.

Jean H. Bloch, 'Rousseau and Helvétius on Innate and Acquired Traits: The Final Stages of the Rousseau-Helvétius Controversy', *Journal of the History of Ideas* 40:1 (1979): 21–41.

Christopher Brooke, 'Aux limites de la volonté générale: silence, exil, ruse et désobéissance dans la pensée politique de Rousseau', *Les Études philosophiques* 83:4 (2007): 425–444.

Christopher Brooke, *Philosophic Pride: Stoicism and the Politics of Self-Love from Lipsius to Rousseau* (Princeton, NJ: Princeton University Press, 2012).

Ernst Cassirer, *The Question of Jean-Jacques Rousseau*, trans. Peter Gay (New York, Columbia University Press, 1954).

Joshua Cohen, 'An Epistemic Conception of Democracy', *Ethics* 97 (1986): 26–38.

N. J. H. Dent, *Rousseau: Introduction to his Psychological, Social and Political Theory* (Oxford: Blackwell, 1988).

Robert Derathé, *Jean-Jacques Rousseau et la science politique de son temps* (Paris: PUF, 1950).

SELECTED BIBLIOGRAPHY 213

Robert Derathé, *Le rationalisme de Jean-Jacques Rousseau* (Paris: PUF, 1948).

Jacques Derrida, *Of Grammatology*, trans. Gayatri Charkravorty Spivak (London: Johns Hopkins University Press, 1974).

Norman DeWitt, *Epicurus and his Philosophy* (Minneapolis: University of Minnesota Press, 1964).

Gabriela Domecq, 'L'ordre du goût chez Rousseau', *Astérion: philosophie, histoire des idées, pensée politique* 16 (2017): https://journals.openedition.org/asterion/2977?lang=en

Robin Douglass, *Rousseau and Hobbes: Nature, Free Will, and the Passions* (Oxford: Oxford University Press, 2015).

John Dunn, *The Cunning Of Unreason Making Sense Of Politics* (London: Basic Books, 2000).

John Dunn, 'The Identity of the History of Ideas', *Philosophy* 43:164 (1968): 85–104.

C. A. Fusil, 'Lucrèce et les littérateurs, poètes et artistes du XVIIIe siècle', *Revue d'histoire littéraire de la France* 37 (1930): 161–176.

C. A. Fusil, 'Lucrèce et les philosophes du XVIIIe siècle', *Revue d'histoire littéraire de la France* 35 (1928): 194–210.

David Gauthier, *Rousseau: The Sentiment of Existence* (Cambridge: Cambridge University Press, 2006).

Etienne Gilson, 'La méthode de M. Wolmar', in *Les idées et les lettres*, ed. Etienne Gilson (Paris: Vrin, 1932): 275–298.

Victor Goldschmitt, *La doctrine d'Epicure et le droit* (Paris: Vrin, 1977).

Victor Gourevitch, 'Rousseau on Providence', *Review of Metaphysics* 53 (2000): 565–611.

Victor Gourevitch, 'Rousseau's Pure State of Nature', *Interpretation* 16 (1988): 23–59.

Victor Gourevitch, 'The "First Times" in Rousseau's Essay on the Origin of Languages', *Graduate Philosophy Journal* 11 (1986): 123–146.

Bernard N. Grofman and Scott L. Feld, 'Rousseau's General Will: A Condorcetian Perspective', *American Political Science Review* 82:2 (1988): 567–576.

Pierre Hadot, *Philosophy as a Way of Life: Spiritual Exercises from Socrates to Foucault*, ed. and trans. Michael Chase and Arnold Davidson (Oxford: Blackwell, 1995).

A. O. Hirschman, *The Passions and the Interests: Political Arguments for Capitalism Before Its Triumph* (Princeton, NJ: Princeton University Press, 1977).

Istvan Hont, *Jealousy of Trade: International Competition and the Nation-state in Historical Perspective* (Cambridge, MA: Harvard University Press, 2005).

Istvan Hont, *Politics in Commercial Society* (London: Harvard University Press, 2015).

SELECTED BIBLIOGRAPHY

Istvan Hont, 'The Early Enlightenment Debate on Commerce and Luxury', in *The Cambridge History of Eighteenth-Century Political Thought*, ed. Mark Goldie and Robert Wokler (Cambridge: Cambridge University Press, 2006): 377–418.

Istvan Hont and Michael Ignatieff, *Wealth and Virtue: The Shaping of Political Economy in the Scottish Enlightenment* (Cambridge: Cambridge University Press, 1986).

Christopher Kelly, *Rousseau's Exemplary Life: The Confessions as Political Philosophy* (Ithaca, NY: Cornell University Press, 1987).

Duncan Kelly, *Propriety of Liberty: Persons, Passions and Judgement in Modern Political Thought* (Oxford: Princeton University Press, 2011).

Nannerl Keohane, *Philosophy and the State in France: The Renaissance to the Enlightenment* (Princeton, NJ: Princeton University Press, 1980).

Paul Oskar Kristeller, 'The Modern System of the Arts: A Study in the History of Aesthetics Part I', *Journal of the History of Ideas* 12:4 (1951): 496–527.

Paul Oskar Kristeller, 'The Modern System of the Arts: A Study in the History of Aesthetics (II)', *Journal of the History of Ideas* 13:1 (1952): 17–46.

Jean Lafond, 'Augustinisme et épicurisme au XVIIe siècle', in *L'homme et son image: morales et littératures de Montaigne à Mandeville* (Paris: Champion, 1996): 345–368.

Jean Lafond, *La Rochefoucauld, augustinisme et littérature* (Paris: Klincksieck, 1977).

John Lough, *Essays on the Encyclopédie of Diderot and D'Alembert* (Oxford: Oxford University Press, 1968).

Pierre-Maurice Masson, 'Rousseau Contre Helvétius', *Revue d'histoire Littéraire de La France* 18:1 (1911): 103–124.

Roger D. Masters, *The Political Philosophy of Rousseau* (Princeton, NJ: Princeton University Press, 1968).

Robert Mauzi, *La philosophie de l'inquiètude dans la literature et philosophie francaise au XVIIIe siècle* (Paris: A. Colin, 1960).

Phillip Mitsis, *Epicurus' Ethical Theory: The Pleasures of Invulnerability* (Ithaca, NY: Cornell University Press, 1988).

James Moore, 'Utility and Humanity: The Quest for the Honestum in Cicero, Hutcheson, and Hume', *Utilitas* 14:3 (2002): 365–386.

Jean Morel, 'Recherches sur les sources du Discours de l'inégalité', *Annales de la Société J.-J. Rousseau* V (1909): 119–198.

Frederick Neuhouser, 'Freedom, Dependence, and the General Will', *The Philosophical Review* 102:3 (1993): 363–395.

Frederick Neuhouser, *Rousseau's Theodicy of Self-Love: Evil, Rationality, and the Drive for Recognition* (Oxford: Oxford University Press, 2008).

SELECTED BIBLIOGRAPHY

Helen F. North, *Sophrosyne: Self-Knowledge and Self-Restraint in Greek Literature* (Ithaca, NY: Cornell University Press, 1966): 150.

Ada Palmer, *Reading Lucretius in the Renaissance* (Cambridge, MA: Harvard University Press, 2014).

John Pocock, *The Machiavellian Moment: Florentine Political Thought and the Atlantic Republican Tradition* (Princeton, NJ: Princeton University Press, 2016).

Jacques Proust, *Diderot et l'Encyclopédie* (Paris: A. Colin, 1962).

Gabriella Radica, 'Le vocabulaire mathématique dans le Contrat social, II, 3', in *Rousseau et les sciences*, ed. B. Bensaude-Vincent and B. Bernardi (Paris: L'Harmattan, 2003): 257–275.

Helena Rosenblatt, *Rousseau and Geneva: From the First Discourse to the Social Contract, 1749–1762* (Cambridge: Cambridge University Press, 1997).

Paul Sagar, *Adam Smith Reconsidered: History, Liberty and the Foundations of Modern Politics* (Princeton, NJ: Princeton University Press, 2022).

Stephen G. Salkever, 'Rousseau & the Concept of Happiness', *Polity* 11:1 (1978): 27–45.

Denise Schaeffer, *Rousseau on Education, Freedom, and Judgment* (University Park: Pennsylvania State University Press, 2014).

David Sedley, *Lucretius and the Transformation of Greek Wisdom* (Cambridge: Cambridge University Press, 1998).

Larry Shiner, *The Invention of Art: A Cultural History* (Chicago: University of Chicago Press, 2003).

Judith N. Shklar, *Men and Citizens: A Study of Rousseau's Social Theory* (Cambridge: Cambridge University Press, 1969).

Quentin Skinner, 'Meaning and Understanding in the History of Ideas', *History and Theory* 8:1 (1969): 3–53.

Quentin Skinner, 'The State', in *Political Innovation and Conceptual Change*, ed. Terence Ball, James Farr, and Russell L. Hanson (Cambridge: Cambridge University Press, 1989): 90–131.

Michael Sonenscher, *Jean-Jacques Rousseau: The Division of Labour, the Politics of the Imagination and the Concept of Federal Government* (Leiden: Brill, 2020).

Michael Sonenscher, *Sans-Culottes: An Eighteenth-Century Emblem in the French Revolution* (Princeton, NJ: Princeton University Press, 2008).

Michael Sonenscher, 'Sociability, Perfectibility and the Intellectual Legacy of Jean-Jacques Rousseau', *History of European Ideas* 41:5 (2015): 683–698.

Céline Spector, 'De Rousseau à Smith: Esthétique démocratique de la sensibilité et théorie économiste de l'esthétique', in *La valeur de l'art. Exposition, marché, critique et public au dix-huitième siècle*, ed. J. Rasmussen (Paris: Champion, 2009): 215–244.

Gopal Sreenivasan, 'What Is the General Will?', *The Philosophical Review* 109:4 (2000): 545–581.

Jean Starobinski, *Jean-Jacques Rousseau, Transparency and Obstruction*, trans. Arthur Goldhammer (Chicago: Chicago University Press, 1988).

Jean Starobinski, *Le remède dans le mal* (Paris: Gallimard, 1989).

Leo Strauss, *Natural Right and History* (Chicago: University of Chicago Press, 1953).

Leo Strauss, 'On the Intention of Rousseau', *Social Research* 14:4 (1947): 455–487.

Leo Strauss, *Seminar in Political Philosophy: Rousseau*, ed. J. Marks (Estate of Leo Strauss, 2014), (online): https://leostrausscenter.uchicago.edu/

Ann Thomson, *Bodies of Thought: Science, Religion, and the Soul in the Early Enlightenment* (Oxford: Oxford University Press, 2008).

Richard Tuck, 'Rousseau and Hobbes: The Hobbesianism of Rousseau', in *Thinking with Rousseau*, ed. Helena Rosenblatt and Paul Schweigert (Cambridge: Cambridge University Press, 2017): 37–62.

Richard Tuck, *The Rights of War and Peace: Political Thought and the Intellectual Order from Grotius to Kant* (Oxford: Oxford University Press, 1999).

Richard Tuck, *The Sleeping Sovereign: The Invention of Modern Democracy* (Cambridge: Cambridge University Press, 2015).

James Warren, *The Pleasures of Reason in Plato, Aristotle, and the Hellenistic Hedonists* (Cambridge: Cambridge University Press, 2014).

Richard Whatmore, *Against War and Empire: Geneva, Britain, and France in the Eighteenth* (New Haven, CT: Yale University Press, 2012).

David Lay Williams, *Rousseau's Platonic Enlightenment* (University Park: Pennsylvania State University Press, 2007).

Robert Wokler, 'Rousseau's Pufendorf: Natural Law and the Foundations of Commercial Society', *History of Political Thought* 15:3 (1994): 373–402.

Index

aesthetic judgement
  aesthetic judgement-political
    judgement distinctions, 136–7,
    163–5
  amour-propre's origins in, 93, 130,
    137–45
  censorship and, 146–7, 162–3
  in *D'Alembert*, 118–19, 144–5
  general taste and, 136, 148–9,
    150–1, 152–3, 162
  Kantian readings of, 118, 135–6,
    164
  moral freedom and, 4–5, 116–17,
    118–19
  political freedom and, 4–5
  sentiment in, 136
  in state theory, 131
aesthetics
  aesthetic dimensions of political
    theory, 17, 91, 203
  of *amour-propre*, 93, 130, 137–45
  emergence of, 16
  Epicureanism's shift from atheism to
    aesthetics, 55, 67, 89
  philosophical importance of, 68–9
  and the reception of Epicureanism,
    55, 67
  temperate sensuality and, 172–3
agreeableness
  judgements of utility and

agreeableness, 99–100, 132, 136,
  146
of the practice of reverie, 167–8
useful-agreeable distinction in
  commercial societies, 98–100,
  101–2, 103–4, 110–11
useful-agreeable distinction in public
  settings, 124–5
useful-agreeable relationship, 92–3,
  95–6, 117
amour de soi, 138, 139, 141
amour-propre
  aesthetic dimension, 20, 93, 130,
    137–45
  competitive psychological dynamics,
    110–11, 139
  corrupt/inflamed form of, 139,
    141
  in *Emile*, 138, 140–1, 142, 143
  in *Julie*, 141–3
  pity's tempering of, 58–9, 70, 112
  Pope's account of, 76
  relationship to pleasure, 110–11,
    137
  revisionist readings of, 139–41, 142,
    143–4, 202
  in the second *Discourse*, 137, 139
  and self-liking in Mandeville, 70–1
  simple/basic form of, 139, 141
  vanity-pride distinction, 138–9

INDEX

Ancients
    ancient/modern periodisation,
       14–16, 91, 120, 201
    ancient-modern theatre distinction,
       120–2
    as distinct from the moderns, 13–14
    Epicurean morals and the collapse of
       Rome, 30–1
    Greek *sophrosyne*, 21–4
    imaginative return to in political
       theory, 11–14
    as sources for Rousseau, 18–19
    sovereignty/government distinction,
       15
Arendt, Hannah, 9, 129, 136, 164
Aristotle, 120
ataraxia, 177, 181, 196
atheism
    atheistic materialism, 59
    an Epicurean society of, 46
    Epicureanism's shift from atheism to
       aesthetics, 55, 67, 89
autobiographies
    accounts of happiness, 174–8
    community of readers for, 194–5
    as an Epicurean memorial practice,
       168–70, 176–7, 178, 189, 192–3,
       197
    the 'Fifth Walk' (*Reveries*), 188–91,
       192, 197
    happiness on the Île de Saint-Pierre
       (Book XII), 189–90, 191–2
    individual flourishing, 167, 169
    interpretations of, 167
    pedagogical aims, 174, 179, 195
    presentations of *inquiétude*, 181–2,
       189, 190–1
    refined Epicureanism, 166–7, 169,
       172
    within Rousseau's *oeuvre*, 167
    sentiments accessed through,
       188–9
    see also Confessions, The

Barbeyrac, Jean, 36–7
Bayle, Pierre, 28, 41, 45–7, 48–9
Bernier, François, 33
Boucher d'Argis, Antoine-Gaspard,
    37, 39
Brown, John, 34, 35–6, 37
Brucker, Johann Jakob
    as Diderot's source material, 28, 41,
       44–5, 47–8, 51
    divine happiness and denial of
       providence, 47–8
    immortal soul/corporeal soul
       debates, 49–50

Castel, Louis Bertrand, 56, 57–9, 64
Castillon, Jean de
    natural law critique of the second
       Discourse, 56, 59–63, 66, 105–6
    reaffirmation of sociability, 60–1,
       93–4
censorship
    aesthetic judgement and, 146–7,
       162–3
    as an articulation of the general
       taste, 131, 147
    censorial institutions, 6
    in *D'Alembert*, 73
    popular judgements of beauty, 137,
       146
    in the *Social Contract*, 131, 137,
       146–7, 162–3
Charon, Pierre, 33
Chaumeix, Abraham-Joseph de, 50, 51
Cicero, 94, 99, 105, 193
commercial society
    agriculture and industry imbalance,
       92, 96–7
    challenges of moral obligation and
       social cohesion, 31–2
    economics as a matter of state, 14
    first *Discourse* critique of, 92, 103–4
    in modern state theories, 90–2,
       99–100

INDEX

219

and Rousseau's critique of vulgar
   Epicureanism, 97–8
sociability in, 55, 91
useful-agreeable distinction, 98–100,
   101–2, 103–4, 110–11
utility and commercial sociability in
   the second *Discourse*, 104–13
see also luxury debates
Condillac, Etienne Bonnot de, 40, 168
Confessions, The
   comparison and self-knowledge, 174
   happiness on the Île de Saint-Pierre,
      189–90, 191–2
   Rousseau's methodology, 17–18
   Rousseau's personal and authorial
      originality, 17
Conzié, François Joseph de, 75–6
Corsica, 138, 139, 162, 203–4
Costa, Uriel da, 32–3
Crousaz, Jean-Pierre de, 78, 79, 80,
   81–2

D'Alembert see Letter to d'Alembert on the
   Theatre
democracy
   democratic accounts of general will,
      93, 153–4, 155–6, 158–9, 160–1,
      162
   political judgement in Rousseau's
      thought, 129–30, 131
   theories of democracy and
      judgement, 128–9
Dialogues see Rousseau, Judge of Jean-
   Jacques: Dialogues
Dictionary of Music, 147–8, 159
Diderot, Denis
   critiques of the *Encyclopédie*, 50–2
   deism, 42–3
   divine happiness and denial of
      providence, 47–9
   Encyclopédie entry on 'Epicuréisme',
      28, 44–52, 89
   human natural sociability, 39

immortal soul/corporeal soul
   debates, 41–2, 44, 45, 49–50
intelligent design debates, 42–3
Letter on the Blind, 43
Lucretius's influence on, 41
materialism, 39–40, 41–4, 48–9
as a modern Epicurean, 35, 41–4
Pensées philosophiques, 41–2, 47
use of Brucker as source, 28, 41,
   44–5, 47–8, 51
Discourse on the Origin and Foundations
   of Inequality Among Men see
   second *Discourse*
Discourse on the Sciences and the Arts see
   first *Discourse*
Douglas, Robin, 72

economics
   ancient/modern periodisation,
      14–16, 91
   as a matter of state, 14, 16
   the modern's focus on private
      interest, 15
education
   civic education, 132, 143
   and the cultivation of refined
      Epicureans, 201–2
   in *Emile*, 132, 143, 166
   judgements of utility and
      agreeableness, 99–100, 132
   in *Julie*, 114–15
   as a path to happiness, 95
   public education, 132, 144, 200–1
Emile
   account of judgement, 84, 133–4,
      136
   account of personal identity, 176–7
   and accusations of plagiarism of
      Seneca, 18
   amour-propre in, 138, 140–1, 142,
      143
   the criterion of voluptuousness in
      general taste, 150, 159

Emile (cont.)
education in, 132, 143, 166
general taste's formation, 148–50
path to happiness, 113–14, 175
within Rousseau's *oeuvre*, 6, 171
Rousseau's utilitarian intentions for,
    10–11, 195
vulgar/refined distinction, 94–5
Epicurean, term, 28
Epicureanism
account of temperance, 23–4, 27
ataraxia, 177, 181, 196
Diderot on 'Epicuréisme', 28,
    44–52
divine happiness and denial of
    providence, 45–9, 52, 54
in eighteenth-century French
    thought, 30–40, 52, 67
in eighteenth-century thought,
    25–9, 30, 89
eighteenth-century use of the term,
    20–1
Epicureans as Stoics, 4, 27
epistemology, 29
essentialist claims of an Epicurean
    tradition, 25–7, 28, 40, 54, 89
in foreign thought, 34–6
hedonistic moral psychology, 28
historiographical debates, 29–30,
    52–3
and human natural sociability, 28,
    36–9, 40, 52
intellectual history of, 29–30
as irreligious, 34–5, 40, 41–2
isonomia concept, 105
materialist natural philosophy, 28,
    41–4
materiality of the soul, 49–50, 52
the nature and the condition of the
    Gods, 45–6
physics, 29, 32–3
pursuit of pleasure, 30–1, 40, 67
recollected pleasure, 183–4

Rousseau's reception as, 53, 54–5,
    56–67
Rousseau's relationship with, 19–24,
    85–6, 161–2
secular political authority and, 54
in seventeenth-century thought,
    32–4
shift from atheism to aesthetics, 55,
    67, 89
sources, 29–30
see also refined Epicureanism; vulgar
    Epicureanism
Epicureanism of reason, 4, 21, 23–4,
    27
Epicurus of Samos, 29

Fénelon, Archbishop, 71–2
first *Discourse*
Castel's critique, 57
criterion of political judgement,
    110, 132
critique of commerce, 92, 103–4
critique of modern luxury, 18
critiques of, 102
excerpts of *Essais* in, 18
as part of Rousseau's system of
    writing, 6
Rousseau's utilitarian intentions for,
    10, 195
theory of taste, 98–104
useful-agreeable distinction in
    commercial societies, 101–2,
    103–4, 116
utility of cultural productions, 103,
    123

Gassendi, Pierre, 33–4, 45, 51
general taste
aesthetic judgement and, 136,
    148–9, 150–1, 152–3, 162
analogy with general will, 127,
    130–2, 147, 151–2, 156, 159,
    161, 162, 163, 164–5

censorship as an articulation of, 131,
147
in *D'Alembert*, 120–2, 130–1
democratic reading of, 145–6
fashion's corruption of, 150–1, 152,
154
formation of, 148–52
the majority vote and, 147–8, 159
and the people's judgement, 120,
128
Rousseau's account of, 147–8
transcendent interpretation of,
152–3
voluptuousness and, 149–51, 159
general will
analogy with general taste, 127,
130–2, 147, 151–2, 156, 159,
161, 162, 163, 164–5
conventionalist, Epicurean reading
of, 20, 39, 91
democratic accounts, 93, 153–4,
155–6, 158–9, 160–1, 162
as distinct from the will of all,
156–7, 158
faction's corruption of, 150, 151,
159–61
interpretations of, 153–4
and the legal standard of justice, 90,
147, 157–8
as a model of popular political
judgement, 128
political freedom and, 21, 113,
166
political judgement and, 113, 128,
130, 135, 136, 150–1, 161–2,
163
problem of outvoted minorities,
148, 154–6
role of reason, 136
self-love in human motivation,
34–5, 37
transcendent interpretation of, 153,
155–6, 157–9, 161, 162

Geneva
citizen-women's role as moderators
of taste, 112–13
compared to Paris, 3, 5, 122, 124
compared to Sparta, 123, 124
judgement of pleasure, 75, 92–3,
96–7
modern citizens of, 13–14
political constitution, 12
republican festivals, 124–5
republican politics, 3, 11, 12, 107
as a site of refined Epicurean
patriotism, 123–4
women's moral authority, 96,
112–13, 116
*see also Letter to d'Alembert on the
Theatre*
Genlis, Stéphanie Félicité, Comtesse
de, 83

happiness
to combat vulgar Epicureanism,
169, 197
divine happiness and denial of
providence, 45–9, 52, 54
as an Epicurean memorial practice,
168–70, 176–7, 184–7, 192–3,
197
equilibrium of desires and faculties,
114, 175–6, 178, 182, 183,
189–90
freedom-happiness relationship,
179–80, 182–3
individual flourishing in the
autobiographies, 167, 169, 179
and personal solitude, 178, 182–3,
185, 189–90, 193, 196–8
the practice of reverie, 167–9, 184
removal of pain and *inquiétude*,
180–3, 189, 190–1
and the restriction of the
imagination, 168–9, 175–6, 178,
184–7

222 INDEX

happiness (*cont.*)
  Rousseau's paths to, 95, 113–14,
    167, 169, 179, 182–3, 191–2
  secured through writing, 188–93
  sentiments of, 169, 188–9
  state power and, 196–7
  temperate sensuality's role in, 174–5
Hayer, Jean-Nicolas, 50–1
hedonism
  Epicurean hedonism, 26, 28, 29, 31,
    53
  and human agency, 73–4
  refined Epicureanism and, 55–6, 70,
    96, 113–14, 116, 128, 169
  Rousseau's paradoxical exploration
    of, 204
  temperate sensuality and, 169, 173
  theory of temperance, 4, 23–4
Helvétius, Claude Adrien
  De L'Ésprit, 50, 51, 85, 133
  on judgement, 133
  on memory, 183
  as a modern Epicurean, 26, 35, 50
  vulgar Epicurean materialism, 85,
    188
Hobbes, Thomas
  Epicurean denial of natural
    sociability, 36, 37, 38, 39, 54, 93
  the impiety of humans, 58
  modern Epicureanism, 19, 26, 35–6
  modern state theory, 90
  natural law theory, 38
  the state of nature, 37, 106
  theory of justice, 36–7, 39
Honneth, Axel, 140, 166
Hont, István, 90, 91, 202
Horace, 79
Hume, David, 70, 91

imagination
  anticipation of future pain, 185–6
  anticipation of future pleasures, 169
  as *askesis*, 168–9, 176, 187, 196

  creation of imaginary societies,
    186–7
  and the cultivation of happiness,
    168–9, 175–6, 178, 184–7
  and the experience of reverie, 168,
    184–5
  function of, 6
  generation of something moral from
    something physical, 84
  the importance of a historical
    imagination, 11–14
  memory-imagination relationship,
    184–5, 187
  as a superfluous faculty, 114, 115
isonomia, term, 105

Jaucourt, Chevalier Louis de, 174
judgement
  as an active faculty, 130, 133–5, 183
  in *Emile*, 84, 133–4, 136
  and the general taste of the people,
    120, 128
  judgements of utility and
    agreeableness, 17, 132, 136, 146
  microscope metaphor, 114, 116,
    117
  moral judgement, 11, 17, 99
  politics of taste, 98, 99–100
  Rousseau's account of, 132–3
  theories of democracy and
    judgement, 128–9
  in *Wise Materialism*, 83–4
  see also aesthetic judgement; political
    judgement
Julie
  amour-propre in, 141–3
  balance of reason and sentiment,
    114–15, 166
  Epicureanism of reason, 23, 24
  Julie's moral authority, 116–17
  popular reception of, 195
  refined Epicureanism, 111, 115–17,
    118, 128, 185

INDEX 223

Rousseau's utilitarian intentions for, 11

the simulacrum of virtue, 100, 101

taste for virtue, 117

temperate sensuality, 115–16

town-country tensions, 104, 109

the useful and agreeable in the household, 117, 118, 124, 125

vulgar-refined Epicureanism distinction, 23, 24, 73, 92, 94–5, 97, 115–16

Kant, Immanuel
on aesthetic judgement, 118, 135–6, 164

on modern Epicureans, 26

on political judgement, 135

Rousseau and respect for human nature, 126

La Mettrie, Julien Offray de, 35, 42, 63

language
aesthetics of Rousseau's style, 69–70, 91

origin of, 62–3, 75, 204

Smith's political language, 69

laws
Athenian moral corruption and, 13

general will and the legal standard of justice, 90, 147, 157–8

Spartan political austerity, 13

Lenclos, Ninon de, 33

Letter on French Music, 57

Letter to d'Alembert on the Theatre
aesthetic judgements, 118–19, 144–5

ancient-modern theatre distinction, 120–2

censorship in, 73

defence against the spread of vulgar Epicureanism, 118–19, 122

education of Genevans's judgements of pleasure, 75, 92–3, 96–7, 196

Geneva as a site of refined Epicurean patriotism, 123–4

luxury debates, 74, 96–7

the people's general taste, 120–2, 130–1

personal taste and public morality, 73, 75, 125

and Platonic aesthetics, 118–19

political-economic critique of the theatre, 122–4

references to Vernet's *Instruction*, 73

threat of fashionable Epicureanism in Geneva, 73–4, 122–3, 138

utility and agreeableness in public harmony, 124–5

Letters from the Mountain, 13–14, 179

Letters to Malesherbes, 179, 188, 195, 197

Levasseur, Thérèse, 194

Locke, John
Essay Concerning Human Understanding, 51

on *inquiétude* (uneasiness), 180–1

and modern Epicureanism, 19, 26

role of memory, 176–7

'thinking matter' hypothesis, 39–40, 63

Lucretius
De rerum natura, 18, 30, 35, 61–2, 104, 109, 147

the division of labour, 107

influence in the second *Discourse*, 18, 61–2, 85, 92, 104, 105–6, 109

influence on Diderot, 41

isonomia concept, 105

on pity, 111–12

proto-evolutionary arguments, 43, 61

luxury debates
in *D'Alembert*, 74, 96–7

224 INDEX

luxury debates (*cont.*)
  of the eighteenth century, 14, 32,
    71–2
  fashionable Epicureanism as
    justification for, 74–5
  Montesquieu's defence, 30–1
  in refined Epicureanism, 115
  revisionist debates, 16–17
  Smith's review of the second
    Discourse, 67–73
  women's role as moderators of taste,
    96, 112–13, 116

Malesherbes, Guillaume-Chrétien de
  Lamoignon de, 179, 188, 195,
  197
Mandeville, Bernard
  account of pity, 54, 112
  Fable of the Bees, 16, 68, 70, 76
  humans' 'thin' sociability, 36
  modern Epicureanism, 35–6, 37
  revisionist readings of, 16–17
  on self-love, 70–1
  utility and moral judgement, 17,
    34–5
materialism
  of Diderot, 39–40, 41–4, 48–9
  Genlis's accusation of Epicurean
    materialism, 83
  materialist natural philosophy of the
    second *Discourse*, 56, 59, 61–2,
    63–5, 69
  Rousseau's wise materialism, 83–4
  of the soul in Epicureanism, 49–50,
    52
Melon, Jean-François, 32
memory
  as an active faculty, 183
  and the alleviation of anxieties of
    anticipation, 177–8
  as *askesis*, 168–9, 176, 187, 196
  and the cultivation of happiness,
    168–9, 176, 183

and the experience of reverie, 168,
    184–5
memorial pleasures, 169, 177–8,
    183–4
memory-imagination relationship,
    184–5, 187
microscope metaphor, 5–6, 12, 114
moeurs, concept, 120
Montaigne, Michel de
  Epicureanism and, 26
  Essais, 18, 33, 168
  on memorial pleasure, 184
Montesquieu, Charles Louis de
  Secondat, Baron de La Brède et
  de, 12, 30–1
moral freedom
  freedom-happiness relationship,
    179–80, 182–3
  links with political freedom, 4–6,
    161–2
  the people as moral arbiter, 145–6
  the problem of modern liberty,
    104–5, 107–9, 201
  Rousseau's account of, 179
  temperance and, 21, 22, 113
  through a taste for virtue, 4, 10
  through aesthetic judgement, 4–5,
    116–17, 118–19
  through personal autonomy, 8–10,
    14
  through sensual pleasure, 4–5
Moral Letters, 198–9

natural law theory
  Castillon's critique of the second
    Discourse, 56, 59–63, 66, 105–6
  Hobbesian theory of justice, 36–7,
    39
  human natural sociability, 36–9,
    40
nature
  distinction between natural and
    fashion-based taste, 113–15

the imagination and experiences of
pleasure in, 185, 198
Neuhouser, Frederick, 7, 14, 141, 143,
144
Nicole, Pierre, 37–8, 76
Nihell, Laurence, 34–6, 37, 41

Oakeshott, Michael, 9, 27

perfectibilité, faculty of, 66, 132
pity
in Lucretius, 111–12
Mandeville's account of, 54, 112
as a substitute for sociability, 58–9,
68, 70
tempering of *amour-propre*, 58–9, 70,
112
women as the paradigmatic subjects
of, 112
Plato
account of true philosophical virtue,
22–3
music and pleasure, 146
rationalist account of moderation
(*sophrosyne*), 21–4, 118–19, 126,
173
Republic, 101
Rousseau's marginalia, 22–3
sophrosyne in, 21–3
Symposium, 101
pleasure
amour-propre and, 110–11, 137
as end of virtue, 4–5, 94
Epicurean pursuit of, 30–1, 40, 67
and fashionable Epicureanism, 73–5
the imagination and experiences of
pleasure in, 185, 198
in Pope, 78–9
of the practice of reverie, 168
recollected pleasure, 169, 177–8,
183–4
in refined Epicureanism, 128
rooted in nature, 4

Rousseau's celebration of, 20, 119
the sensation of, 169
as voluptuousness, 149–50
writing as a source of, 188, 192–3
see also agreeableness
Plutarch, 11
Poland, 160, 162
Political Economy, 54, 101, 132, 156–7,
160
political freedom
balance in, 5
under the general will, 21, 113,
166
links with moral freedom, 4–6,
161–2
the mind as both microscope and
telescope, 5–6, 12
the problem of modern liberty,
104–5, 107–9, 201
temperance and, 21, 22
through a taste for virtue, 10
through aesthetic judgement, 4–5
through popular sovereignty, 8–9,
10
through sensual pleasure, 4–5
political judgement
aesthetic judgement-political
judgement distinctions, 136–7,
163–5
criteria of in the *Discourses*, 110,
132, 136
definition, 135
and democracy in political theory,
128–9
general taste and, 150
the general will and, 113, 128, 130,
135, 136, 150–1, 161–2, 163
Kantian readings of, 135
Rousseau's account of, 129–30, 131
political theory
aesthetic dimensions, 17, 91, 203
contemporary liberal-egalitarianism,
9

political theory (*cont.*)
the importance of a historical
imagination, 11–14
the public vs the private good and,
125–6
Rousseau's state theory, 11, 14–17,
89, 90, 91–2, 202–4
solitude and, 170, 178
useless forms of, 11–12
Polybius, 30, 31
Pope, Alexander
account of happiness, 81–2, 95
accusations of Epicureanism, 28, 55,
75, 76, 77–9
impiety, 76, 77, 81
the passions and human agency, 76,
78, 79, 80–1
Rousseau's defence of, 27, 55,
75–9, 81–2, 89, 95, 169, 170–1
vulgar Epicureanism, 79, 80–1, 82
Warburton's defence of, 79–81
Prades, Jean-Martin de, 40
Pufendorf, Samuel von
critique of Hobbes's theory of
justice, 36–7
defence of natural sociability, 32,
38, 39
imbecillitas concept, 93
on justice, 90
Law of Nature and Nations, 36, 63
natural law theory, 38
the physical side of natural man,
63

Quesnay, François, 133

Raynal, Abbé, 98, 103, 104, 120
reason
balance of reason and sentiment,
113–15, 166
Epicureanism of reason, 4, 21, 23–4,
27
in general will, 136

progression to via sensation, 112–13,
134–5
and solitude in the autobiographies,
167
and the transition to civil society,
65–6
refined Epicureanism
in the autobiographies, 166–7, 169,
172
creation of through education,
201–2
in *Julie*, 111, 115–17, 118, 128, 185
of Rousseau, 55, 91–2, 93–8, 203
vulgar-refined Epicureanism
distinction, 23–4, 53, 73, 82, 92,
94–8, 113, 115–16, 118
Reimarus, Hermann Samuel, 56,
63–6
religion
contemporary theological debates,
41–2, 44
de Prades affair, 40
Epicureanism as irreligious, 34–5,
40, 41–2
Epicureanism's denial of providence,
45–9, 52, 54
immortal soul/corporeal soul
debates, 41–2, 44, 45, 49, 52, 54
providence and creation, 46–7
Reveries
the 'Fifth Walk', 188–91, 192
solitude within society, 198
Rousseau, Jean-Jacques
the consistency dilemma, 6–10, 166
engagement with Epicureanism,
19–24, 85–6, 161–2
ethos of critique, 76–8, 169, 170–1
his writings as a system, 6–7, 10, 17,
169, 170–4, 195, 207
the incompatibility thesis and, 7,
9–10, 196
the paradoxical thought of, 3–4, 7,
8, 204–6

INDEX

reception as an Epicurean, 53, 54–5, 56–67

as a refined Epicurean, 55, 91–2, 93–8, 203

retreat from Paris, 182

social autonomy interpretation of, 7, 9–10, 14

sources and influences, 18–19

'thin' human natural sociability, 38–9

utilitarian intentions for his writings, 10–11, 17

Rousseau, Judge of Jean-Jacques: Dialogues

account of temperate sensuality, 23, 172–4

defence of the coherence of his system, 169, 170–4, 207

the ideal world of, 172–3

within Rousseau's *oeuvre*, 171–2

Saint-Évremond, Charles de, 33

second *Discourse*

aesthetic aims, 205–7

amour-propre, 137, 139

Castel's theological critique, 56, 57–9, 64, 66

Castillon's natural law critique, 56, 59–63, 66, 105–6

criterion of political judgement, 110

denial of justice, 62, 68, 90

denial of natural sociability, 54, 56, 58–9, 60–1, 62, 65, 68, 90, 93

denial of providence, 57–8, 59

division of labour in society, 105, 107–10

four-stages theory, 108

justice as an artificial virtue, 54, 56, 59, 90

Lucretius's influence on, 18, 61–2, 85, 92, 104, 105–6, 109

luxury debates, 67–73

materialist natural philosophy, 56, 59, 61–2, 63–5, 69

natural and moral inequality, 107, 110

paradoxical aims, 205–7

path to happiness, 114

perfectibilité, faculty of, 66, 132

the problem of modern liberty, 104–5, 107–9, 201

Reimarus's critique, 56, 63–6

Rousseau's reception as an Epicurean, 27, 54, 56–67, 75

Rousseau's style, 69–70

Rousseau's utilitarian intentions for, 6, 10, 195

the state of nature, 38, 59, 60, 105–7

town-country tensions, 104, 108–10

utility and commercial sociability, 104–13

utility-agreeableness balance, 110–11

vulgar materialist readings of, 54–5, 102, 134, 182

Seneca, 18

sensation

as distinct from sentiment, 188

Epicurean account of sensation and error, 134

in Epicureanism, 23, 29, 51

errors in judgement and, 134

the microscope of judgment metaphor and, 5, 6

of pleasure, 169

progression to reason, 112–13, 134–5

as the union of body and soul, 49–50

sensationalism, 39–40, 51

sentiment

in aesthetic judgement, 136

awareness of beauty, 55–6

balance of reason and sentiment, 113–15, 166

communicability of, 193–6

sentiment (*cont.*)
  as distinct from sensation, 188
  of happiness, 169, 188–9
  in refined Epicureanism, 113–15
  and solitude in the autobiographies,
    167, 185, 189–90
Shaftesbury, Anthony Ashley-Cooper,
  16–17, 26, 32, 71
Shklar, Judith, 7, 14, 117, 161
Smith, Adam
  aesthetic dimensions of political
    theory, 91
  on commercial society, 91
  discussion of commercial society,
    103–4
  parallels between Rousseau and
    Mandeville, 68, 70
  translation of the second *Discourse*,
    55
sociability
  Castel's critique of the second
    Discourse, 58–9
  Castillon's reaffirmation of, 60–1,
    93–4
  in commercial societies, 55, 91
  denial of natural sociability in the
    second *Discourse*, 54, 56, 58–9,
    60–1, 62, 65, 68, 90, 93
  of friendship, 170, 179–80, 193
  Hobbe's Epicurean denial of natural
    sociability, 36, 37, 38, 39, 54, 93
  and modern state theory, 89–91
  as a natural human condition, 36
  the origin of language, 62, 63
  pity as a substitute for, 58–9, 68,
    70
  Pufendorf's defence of natural
    sociability, 32, 38, 39
  reverie's threat to, 168, 184
  sociability-solitude relationship,
    193–9
  'thin' human natural sociability, 36,
    38–9

utility and commercial sociability in
  the second *Discourse*, 104–13
Social Contract
  aesthetic dimensions of political
    theory, 91, 161–2
  censorship and, 131, 137, 146–7,
    162–3
  critique of direct democracy, 13
  dangers of factional interests, 150
  general will as distinct from the will
    of all, 156–7, 158
  and Geneva's republicanism, 12
  legal hierarchies of rank, 111
  principles of political right, 149
  problem of modern liberty, 15–17,
    91–2
  problem of outvoted minorities,
    148, 154–6
  sovereignty/government distinction,
    15
  state theory, 11, 12, 14, 90
solitude
  freedom-happiness relationship,
    179–80, 182–3
  friendship-solitude relationship,
    193–9
  moral and political utility of, 198–9
  and personal happiness, 178, 182–3,
    185, 189–90, 193, 196–8
  political theory and, 170, 178
  and sentiment in the
    autobiographies, 167, 185,
    189–90
Sonenscher, Michael, 10
soul
  the composite soul, 66
  in Epicureanism, 49–50, 52
  immortal soul/corporeal soul
    debates, 41–2, 44, 45, 49–50, 52,
    54
sovereignty
  natural sociability arguments and,
    54

INDEX

political commitments of popular
   sovereignty, 196–7
separation from government, 13
sovereignty/government distinction,
   15
Sparta, 13–14
state theory
   modern concept of the state, 89–90
   personal happiness and, 196–7
   role of aesthetic judgement, 131
   Rousseau's state theory, 11, 202–4
   sociability and, 89–91
   of *Social Contract*, 11, 12, 14, 90
Stoicism
   anticipation of future pain, 186
   Epicureans as, 4, 27
   natural law theory, 27
   Rousseau's rejection of asceticism,
      20
Strauss, Leo, 7, 9, 52, 193, 196

taste
   distinction between natural and
      fashion-based taste, 113–15
   eighteenth-century discourse of, 16
   in the first *Discourse*, 98–104
   the politics of taste, 6, 16, 99, 100
   Rousseau's metaphorical description
      of, 5–6, 12, 114, 116, 117
   temperance grounded in, 4
   temperate sensuality, 27, 56
   useful-agreeable distinction, 98–9
   women's natural moral authority,
      96, 112–13, 116
   see also general taste
taste for virtue
   concept, 99–101
   Epicureanism of reason, 4, 21, 23–4,
      27
   in *Julie*, 117
   moral and political freedom and, 4,
      10
   phrase, 4

temperate sensuality, 21, 23–4, 56,
   113, 169, 172–3
temperance
   Epicureanism and, 22–4, 113
   Greek *sophrosyne*, 21–4
   grounded in taste, 4
   hedonist theory of, 4, 23–4
   for moral and political freedom, 21,
      22, 113
temperate sensuality
   aesthetics and, 172–3
   in *Dialogues*, 23, 172–4
   happiness and, 174–5
   hedonism and, 169, 173
   of refined Epicureanism, 115–16
   and the taste for virtue, 21, 23–4,
      56, 113, 169
Tronchin, Théodore, 201, 203, 204

utility
   commercial sociability of the second
      Discourse, 104–13
   judgements of utility and
      agreeableness, 17, 99–100, 132,
      136, 146
   and moral judgement, 17, 34–5
   Rousseau's utilitarian intentions for
      his writings, 10–11, 204
   useful-agreeable distinction in
      commercial societies, 98–100,
      101–2, 103–4, 110–11
   useful-agreeable distinction in public
      settings, 124–5
   useful-agreeable relationship, 92–3,
      95–6, 117
utopianism, 12

vanity, 138–9
Vernet, Jacob
   on fashionable Epicureanism, 73–5
   practical Epicureanism, 74
   Rousseau and the luxury debates,
      55, 67

230 INDEX

Vernet, Jacob (*cont.*)
  speculative Epicureanism, 74
  on vulgar Epicureanism, 96, 118, 201
virtue
  justice as an artificial virtue, 54, 56, 59, 90
  the simulacrum of virtue, 100–1, 120
  as a supplement to taste, 100
  through pleasure, 4–5, 94
  see also taste for virtue
Voltaire, 32, 40, 46, 122, 126
vulgar Epicureanism
  amour-propre and, 137, 138
  in *D'Alembert*, 118–19, 122
  in Geneva, 201, 203

Helvétius's vulgar Epicurean materialism, 85, 188
Hobbesian denial of natural sociability, 36–8, 93, 94
and Pope, 78–82
temperance and, 22–4
vulgar-refined Epicureanism distinction, 23–4, 53, 73, 82, 92, 94–8, 113, 115–16, 118

Warburton, William, 79–80
Wise Man's Materialism, 135
Wise Materialism, 83–4
Wolff, Christian, 64
women
  moral authority, 96, 112–13, 116
  as paradigmatic subjects of pity, 112

www.ingramcontent.com/pod-product-compliance
Lightning Source LLC
LaVergne TN
LVHW011556100225
803225LV00068B/396